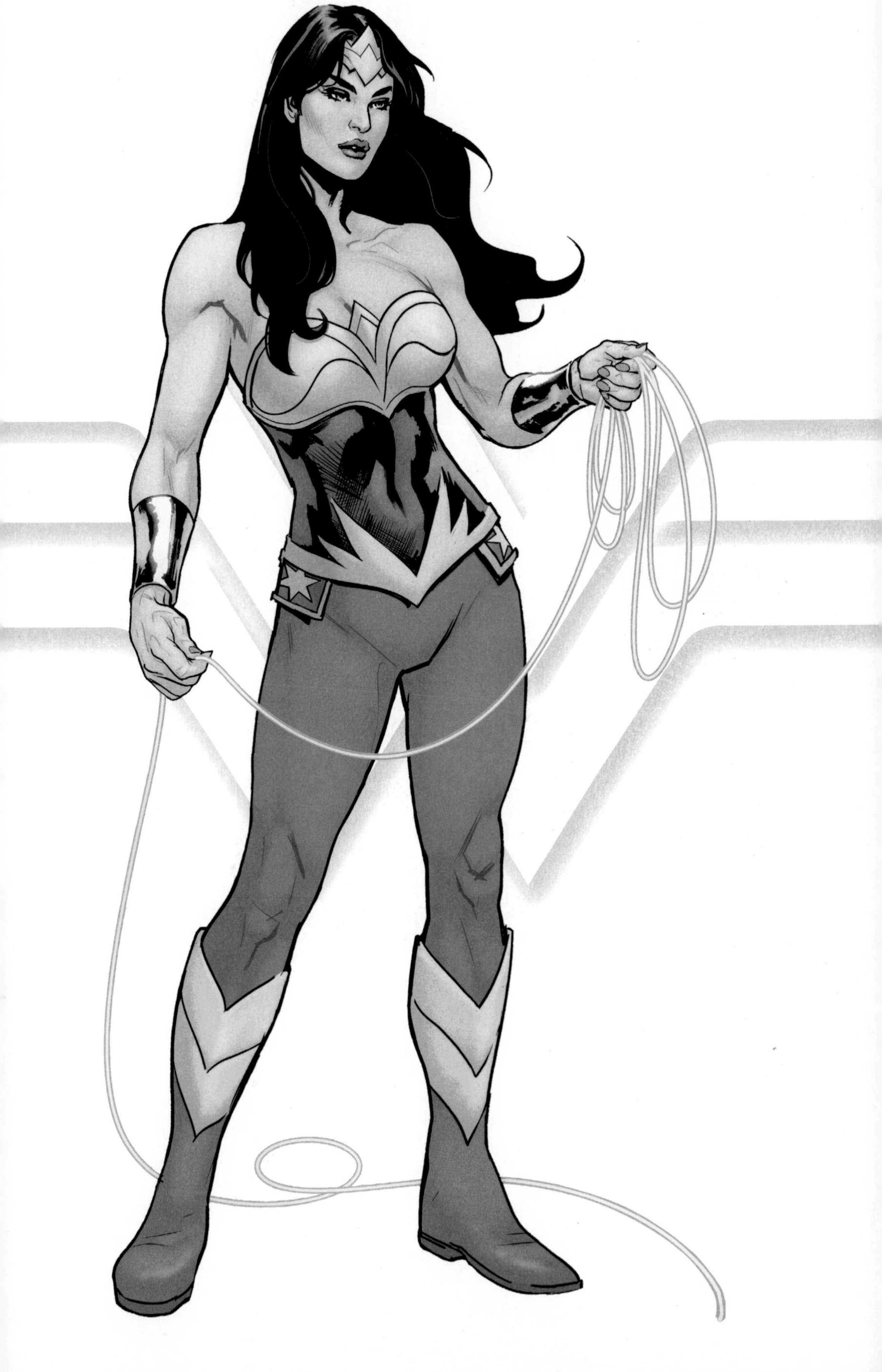

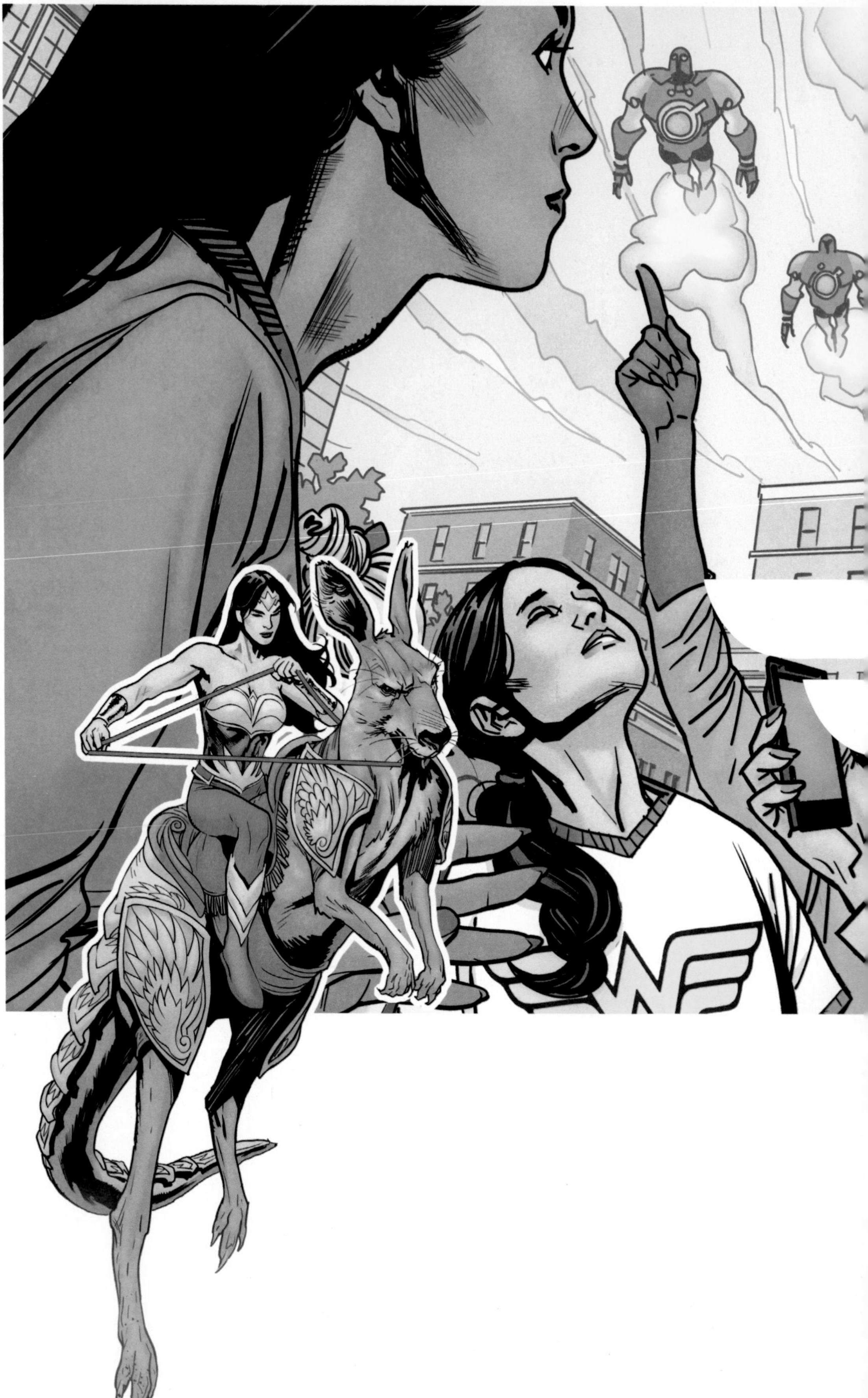

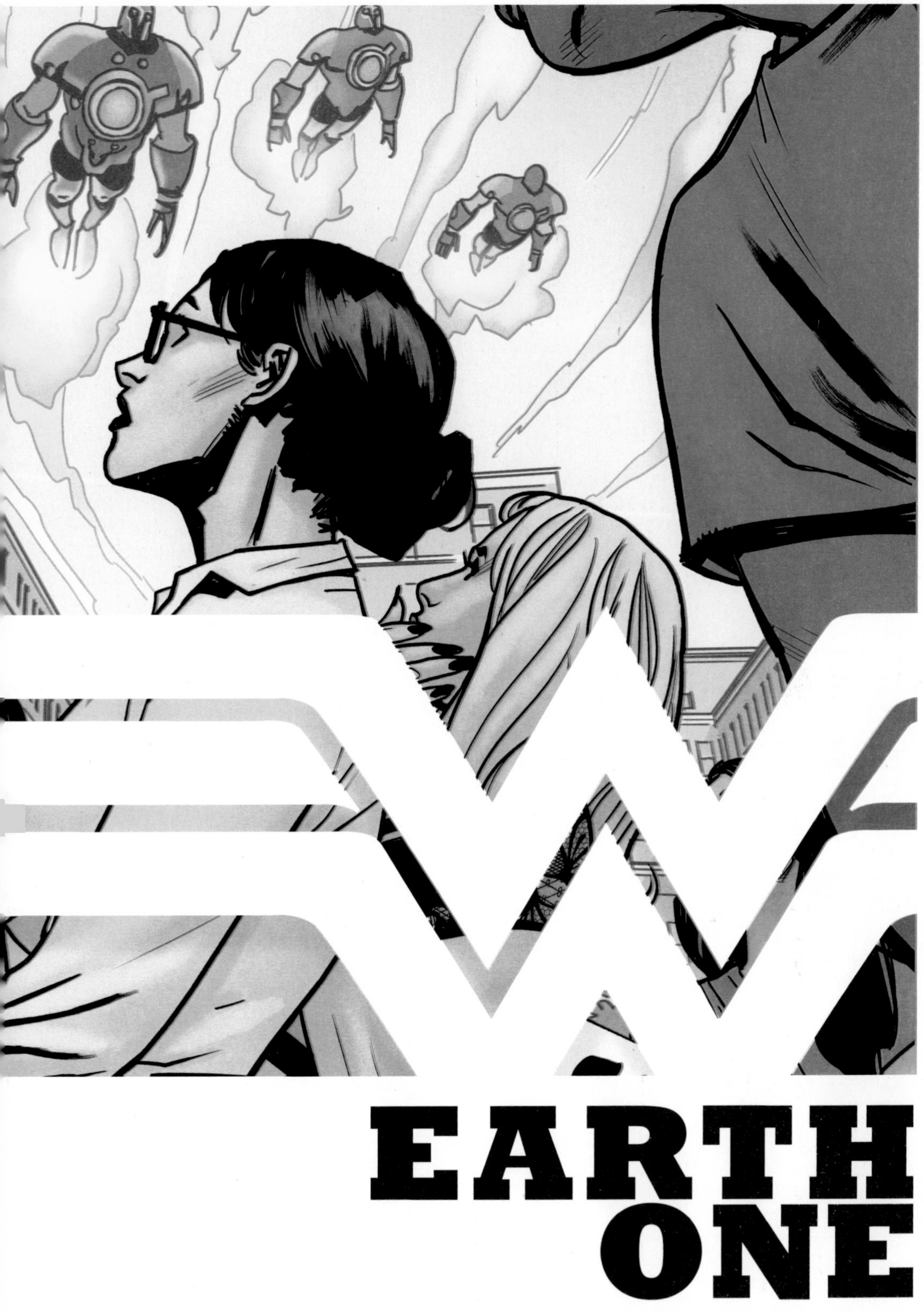

EARTH ONE

Written by Grant Morrison

Art and Cover by Yanick Paquette

Colors by Nathan Fairbairn

Letters by Todd Klein

Wonder Woman created by William Moulton Marston

Andrew Marino Editor – Original Series
Steve Cook Design Director – Books
Louis Prandi Publication Design
Sandy Alonzo Publication Production

Marie Javins Editor-in-Chief, DC Comics

Daniel Cherry III Senior VP – General Manager
Jim Lee Publisher & Chief Creative Officer
Don Falletti VP – Manufacturing Operations & Workflow Management
Lawrence Ganem VP – Talent Services
Alison Gill Senior VP – Manufacturing & Operations
Nick J. Napolitano VP – Manufacturing Administration & Design
Nancy Spears VP – Revenue
Michele R. Wells VP & Executive Editor, Young Reader

WONDER WOMAN: EARTH ONE VOLUME THREE

Published by DC Comics. Copyright © 2021 DC Comics. All Rights Reserved. All characters, their distinctive likenesses, and related elements featured in this publication are trademarks of DC Comics. The stories, characters, and incidents featured in this publication are entirely fictional. DC Comics does not read or accept unsolicited submissions of ideas, stories, or artwork.

DC Comics, 2900 West Alameda Ave., Burbank, CA 91505

Printed by LSC Communications, Willard, OH, USA. 1/29/21. First Printing. ISBN: 978-1-77950-207-0

Library of Congress Cataloging-in-Publication Data is available.

PEFC Certified

This product is from sustainably managed forests and controlled sources

PEFC/29-31-337   www.pefc.org

DEDICATIONS

For Leigh, my sister
Grant Morrison

For diversity, love, and equity
Yanick Paquette

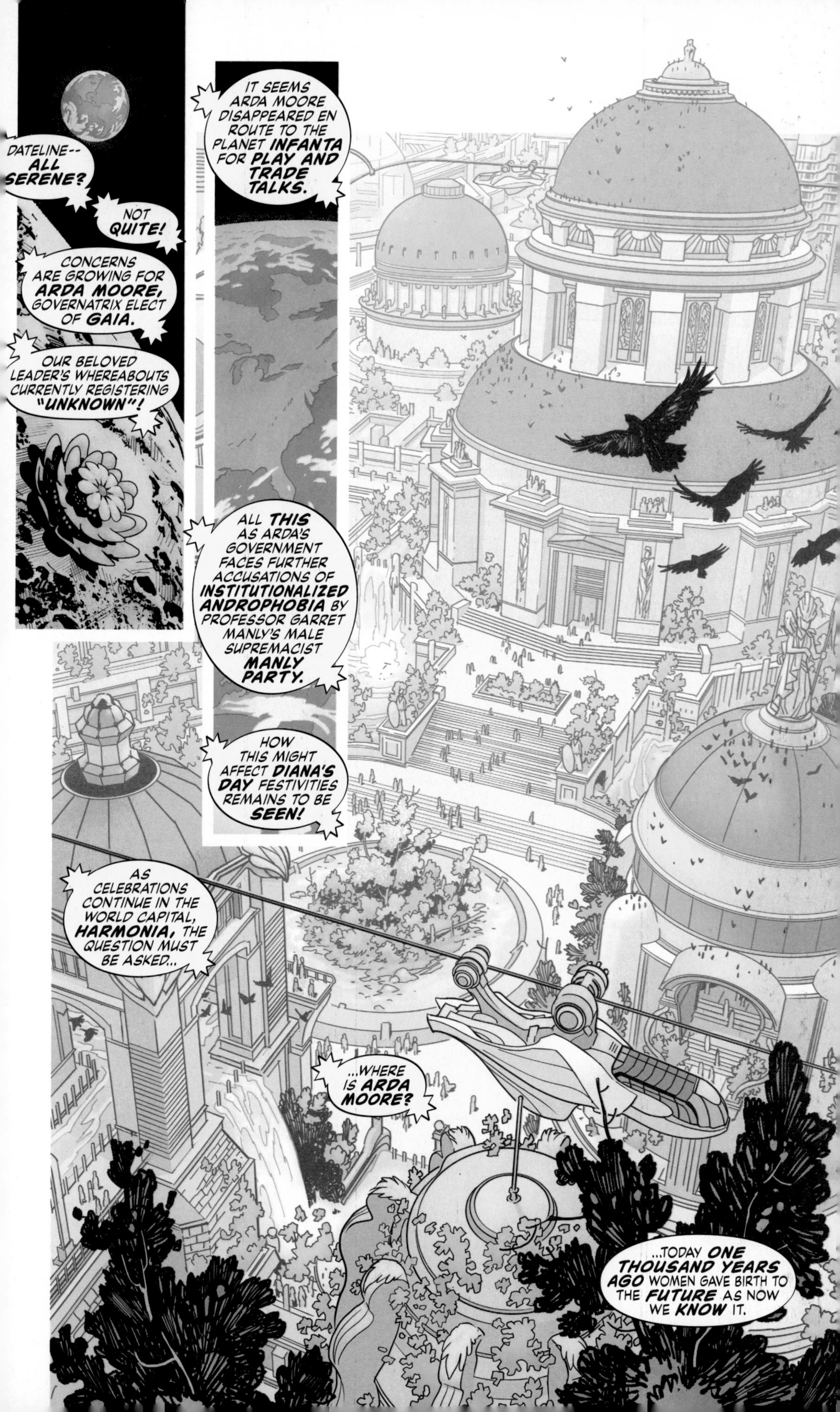
DATELINE-- ALL SERENE?
NOT QUITE!
CONCERNS ARE GROWING FOR ARDA MOORE, GOVERNATRIX ELECT OF GAIA.
OUR BELOVED LEADER'S WHEREABOUTS CURRENTLY REGISTERING "UNKNOWN"!
IT SEEMS ARDA MOORE DISAPPEARED EN ROUTE TO THE PLANET INFANTA FOR PLAY AND TRADE TALKS.
ALL THIS AS ARDA'S GOVERNMENT FACES FURTHER ACCUSATIONS OF INSTITUTIONALIZED ANDROPHOBIA BY PROFESSOR GARRET MANLY'S MALE SUPREMACIST MANLY PARTY.
HOW THIS MIGHT AFFECT DIANA'S DAY FESTIVITIES REMAINS TO BE SEEN!
AS CELEBRATIONS CONTINUE IN THE WORLD CAPITAL, HARMONIA, THE QUESTION MUST BE ASKED...
...WHERE IS ARDA MOORE?
...TODAY ONE THOUSAND YEARS AGO WOMEN GAVE BIRTH TO THE FUTURE AS NOW WE KNOW IT.

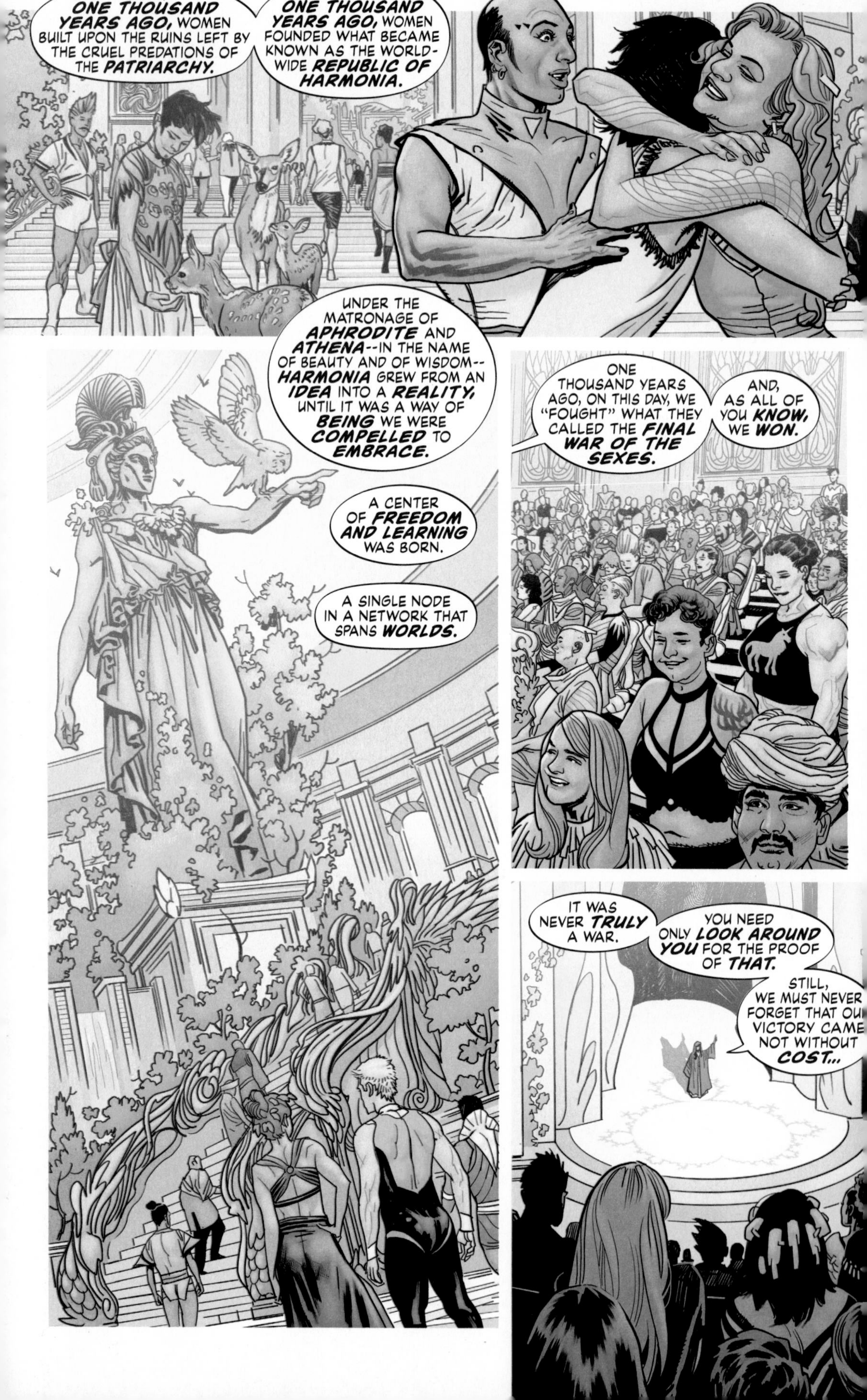
TODAY, ONE THOUSAND YEARS AGO, WOMEN BUILT UPON THE RUINS LEFT BY THE CRUEL PREDATIONS OF THE PATRIARCHY.
TODAY, ONE THOUSAND YEARS AGO, WOMEN FOUNDED WHAT BECAME KNOWN AS THE WORLD-WIDE REPUBLIC OF HARMONIA.
UNDER THE MATRONAGE OF APHRODITE AND ATHENA--IN THE NAME OF BEAUTY AND OF WISDOM--HARMONIA GREW FROM AN IDEA INTO A REALITY, UNTIL IT WAS A WAY OF BEING WE WERE COMPELLED TO EMBRACE.
A CENTER OF FREEDOM AND LEARNING WAS BORN.
A SINGLE NODE IN A NETWORK THAT SPANS WORLDS.
ONE THOUSAND YEARS AGO, ON THIS DAY, WE "FOUGHT" WHAT THEY CALLED THE FINAL WAR OF THE SEXES.
AND, AS ALL OF YOU KNOW, WE WON.
IT WAS NEVER TRULY A WAR.
YOU NEED ONLY LOOK AROUND YOU FOR THE PROOF OF THAT.
STILL, WE MUST NEVER FORGET THAT OU VICTORY CAME NOT WITHOUT COST...

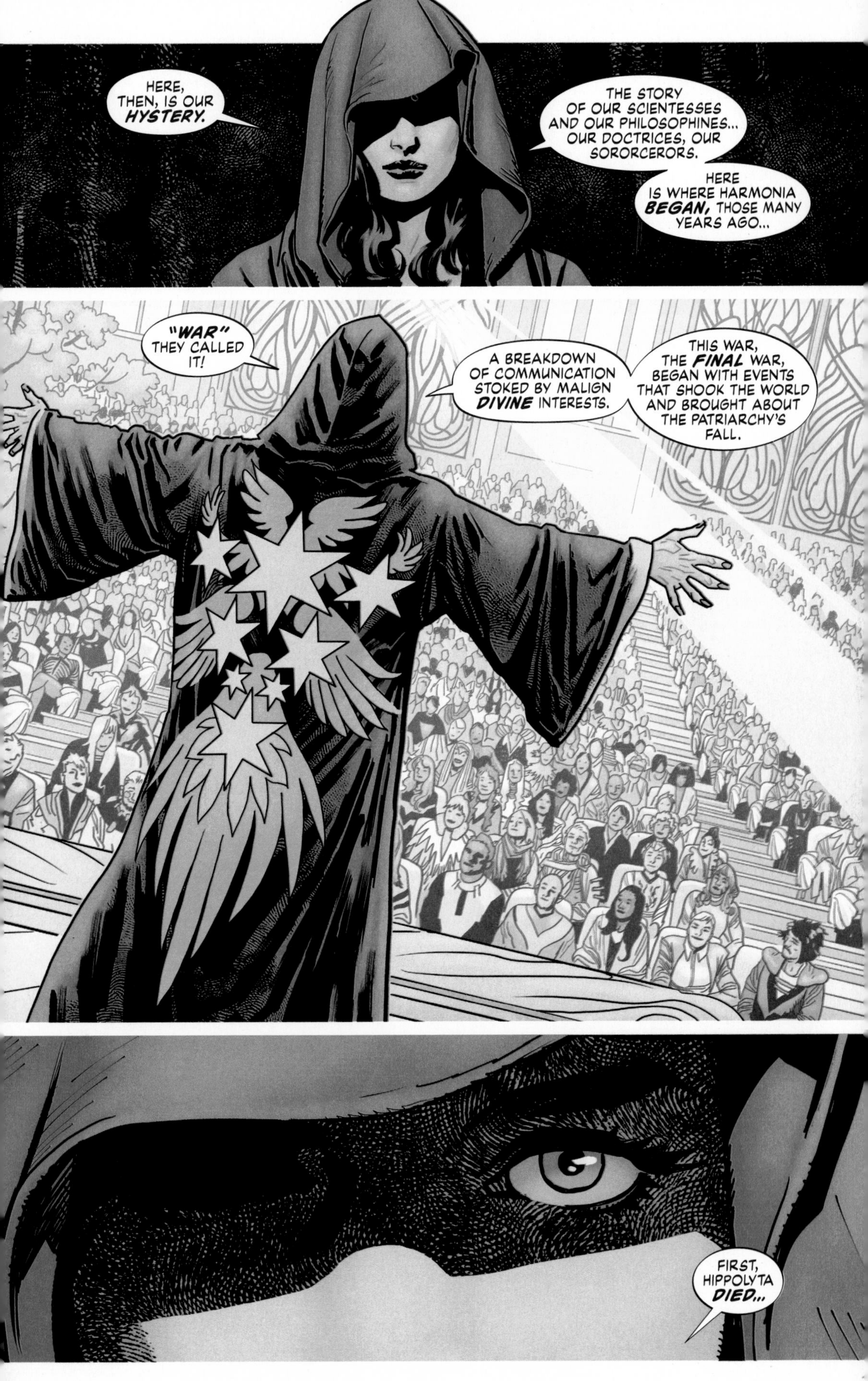
HERE, THEN, IS OUR HYSTERY.
THE STORY OF OUR SCIENTESSES AND OUR PHILOSOPHINES... OUR DOCTRICES, OUR SORORCERORS.
HERE IS WHERE HARMONIA BEGAN, THOSE MANY YEARS AGO...
"WAR" THEY CALLED IT!
A BREAKDOWN OF COMMUNICATION STOKED BY MALIGN DIVINE INTERESTS.
THIS WAR, THE FINAL WAR, BEGAN WITH EVENTS THAT SHOOK THE WORLD AND BROUGHT ABOUT THE PATRIARCHY'S FALL.
FIRST, HIPPOLYTA DIED...

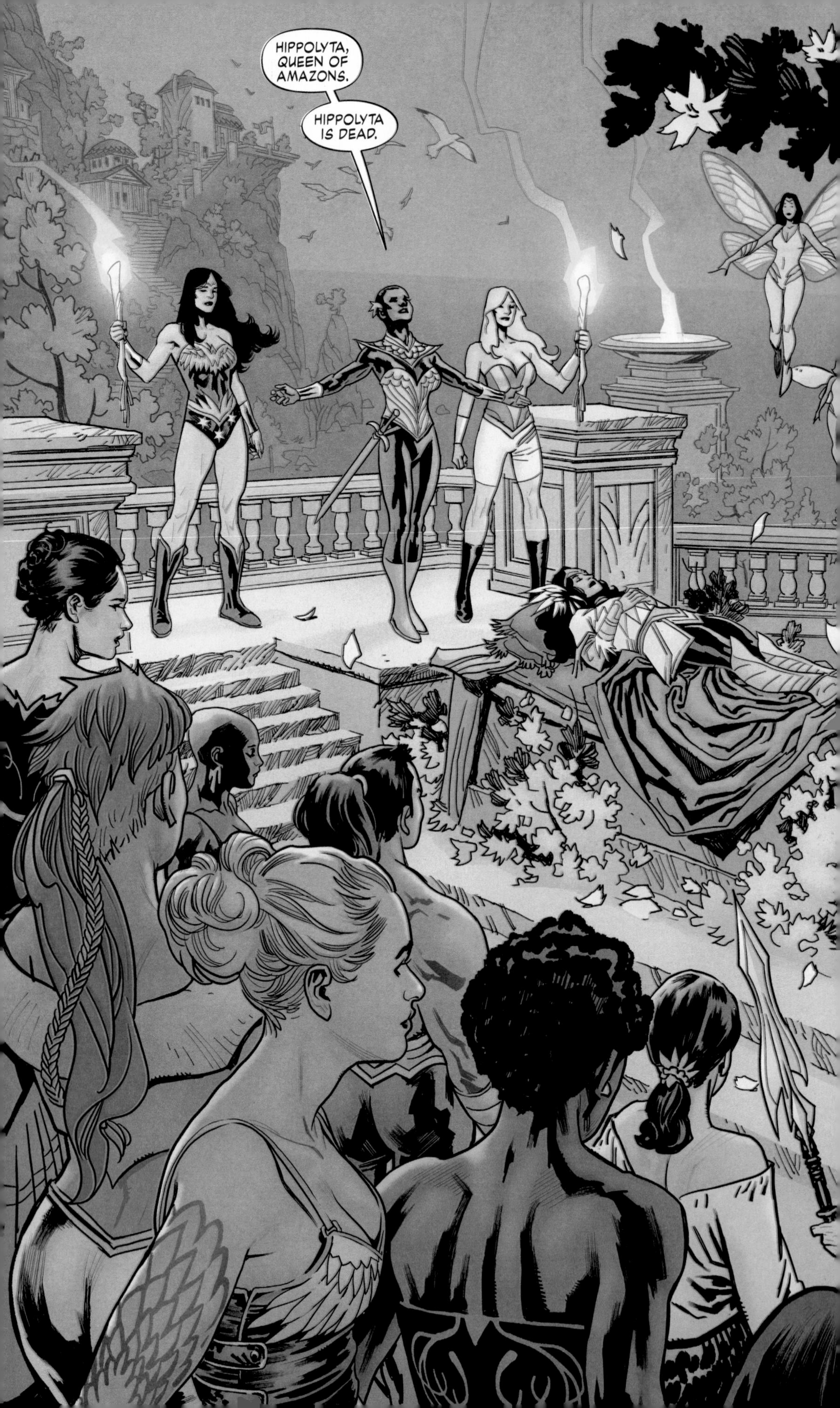
HIPPOLYTA, QUEEN OF AMAZONS.
HIPPOLYTA IS DEAD.

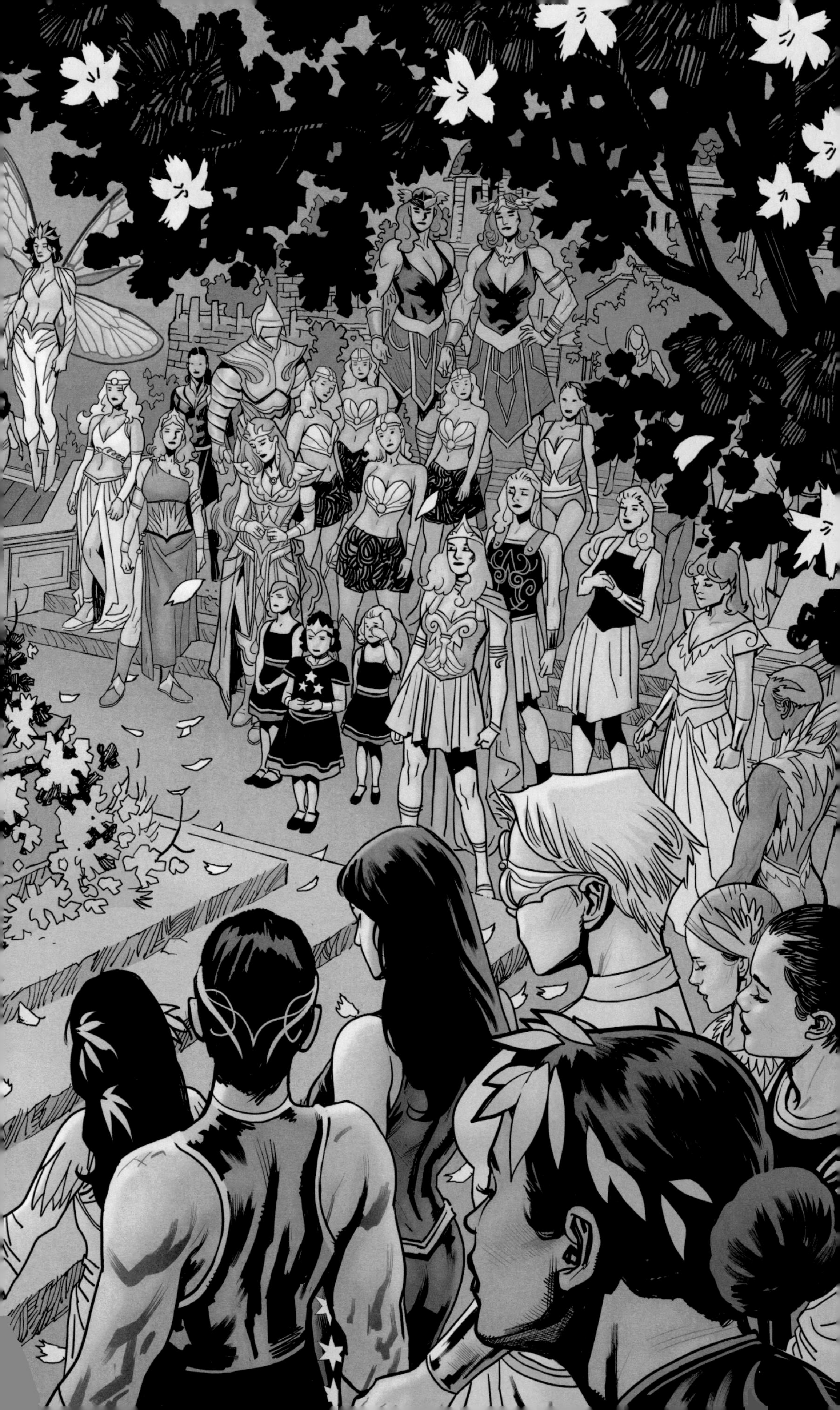

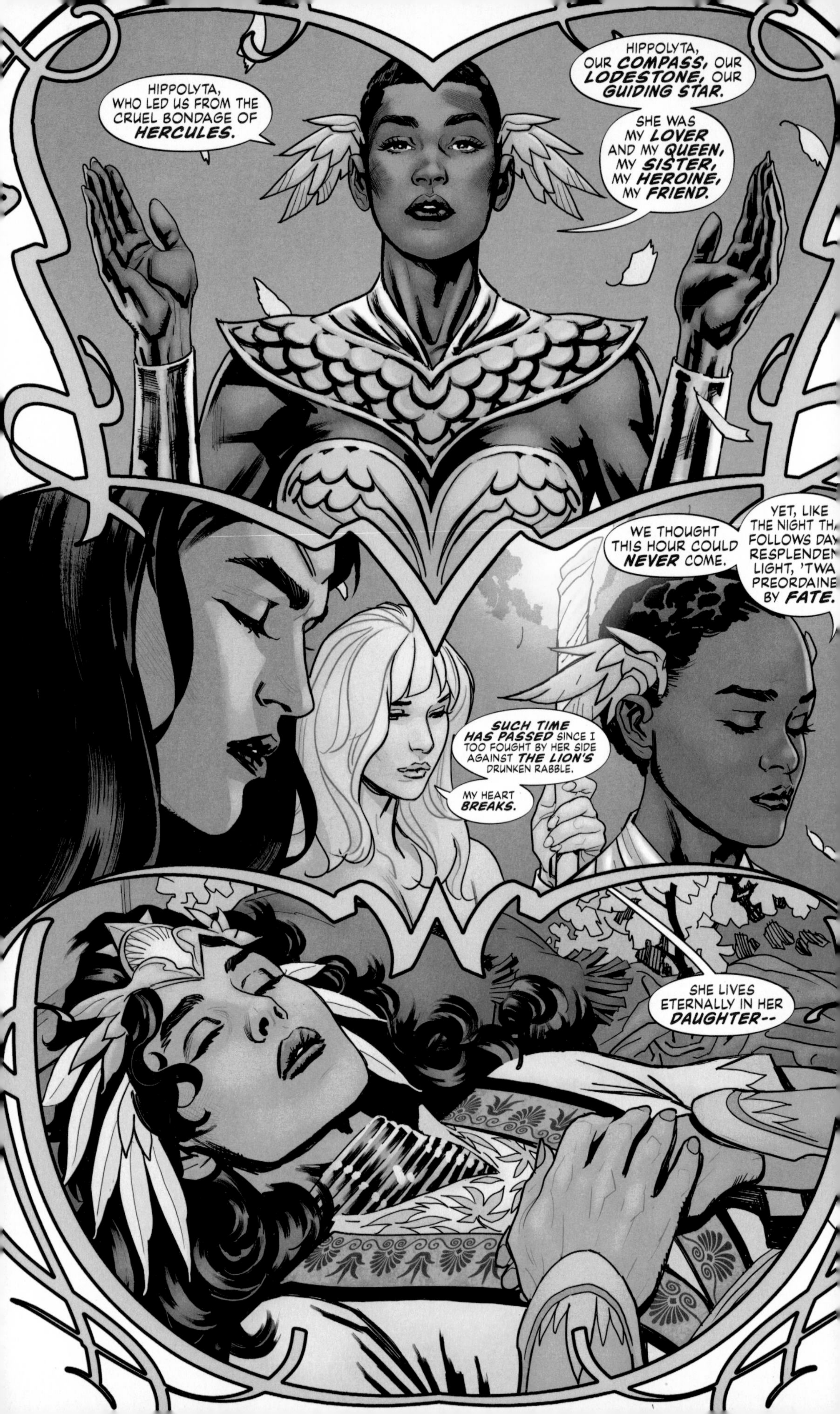
HIPPOLYTA, WHO LED US FROM THE CRUEL BONDAGE OF HERCULES.
HIPPOLYTA, OUR COMPASS, OUR LODESTONE, OUR GUIDING STAR.
SHE WAS MY LOVER AND MY QUEEN, MY SISTER, MY HEROINE, MY FRIEND.
WE THOUGHT THIS HOUR COULD NEVER COME.
SUCH TIME HAS PASSED SINCE I TOO FOUGHT BY HER SIDE AGAINST THE LION'S DRUNKEN RABBLE.
MY HEART BREAKS.
SHE LIVES ETERNALLY IN HER DAUGHTER--

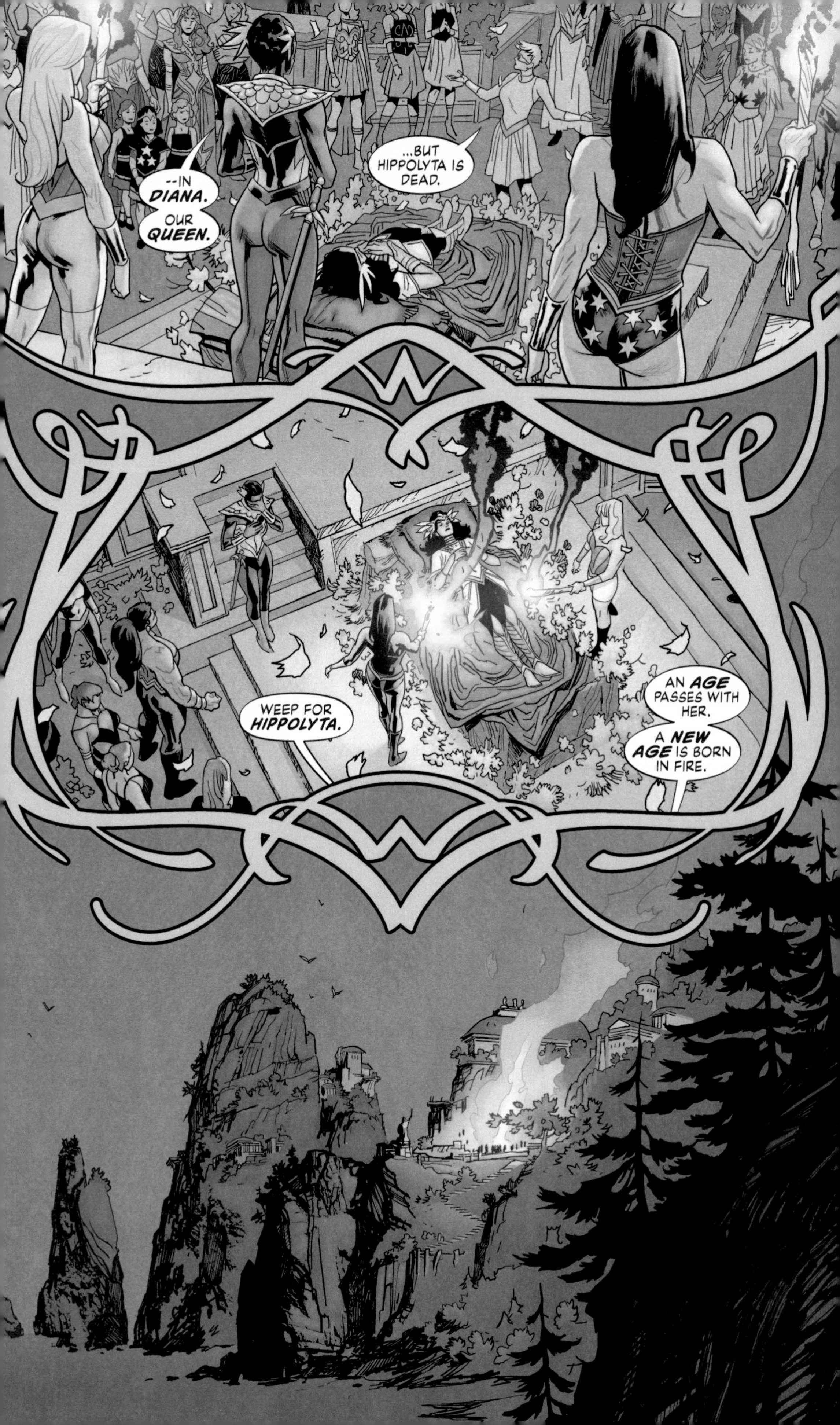
--IN DIANA.
OUR QUEEN.
...BUT HIPPOLYTA IS DEAD.
WEEP FOR HIPPOLYTA.
AN AGE PASSES WITH HER.
A NEW AGE IS BORN IN FIRE.

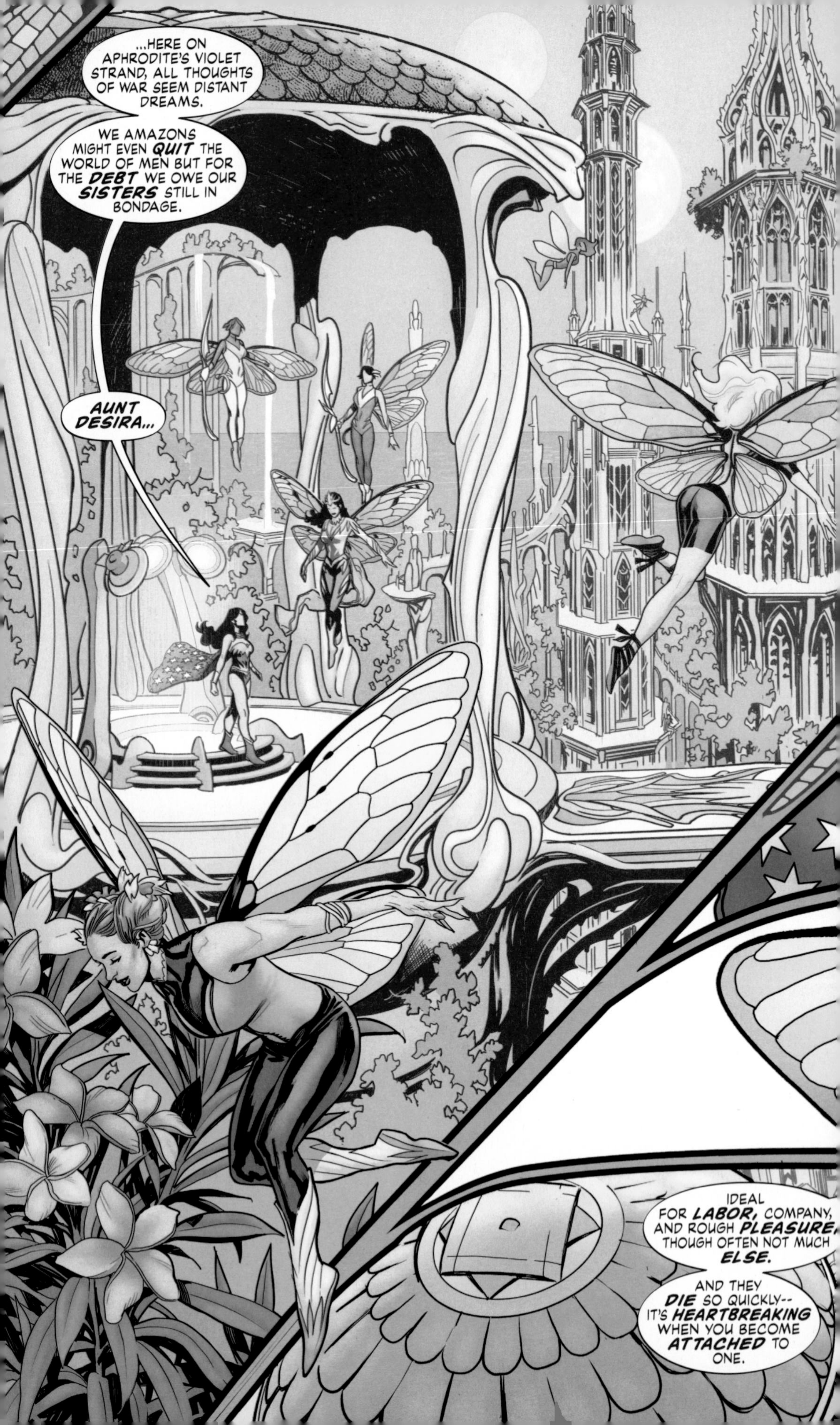

...HERE ON APHRODITE'S VIOLET STRAND, ALL THOUGHTS OF WAR SEEM DISTANT DREAMS.
WE AMAZONS MIGHT EVEN QUIT THE WORLD OF MEN BUT FOR THE DEBT WE OWE OUR SISTERS STILL IN BONDAGE.
AUNT DESIRA...
IDEAL FOR LABOR, COMPANY, AND ROUGH PLEASURE, THOUGH OFTEN NOT MUCH ELSE.
AND THEY DIE SO QUICKLY-- IT'S HEARTBREAKING WHEN YOU BECOME ATTACHED TO ONE.

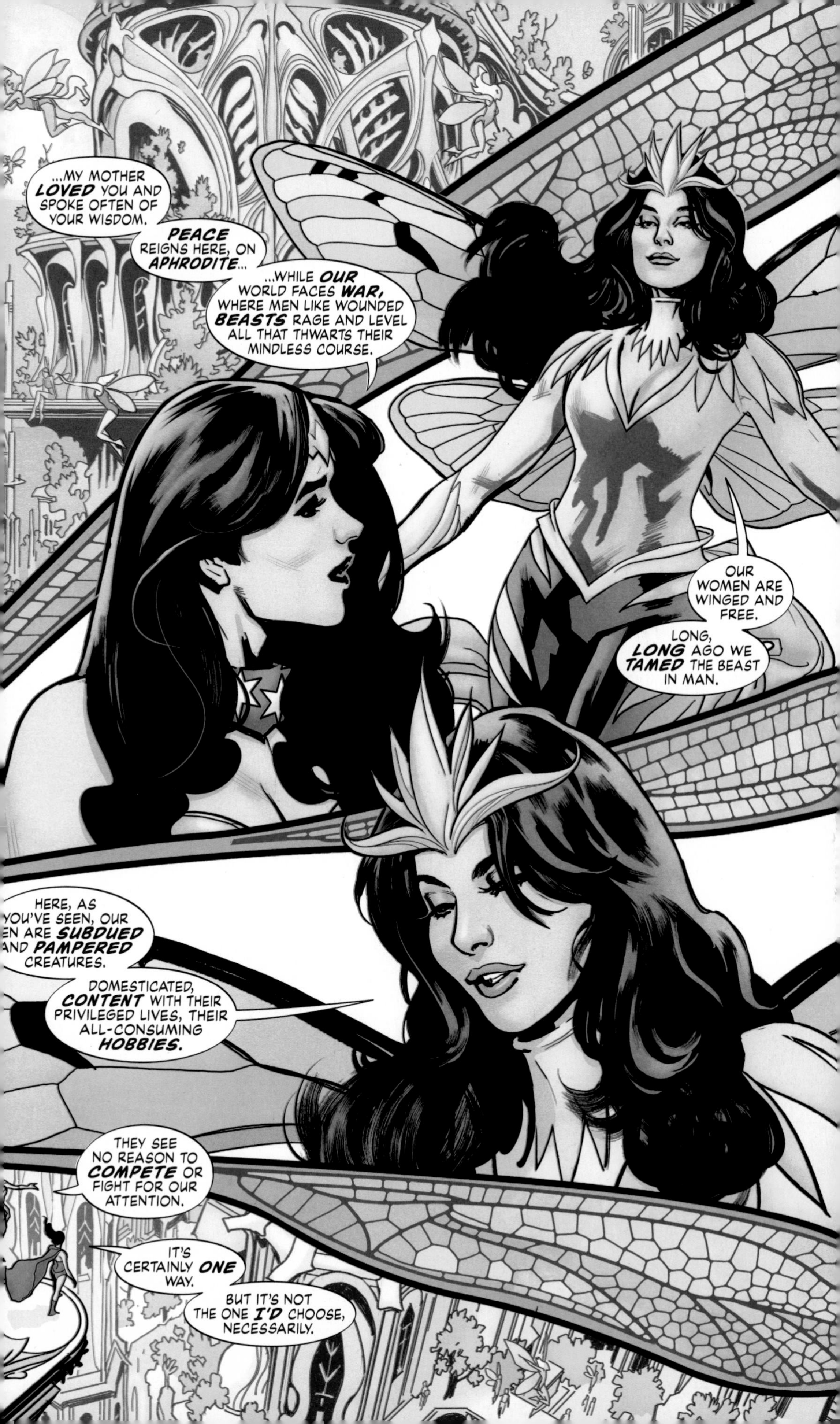
...MY MOTHER LOVED YOU AND SPOKE OFTEN OF YOUR WISDOM.
PEACE REIGNS HERE, ON APHRODITE...
...WHILE OUR WORLD FACES WAR, WHERE MEN LIKE WOUNDED BEASTS RAGE AND LEVEL ALL THAT THWARTS THEIR MINDLESS COURSE.
OUR WOMEN ARE WINGED AND FREE.
LONG, LONG AGO WE TAMED THE BEAST IN MAN.
HERE, AS YOU'VE SEEN, OUR EN ARE SUBDUED AND PAMPERED CREATURES.
DOMESTICATED, CONTENT WITH THEIR PRIVILEGED LIVES, THEIR ALL-CONSUMING HOBBIES.
THEY SEE NO REASON TO COMPETE OR FIGHT FOR OUR ATTENTION.
IT'S CERTAINLY ONE WAY.
BUT IT'S NOT THE ONE I'D CHOOSE, NECESSARILY.

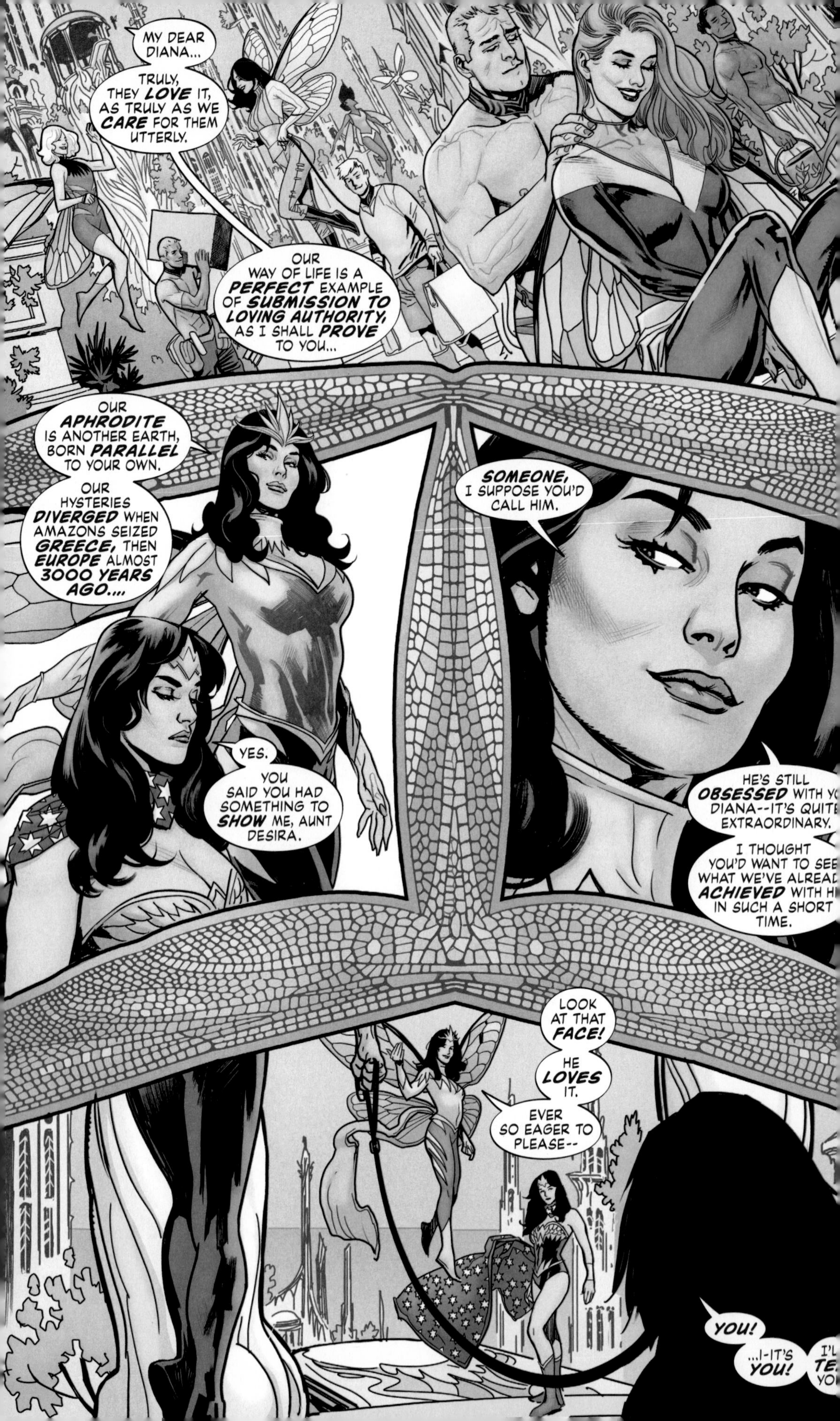
MY DEAR DIANA...
TRULY, THEY LOVE IT, AS TRULY AS WE CARE FOR THEM UTTERLY.
OUR WAY OF LIFE IS A PERFECT EXAMPLE OF SUBMISSION TO LOVING AUTHORITY, AS I SHALL PROVE TO YOU...
OUR APHRODITE IS ANOTHER EARTH, BORN PARALLEL TO YOUR OWN.
OUR HYSTERIES DIVERGED WHEN AMAZONS SEIZED GREECE, THEN EUROPE ALMOST 3000 YEARS AGO....
YES.
YOU SAID YOU HAD SOMETHING TO SHOW ME, AUNT DESIRA.
SOMEONE, I SUPPOSE YOU'D CALL HIM.
HE'S STILL OBSESSED WITH YO DIANA--IT'S QUITE EXTRAORDINARY.
I THOUGHT YOU'D WANT TO SEE WHAT WE'VE ALREAD ACHIEVED WITH HI IN SUCH A SHORT TIME.
LOOK AT THAT FACE!
HE LOVES IT.
EVER SO EAGER TO PLEASE--
YOU!
...I-IT'S YOU!

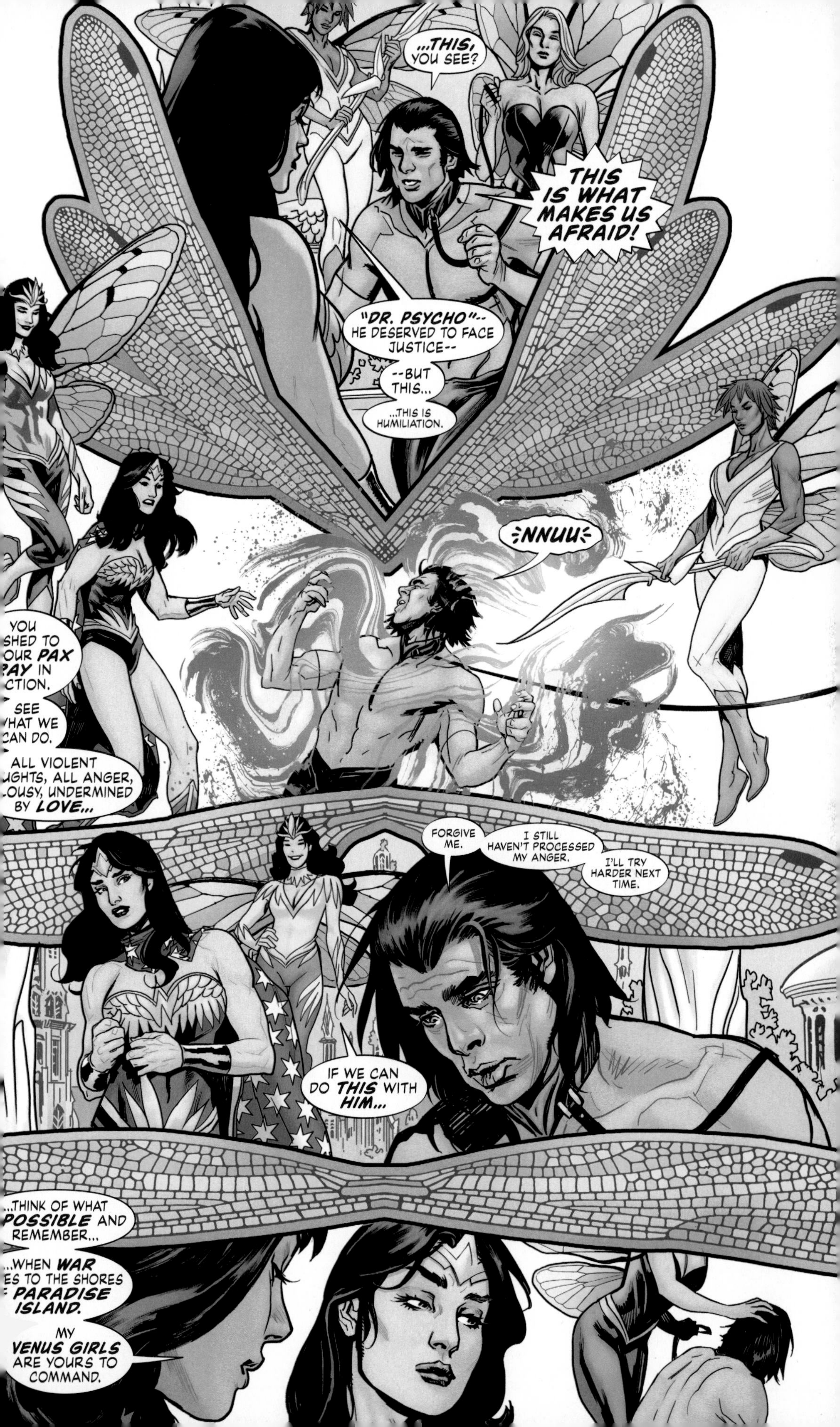
...THIS, YOU SEE?
THIS IS WHAT MAKES US AFRAID!
"DR. PSYCHO"-- HE DESERVED TO FACE JUSTICE--
--BUT THIS...
...THIS IS HUMILIATION.
NNUU
YOU
SHED TO
OUR PAX
AY IN
CTION.
SEE
HAT WE
CAN DO.
ALL VIOLENT
UGHTS, ALL ANGER,
LOUSY, UNDERMINED
BY LOVE...
FORGIVE ME.
I STILL HAVEN'T PROCESSED MY ANGER.
I'LL TRY HARDER NEXT TIME.
IF WE CAN DO THIS WITH HIM...
...THINK OF WHAT
POSSIBLE AND
REMEMBER...
...WHEN WAR
ES TO THE SHORES
PARADISE
ISLAND.
MY VENUS GIRLS ARE YOURS TO COMMAND.

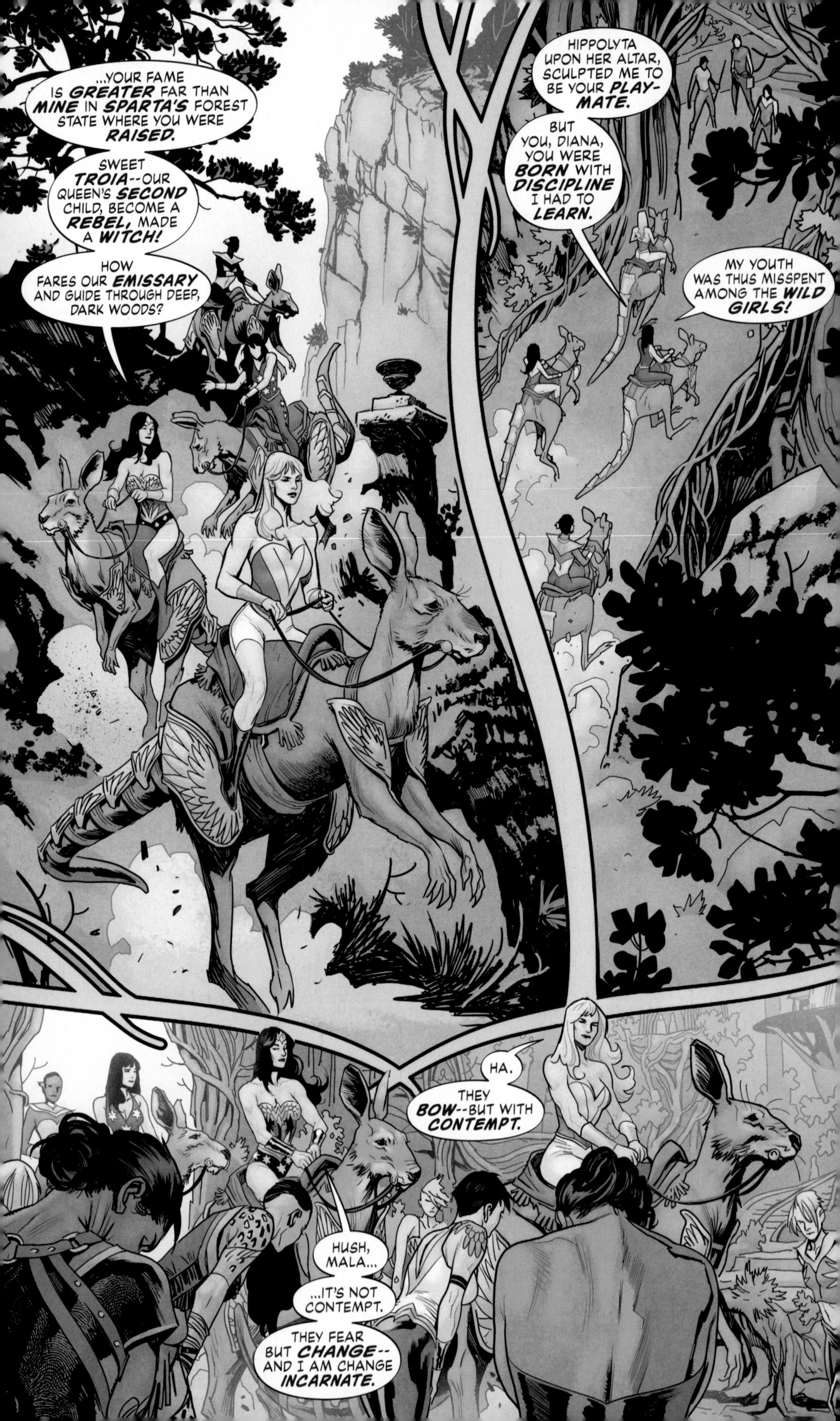
...YOUR FAME IS GREATER FAR THAN MINE IN SPARTA'S FOREST STATE WHERE YOU WERE RAISED.
SWEET TROIA--OUR QUEEN'S SECOND CHILD, BECOME A REBEL, MADE A WITCH!
HOW FARES OUR EMISSARY AND GUIDE THROUGH DEEP, DARK WOODS?
HIPPOLYTA UPON HER ALTAR, SCULPTED ME TO BE YOUR PLAYMATE.
BUT YOU, DIANA, YOU WERE BORN WITH DISCIPLINE I HAD TO LEARN.
MY YOUTH WAS THUS MISSPENT AMONG THE WILD GIRLS!
HA.
THEY BOW--BUT WITH CONTEMPT.
HUSH, MALA...
...IT'S NOT CONTEMPT.
THEY FEAR BUT CHANGE--AND I AM CHANGE INCARNATE.

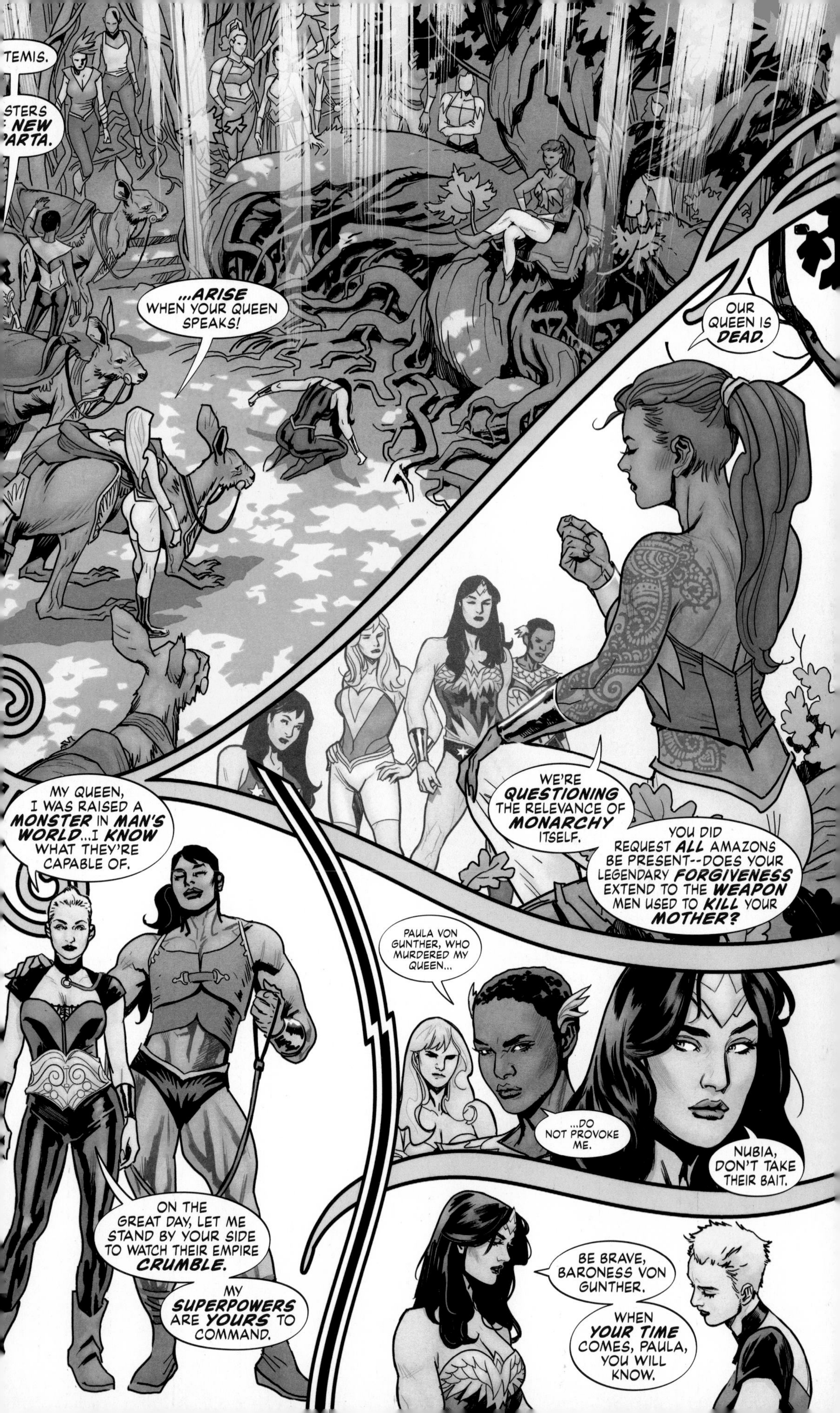
TEMIS.
STERS
NEW
PARTA.
...ARISE WHEN YOUR QUEEN SPEAKS!
OUR QUEEN IS DEAD.
WE'RE QUESTIONING THE RELEVANCE OF MONARCHY ITSELF.
YOU DID REQUEST ALL AMAZONS BE PRESENT--DOES YOUR LEGENDARY FORGIVENESS EXTEND TO THE WEAPON MEN USED TO KILL YOUR MOTHER?
MY QUEEN, I WAS RAISED A MONSTER IN MAN'S WORLD...I KNOW WHAT THEY'RE CAPABLE OF.
ON THE GREAT DAY, LET ME STAND BY YOUR SIDE TO WATCH THEIR EMPIRE CRUMBLE.
MY SUPERPOWERS ARE YOURS TO COMMAND.
PAULA VON GUNTHER, WHO MURDERED MY QUEEN...
...DO NOT PROVOKE ME.
NUBIA, DON'T TAKE THEIR BAIT.
BE BRAVE, BARONESS VON GUNTHER.
WHEN YOUR TIME COMES, PAULA, YOU WILL KNOW.

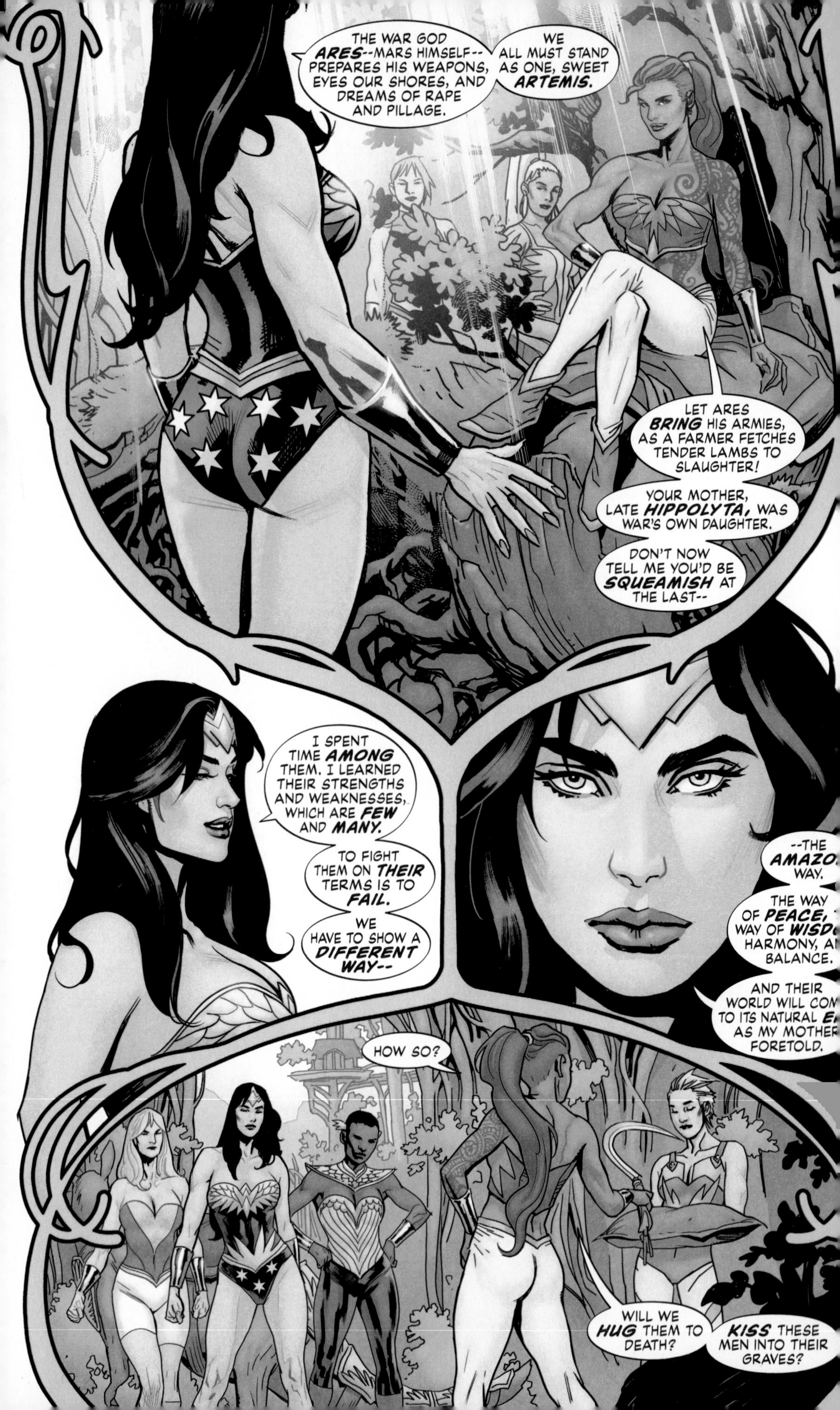

THE WAR GOD ARES--MARS HIMSELF--PREPARES HIS WEAPONS, EYES OUR SHORES, AND DREAMS OF RAPE AND PILLAGE.
WE ALL MUST STAND AS ONE, SWEET ARTEMIS.
LET ARES BRING HIS ARMIES, AS A FARMER FETCHES TENDER LAMBS TO SLAUGHTER!
YOUR MOTHER, LATE HIPPOLYTA, WAS WAR'S OWN DAUGHTER.
DON'T NOW TELL ME YOU'D BE SQUEAMISH AT THE LAST--
I SPENT TIME AMONG THEM. I LEARNED THEIR STRENGTHS AND WEAKNESSES, WHICH ARE FEW AND MANY.
TO FIGHT THEM ON THEIR TERMS IS TO FAIL.
WE HAVE TO SHOW A DIFFERENT WAY--
--THE AMAZO WAY.
THE WAY OF PEACE, WAY OF WISD HARMONY, A BALANCE.
AND THEIR WORLD WILL COM TO ITS NATURAL E AS MY MOTHER FORETOLD.
HOW SO?
WILL WE HUG THEM TO DEATH?
KISS THESE MEN INTO THEIR GRAVES?

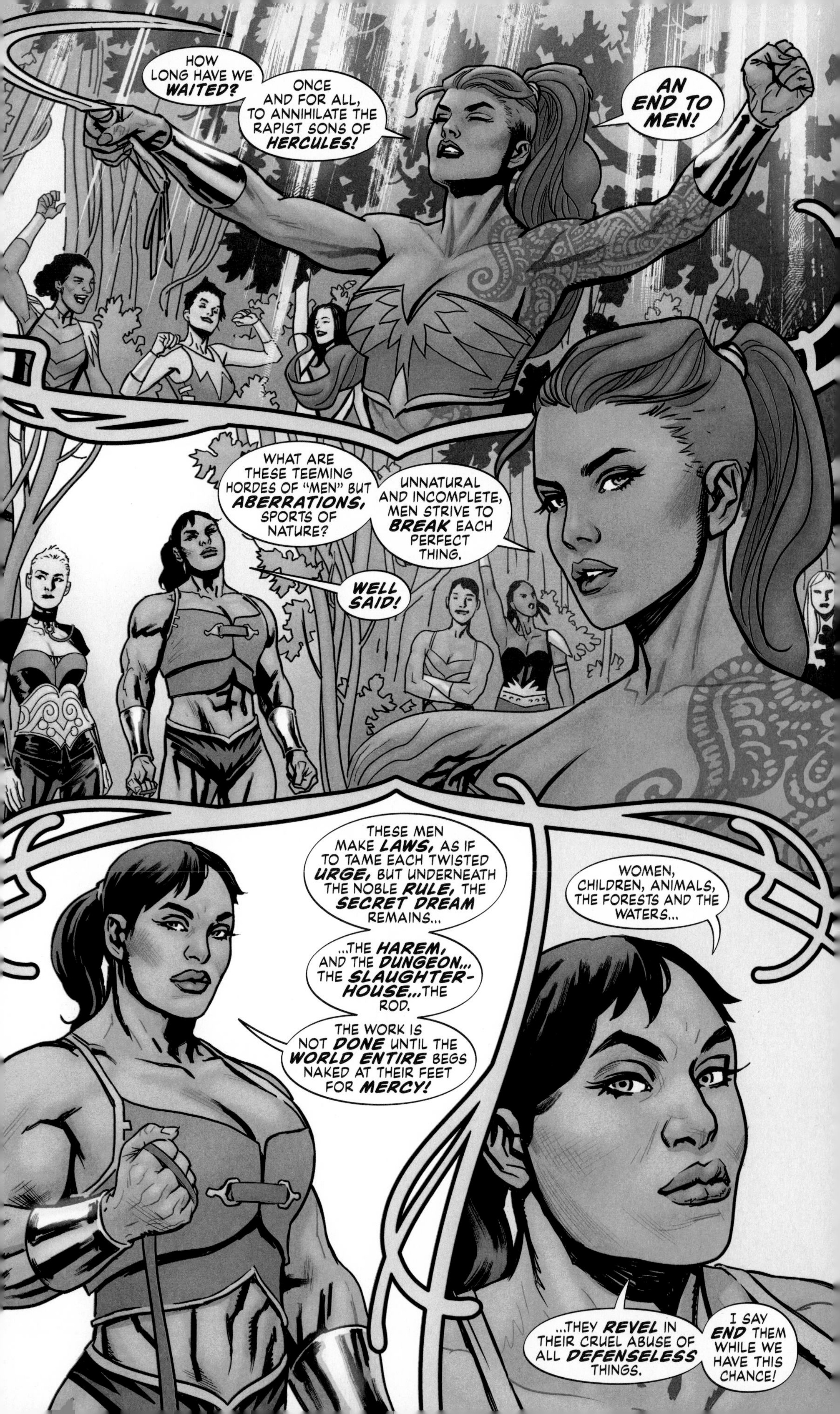
HOW LONG HAVE WE WAITED?
ONCE AND FOR ALL, TO ANNIHILATE THE RAPIST SONS OF HERCULES!
AN END TO MEN!
WHAT ARE THESE TEEMING HORDES OF "MEN" BUT ABERRATIONS, SPORTS OF NATURE?
UNNATURAL AND INCOMPLETE, MEN STRIVE TO BREAK EACH PERFECT THING.
WELL SAID!
THESE MEN MAKE LAWS, AS IF TO TAME EACH TWISTED URGE, BUT UNDERNEATH THE NOBLE RULE, THE SECRET DREAM REMAINS...
...THE HAREM, AND THE DUNGEON... THE SLAUGHTER-HOUSE...THE ROD.
THE WORK IS NOT DONE UNTIL THE WORLD ENTIRE BEGS NAKED AT THEIR FEET FOR MERCY!
WOMEN, CHILDREN, ANIMALS, THE FORESTS AND THE WATERS...
...THEY REVEL IN THEIR CRUEL ABUSE OF ALL DEFENSELESS THINGS.
I SAY END THEM WHILE WE HAVE THIS CHANCE!

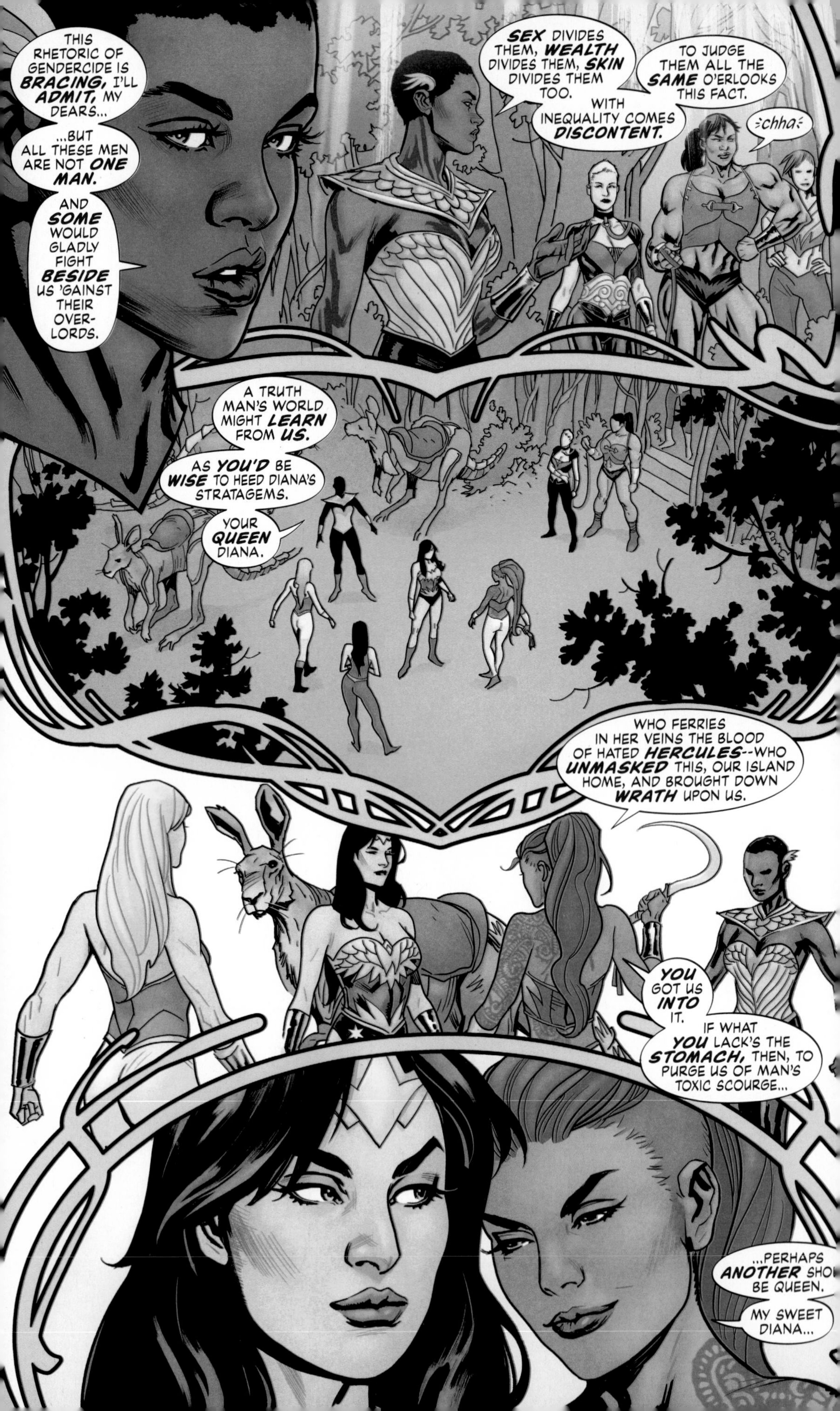
THIS RHETORIC OF GENDERCIDE IS BRACING, I'LL ADMIT, MY DEARS...
...BUT ALL THESE MEN ARE NOT ONE MAN.
AND SOME WOULD GLADLY FIGHT BESIDE US 'GAINST THEIR OVER-LORDS.
SEX DIVIDES THEM, WEALTH DIVIDES THEM, SKIN DIVIDES THEM TOO.
WITH INEQUALITY COMES DISCONTENT.
TO JUDGE THEM ALL THE SAME O'ERLOOKS THIS FACT.
chha
A TRUTH MAN'S WORLD MIGHT LEARN FROM US.
AS YOU'D BE WISE TO HEED DIANA'S STRATAGEMS.
YOUR QUEEN DIANA.
WHO FERRIES IN HER VEINS THE BLOOD OF HATED HERCULES--WHO UNMASKED THIS, OUR ISLAND HOME, AND BROUGHT DOWN WRATH UPON US.
YOU GOT US INTO IT.
IF WHAT YOU LACK'S THE STOMACH, THEN, TO PURGE US OF MAN'S TOXIC SCOURGE...
...PERHAPS ANOTHER SHO
BE QUEEN.
MY SWEET DIANA...

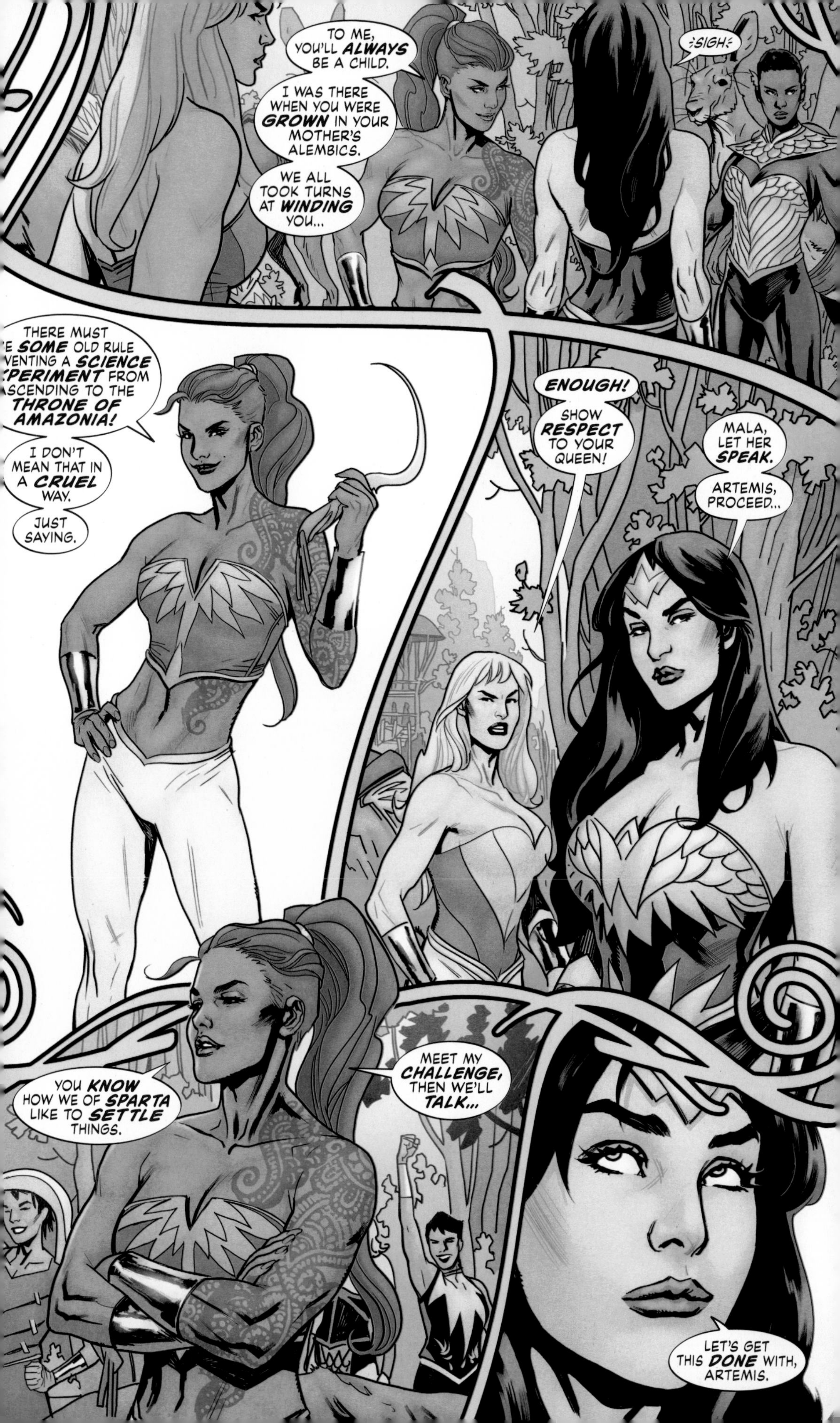
TO ME, YOU'LL ALWAYS BE A CHILD.
I WAS THERE WHEN YOU WERE GROWN IN YOUR MOTHER'S ALEMBICS.
WE ALL TOOK TURNS AT WINDING YOU...
SIGH
THERE MUST BE SOME OLD RULE PREVENTING A SCIENCE EXPERIMENT FROM ASCENDING TO THE THRONE OF AMAZONIA!
I DON'T MEAN THAT IN A CRUEL WAY.
JUST SAYING.
ENOUGH!
SHOW RESPECT TO YOUR QUEEN!
MALA, LET HER SPEAK.
ARTEMIS, PROCEED...
YOU KNOW HOW WE OF SPARTA LIKE TO SETTLE THINGS.
MEET MY CHALLENGE, THEN WE'LL TALK...
LET'S GET THIS DONE WITH, ARTEMIS.

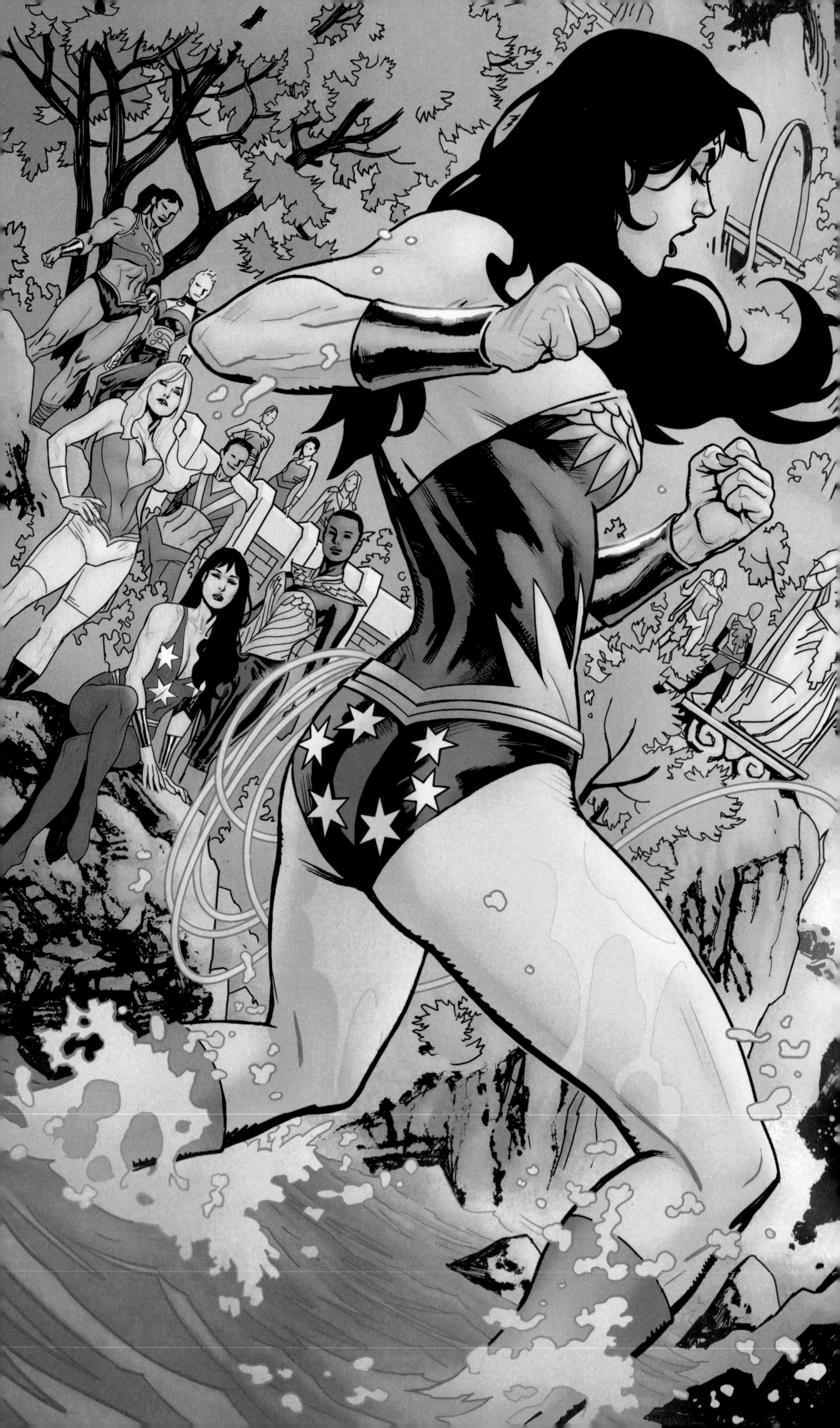

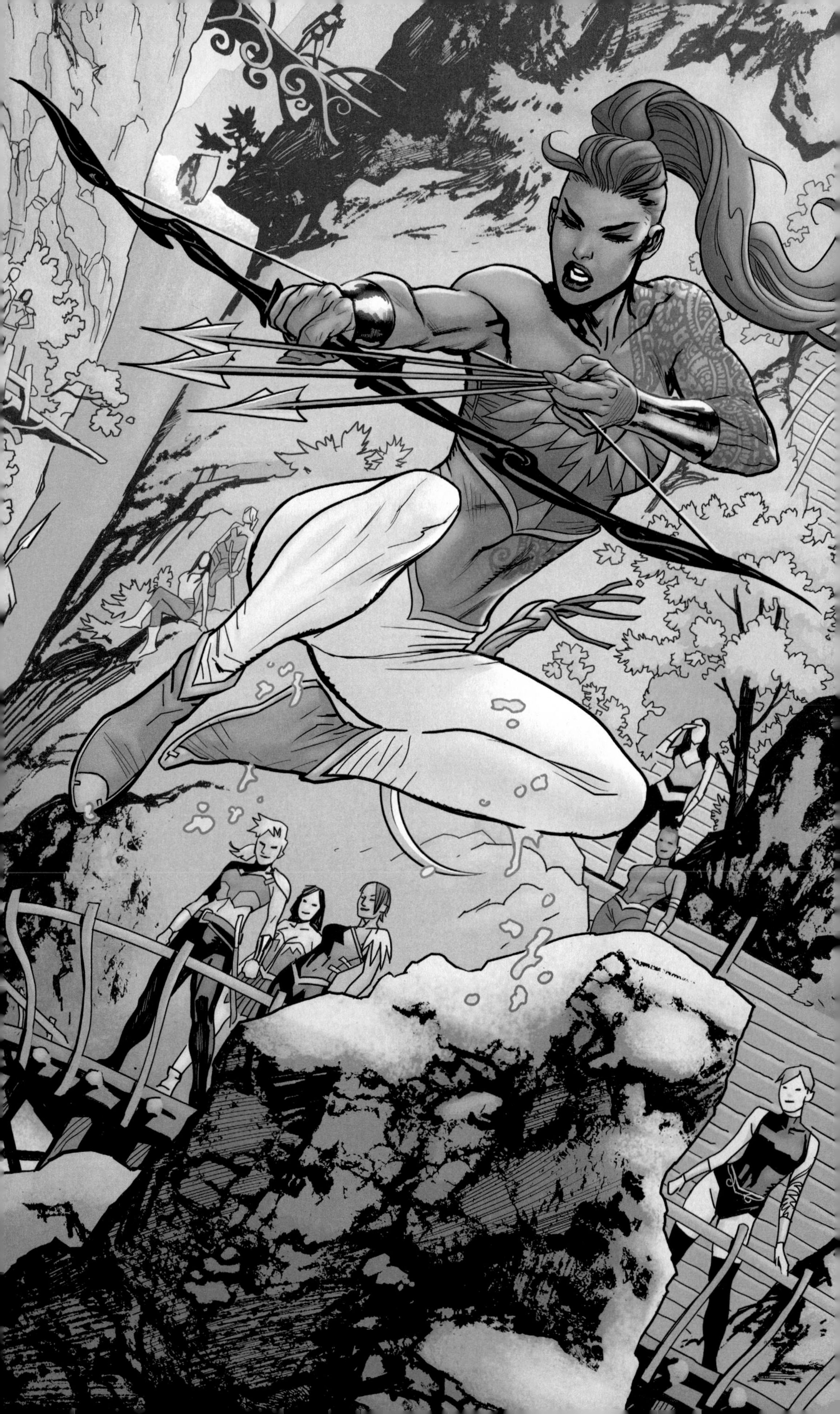

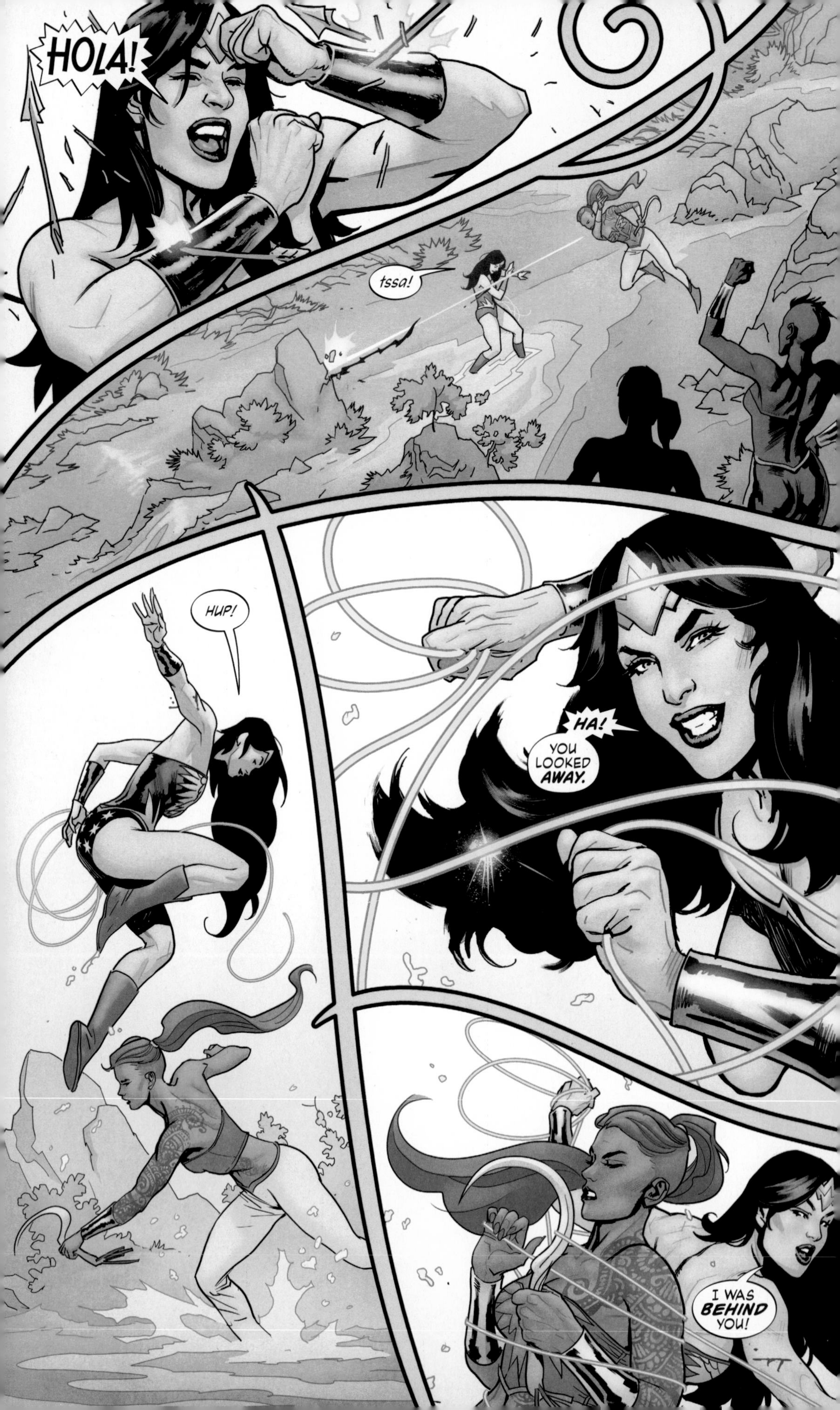
HOLA!
tssa!
HUP!
HA!
YOU LOOKED AWAY.
I WAS BEHIND YOU!

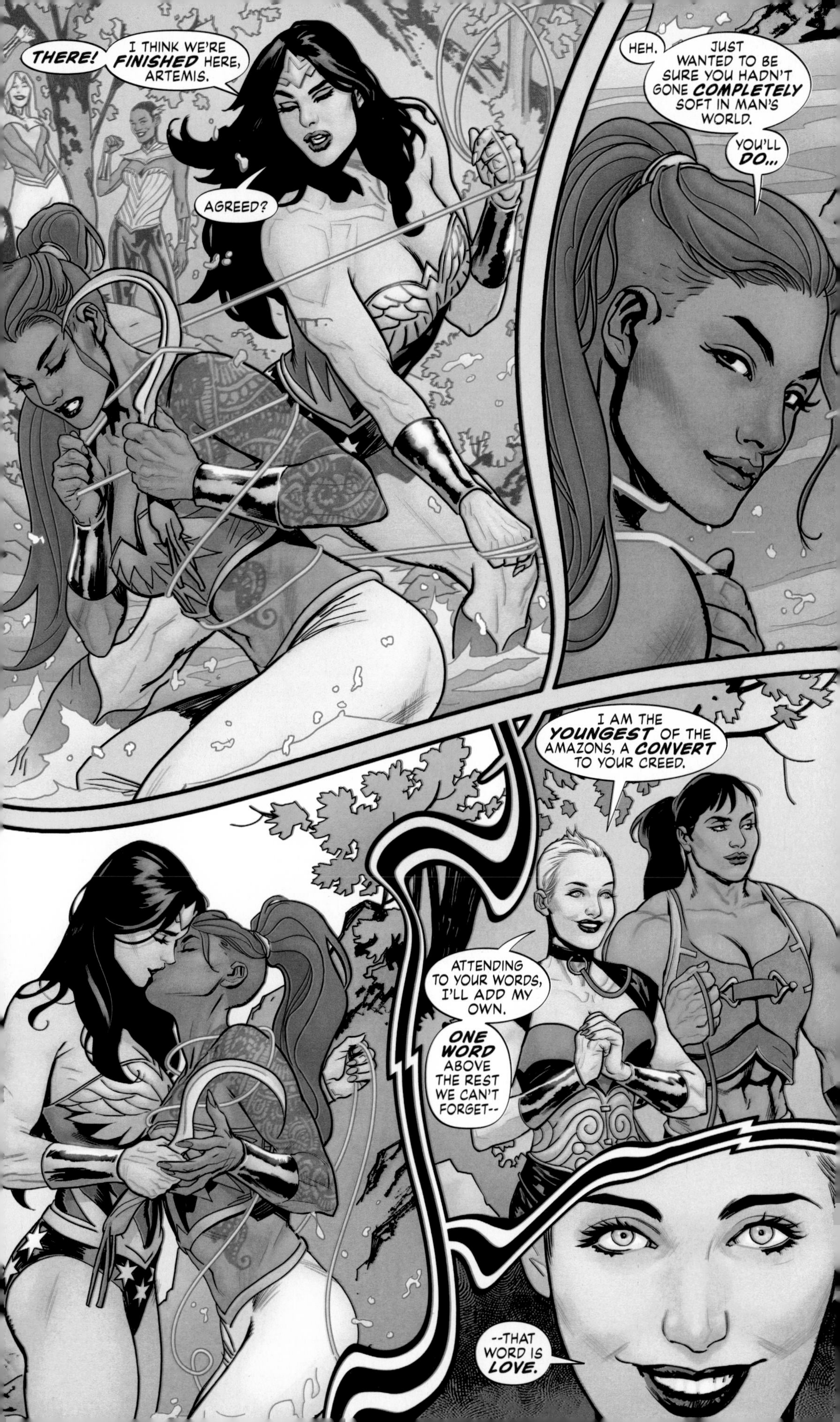
THERE!
I THINK WE'RE FINISHED HERE, ARTEMIS.
AGREED?
HEH.
JUST WANTED TO BE SURE YOU HADN'T GONE COMPLETELY SOFT IN MAN'S WORLD.
YOU'LL DO...
I AM THE YOUNGEST OF THE AMAZONS, A CONVERT TO YOUR CREED.
ATTENDING TO YOUR WORDS, I'LL ADD MY OWN.
ONE WORD ABOVE THE REST WE CAN'T FORGET--
--THAT WORD IS LOVE.

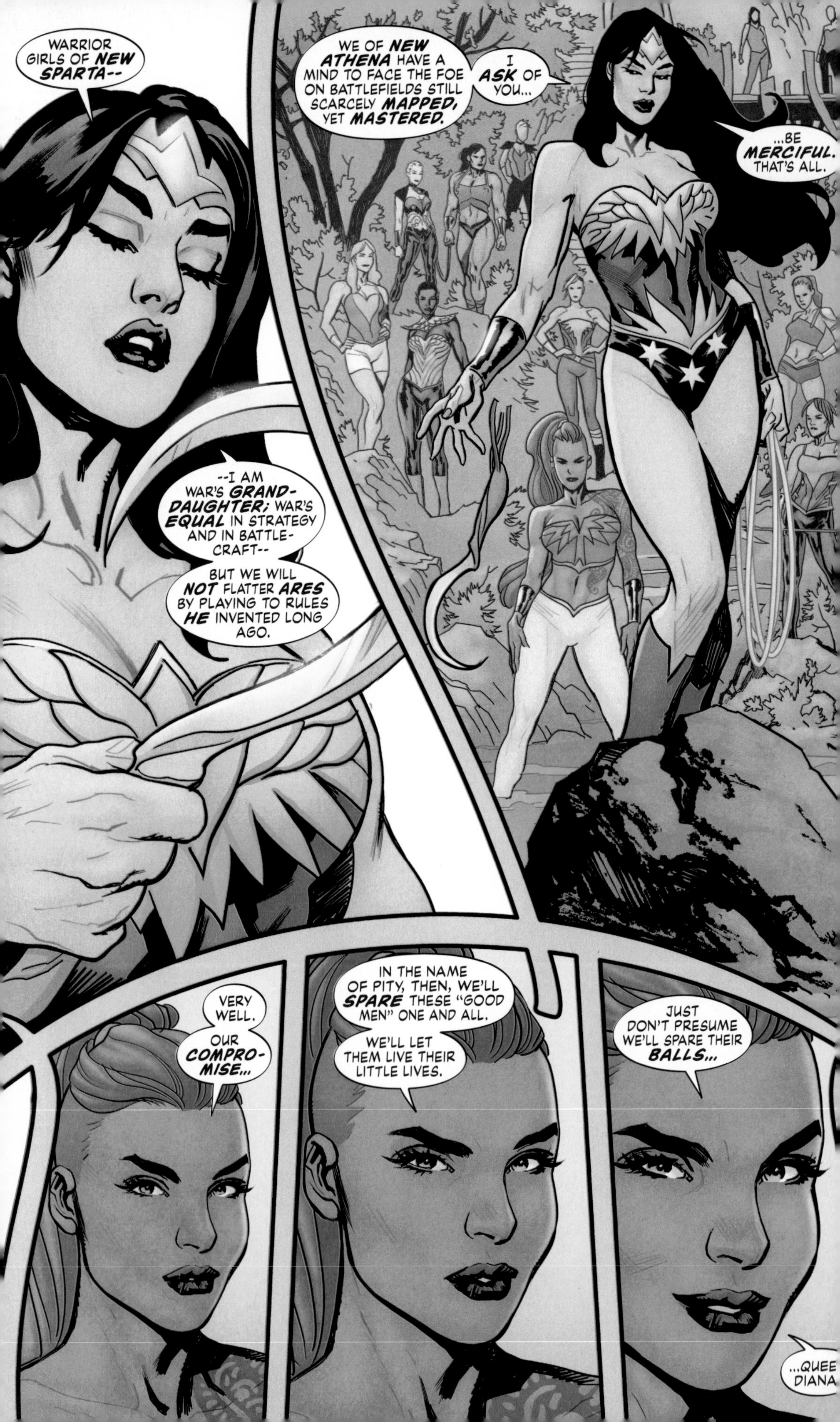
WARRIOR GIRLS OF NEW SPARTA--
--I AM WAR'S GRAND-DAUGHTER; WAR'S EQUAL IN STRATEGY AND IN BATTLE-CRAFT--
BUT WE WILL NOT FLATTER ARES BY PLAYING TO RULES HE INVENTED LONG AGO.
WE OF NEW ATHENA HAVE A MIND TO FACE THE FOE ON BATTLEFIELDS STILL SCARCELY MAPPED, YET MASTERED.
I ASK OF YOU...
...BE MERCIFUL. THAT'S ALL.
VERY WELL.
OUR COMPRO-MISE...
IN THE NAME OF PITY, THEN, WE'LL SPARE THESE "GOOD MEN" ONE AND ALL.
WE'LL LET THEM LIVE THEIR LITTLE LIVES.
JUST DON'T PRESUME WE'LL SPARE THEIR BALLS...

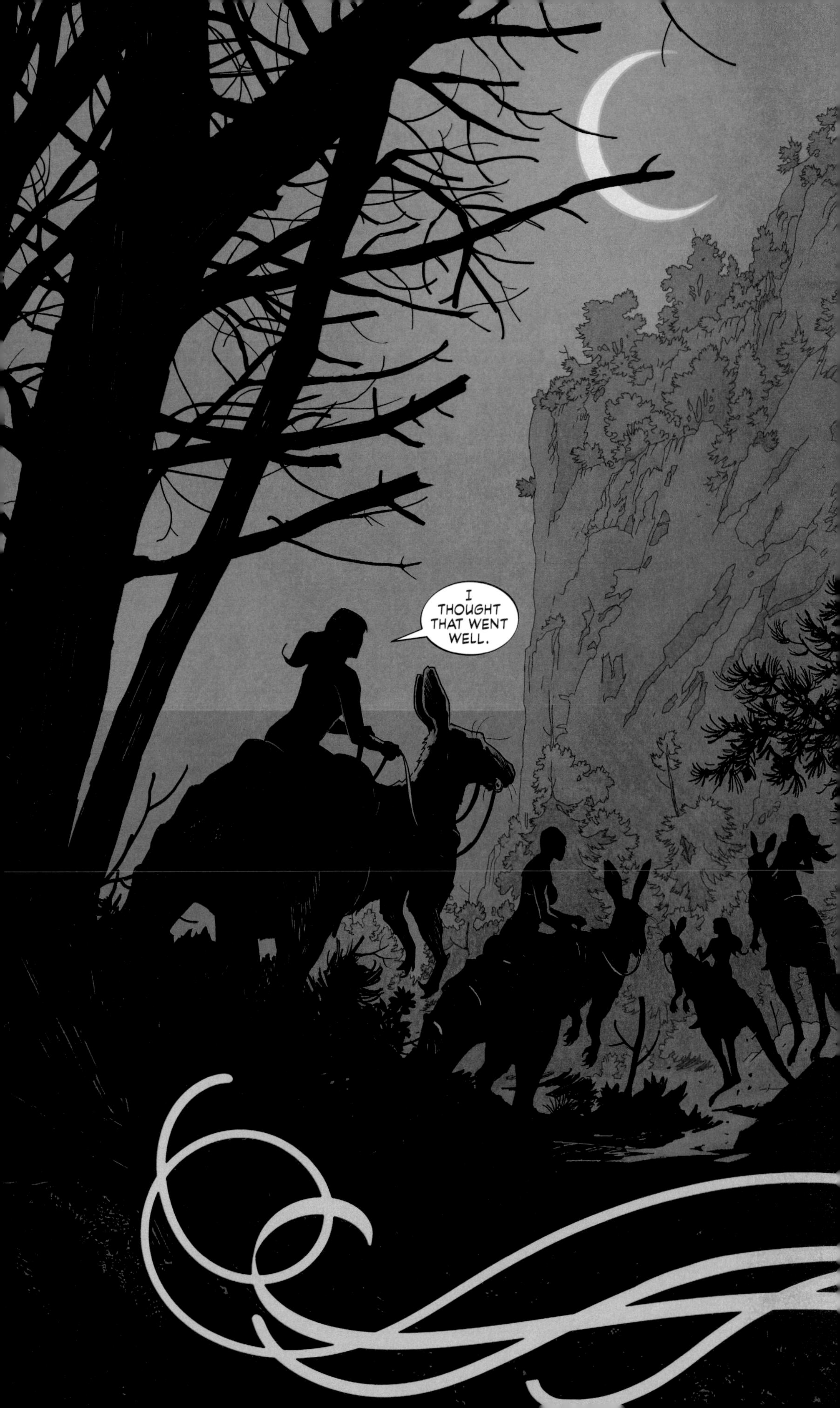
I THOUGHT THAT WENT WELL.

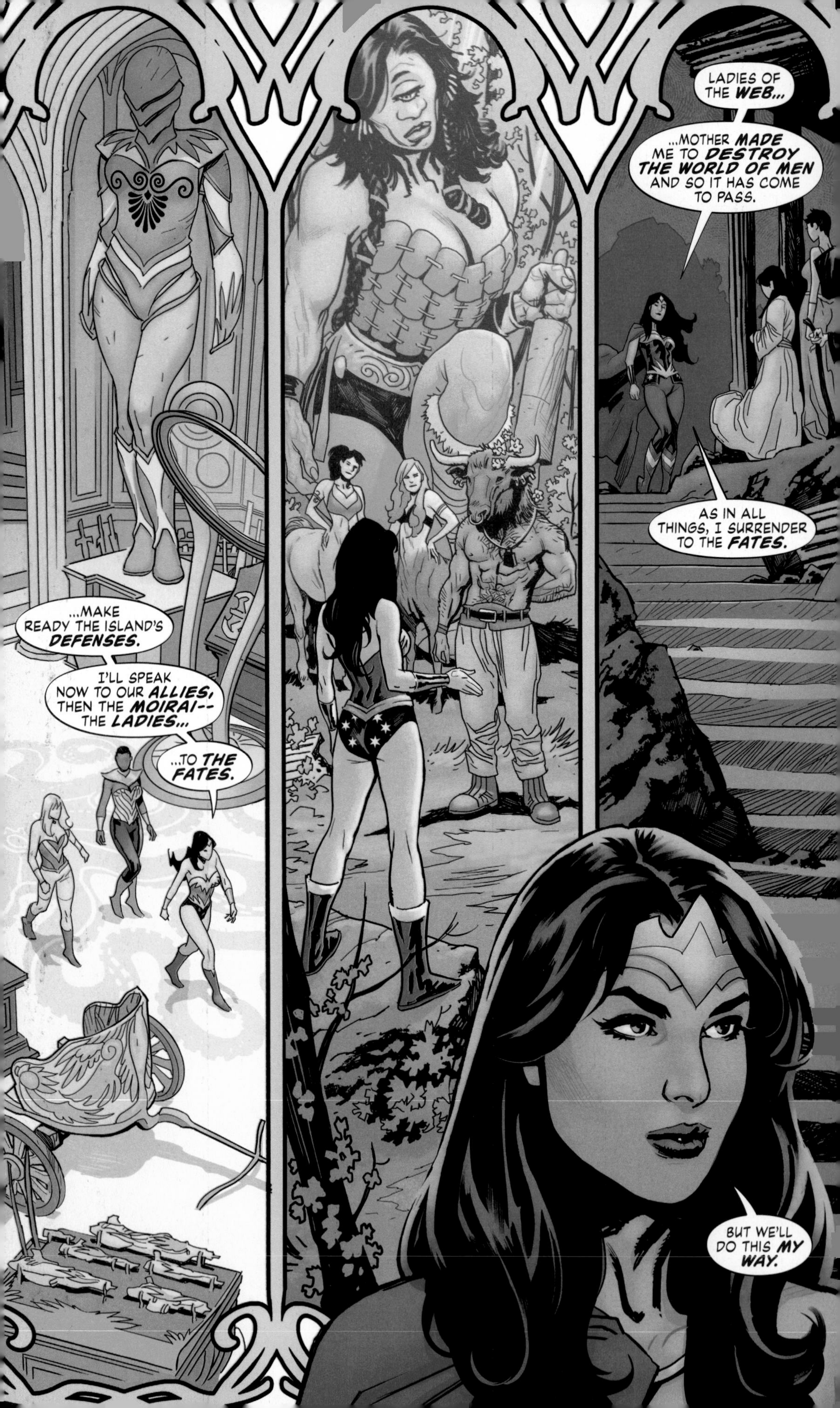
...MAKE READY THE ISLAND'S DEFENSES.
I'LL SPEAK NOW TO OUR ALLIES, THEN THE MOIRAI-- THE LADIES...
...TO THE FATES.
LADIES OF THE WEB...
...MOTHER MADE ME TO DESTROY THE WORLD OF MEN AND SO IT HAS COME TO PASS.
AS IN ALL THINGS, I SURRENDER TO THE FATES.
BUT WE'LL DO THIS MY WAY.

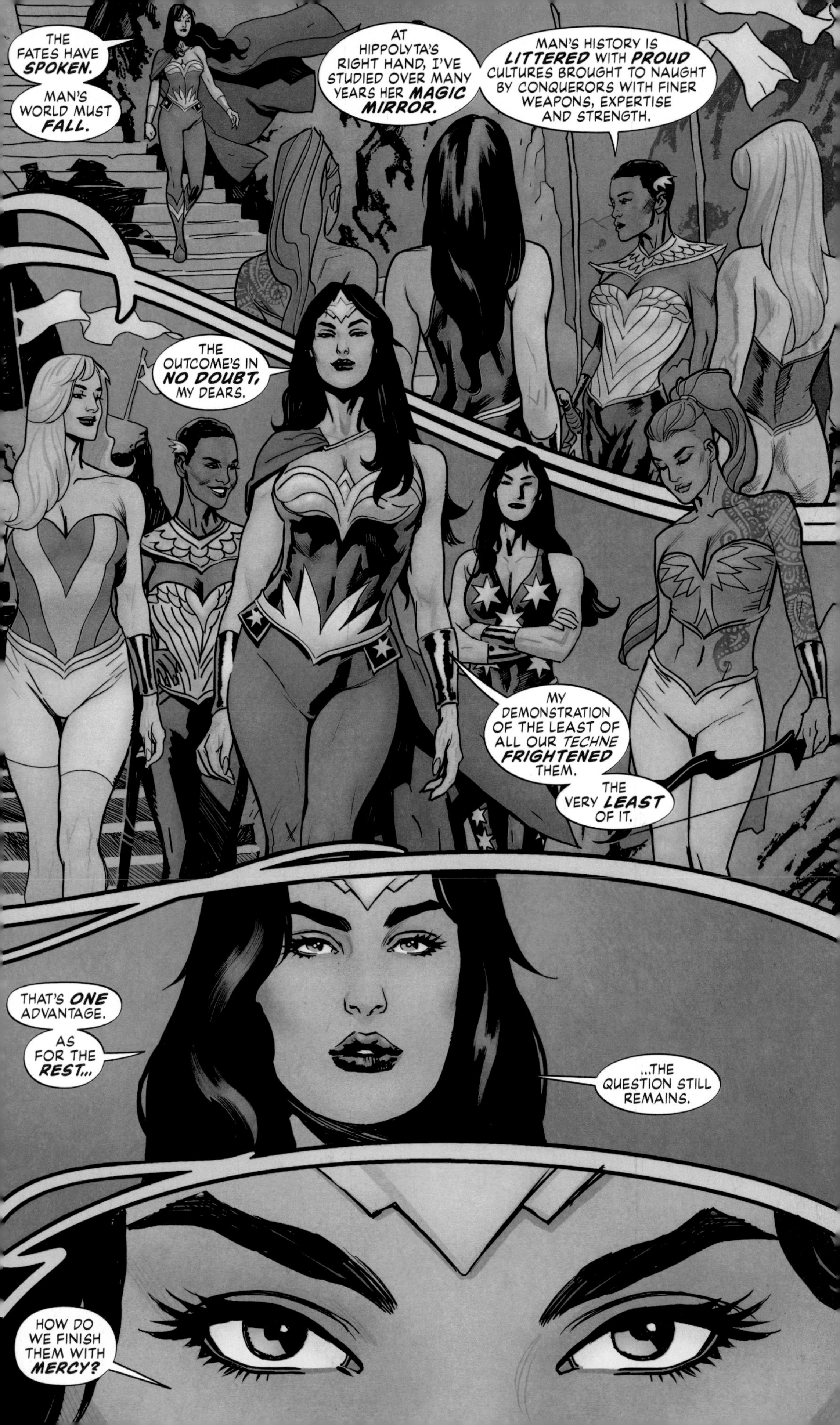

THE FATES HAVE SPOKEN.
MAN'S WORLD MUST FALL.
AT HIPPOLYTA'S RIGHT HAND, I'VE STUDIED OVER MANY YEARS HER MAGIC MIRROR.
MAN'S HISTORY IS LITTERED WITH PROUD CULTURES BROUGHT TO NAUGHT BY CONQUERORS WITH FINER WEAPONS, EXPERTISE AND STRENGTH.
THE OUTCOME'S IN NO DOUBT, MY DEARS.
MY DEMONSTRATION OF THE LEAST OF ALL OUR TECHNE FRIGHTENED THEM.
THE VERY LEAST OF IT.
THAT'S ONE ADVANTAGE.
AS FOR THE REST...
...THE QUESTION STILL REMAINS.
HOW DO WE FINISH THEM WITH MERCY?

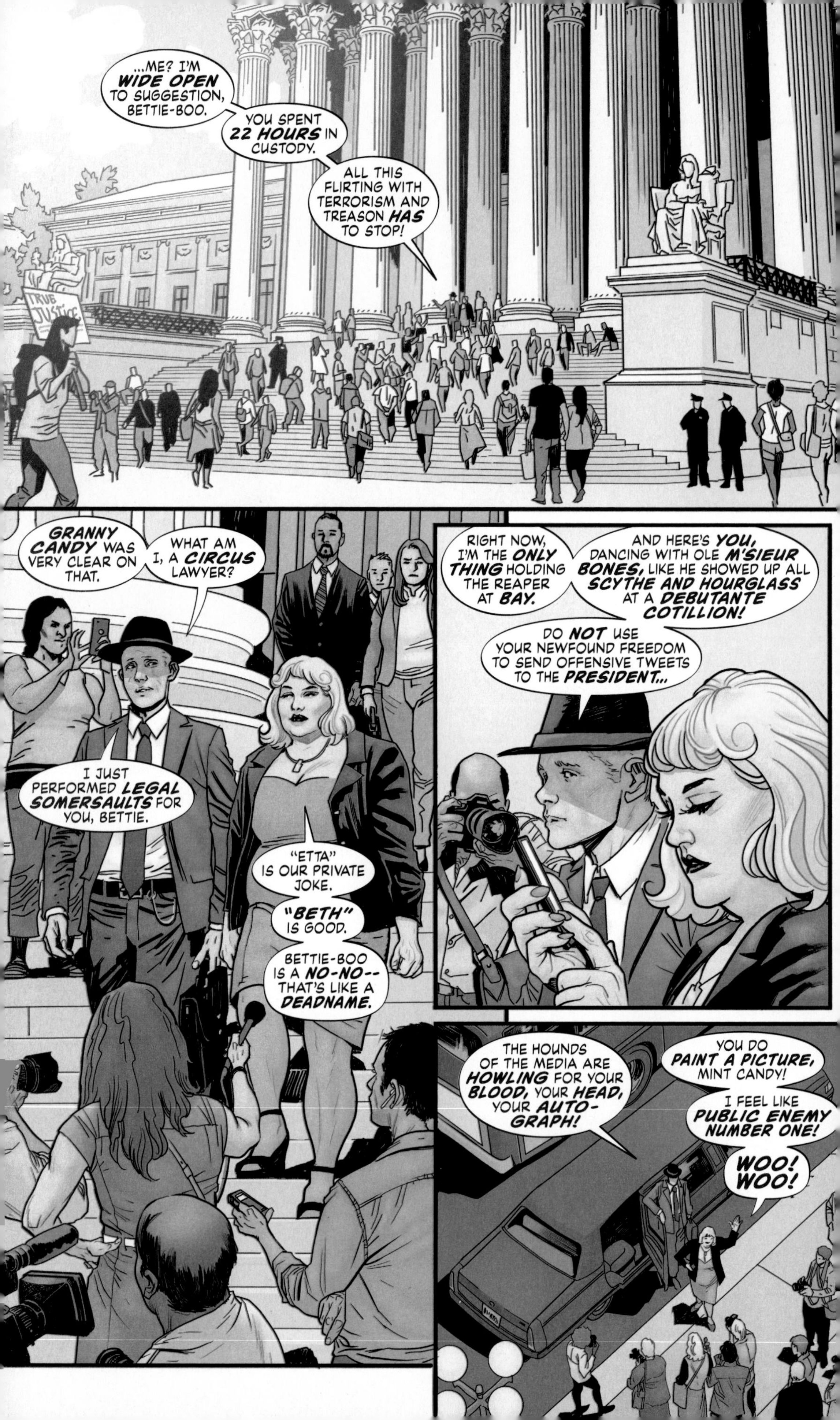

...ME? I'M WIDE OPEN TO SUGGESTION, BETTIE-BOO.
YOU SPENT 22 HOURS IN CUSTODY.
ALL THIS FLIRTING WITH TERRORISM AND TREASON HAS TO STOP!
TRUE JUSTICE
GRANNY CANDY WAS VERY CLEAR ON THAT.
WHAT AM I, A CIRCUS LAWYER?
I JUST PERFORMED LEGAL SOMERSAULTS FOR YOU, BETTIE.
"ETTA" IS OUR PRIVATE JOKE.
"BETH" IS GOOD.
BETTIE-BOO IS A NO-NO-- THAT'S LIKE A DEADNAME.
RIGHT NOW, I'M THE ONLY THING HOLDING THE REAPER AT BAY.
AND HERE'S YOU, DANCING WITH OLE M'SIEUR BONES, LIKE HE SHOWED UP ALL SCYTHE AND HOURGLASS AT A DEBUTANTE COTILLION!
DO NOT USE YOUR NEWFOUND FREEDOM TO SEND OFFENSIVE TWEETS TO THE PRESIDENT...
THE HOUNDS OF THE MEDIA ARE HOWLING FOR YOUR BLOOD, YOUR HEAD, YOUR AUTO-GRAPH!
YOU DO PAINT A PICTURE, MINT CANDY!
I FEEL LIKE PUBLIC ENEMY NUMBER ONE!
WOO! WOO!

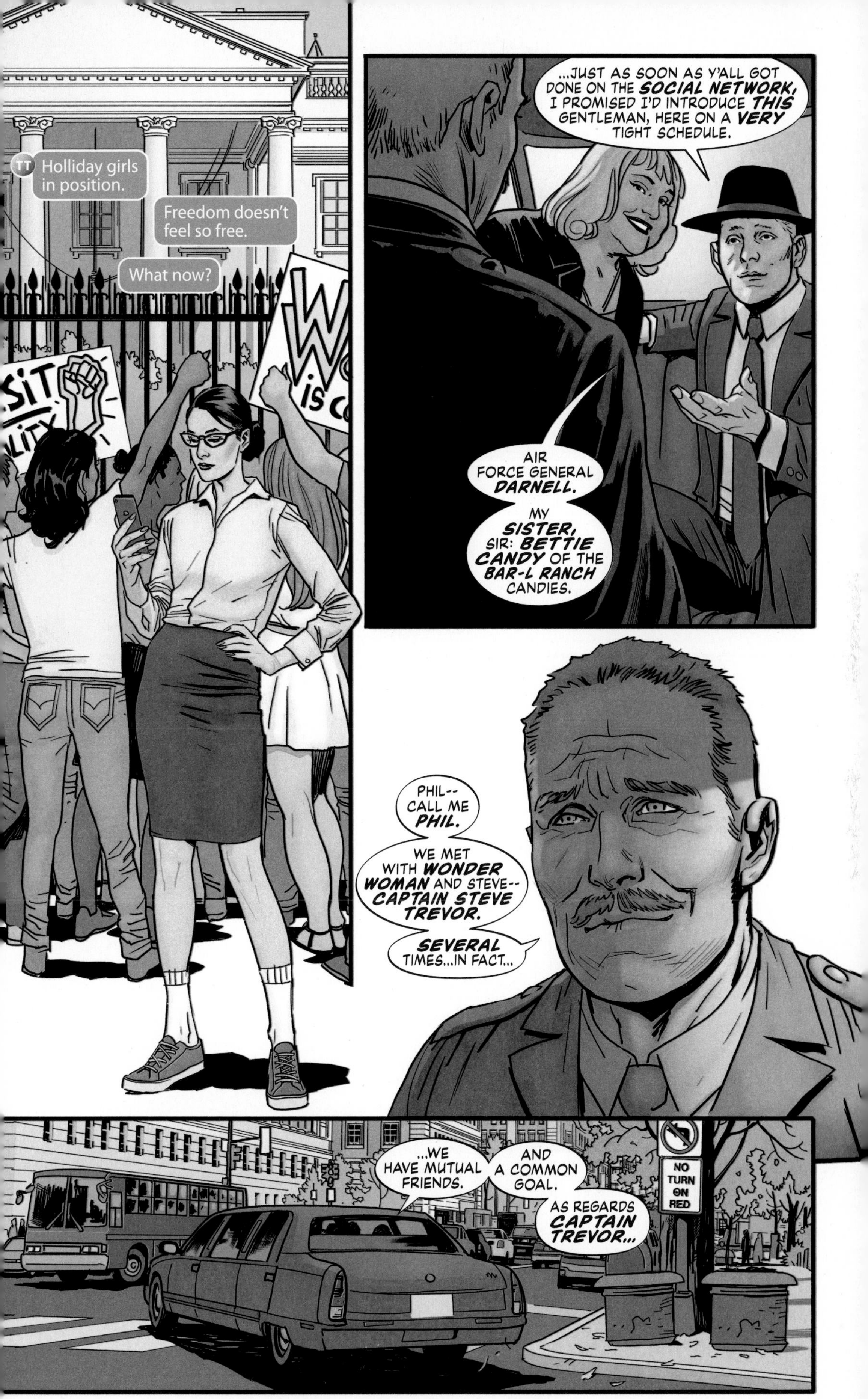
Holliday girls in position.
Freedom doesn't feel so free.
What now?
SIT
IS C
...JUST AS SOON AS Y'ALL GOT DONE ON THE SOCIAL NETWORK, I PROMISED I'D INTRODUCE THIS GENTLEMAN, HERE ON A VERY TIGHT SCHEDULE.
AIR FORCE GENERAL DARNELL.
MY SISTER, SIR: BETTIE CANDY OF THE BAR-L RANCH CANDIES.
PHIL-- CALL ME PHIL.
WE MET WITH WONDER WOMAN AND STEVE-- CAPTAIN STEVE TREVOR.
SEVERAL TIMES...IN FACT...
...WE HAVE MUTUAL FRIENDS.
AND A COMMON GOAL.
AS REGARDS CAPTAIN TREVOR...
NO TURN ON RED

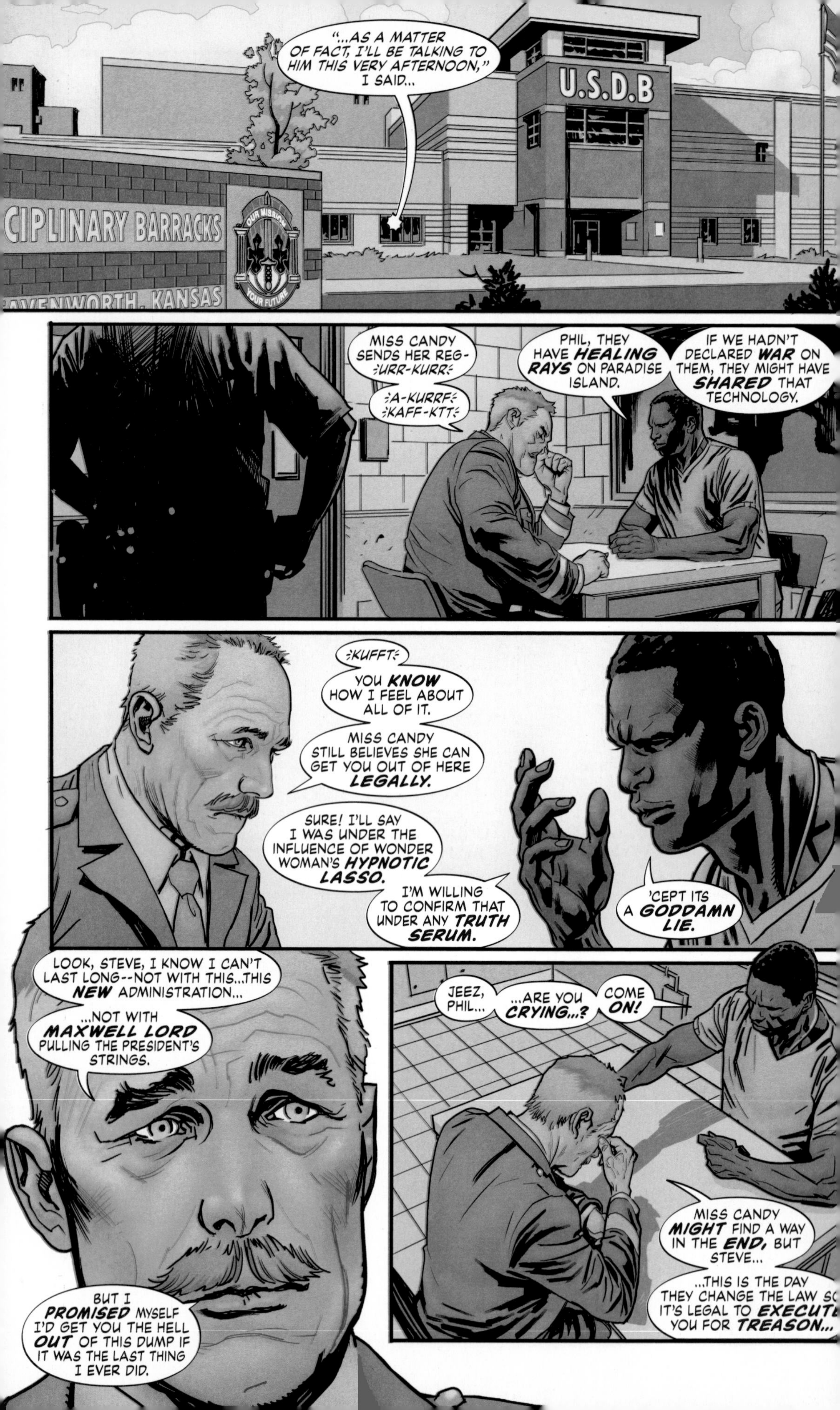
"...AS A MATTER OF FACT, I'LL BE TALKING TO HIM THIS VERY AFTERNOON," I SAID...
U.S.D.B
CIPLINARY BARRACKS
AVENWORTH, KANSAS
OUR MISSION
YOUR FUTURE
MISS CANDY SENDS HER REG- URR-KURR
A-KURRF KAFF-KTT
PHIL, THEY HAVE HEALING RAYS ON PARADISE ISLAND.
IF WE HADN'T DECLARED WAR ON THEM, THEY MIGHT HAVE SHARED THAT TECHNOLOGY.
KUFFT
YOU KNOW HOW I FEEL ABOUT ALL OF IT.
MISS CANDY STILL BELIEVES SHE CAN GET YOU OUT OF HERE LEGALLY.
SURE! I'LL SAY I WAS UNDER THE INFLUENCE OF WONDER WOMAN'S HYPNOTIC LASSO.
I'M WILLING TO CONFIRM THAT UNDER ANY TRUTH SERUM.
'CEPT ITS A GODDAMN LIE.
LOOK, STEVE, I KNOW I CAN'T LAST LONG--NOT WITH THIS...THIS NEW ADMINISTRATION...
...NOT WITH MAXWELL LORD PULLING THE PRESIDENT'S STRINGS.
BUT I PROMISED MYSELF I'D GET YOU THE HELL OUT OF THIS DUMP IF IT WAS THE LAST THING I EVER DID.
JEEZ, PHIL...
...ARE YOU CRYING...?
COME ON!
MISS CANDY MIGHT FIND A WAY IN THE END, BUT STEVE...
...THIS IS THE DAY THEY CHANGE THE LAW SO IT'S LEGAL TO EXECUTE YOU FOR TREASON...

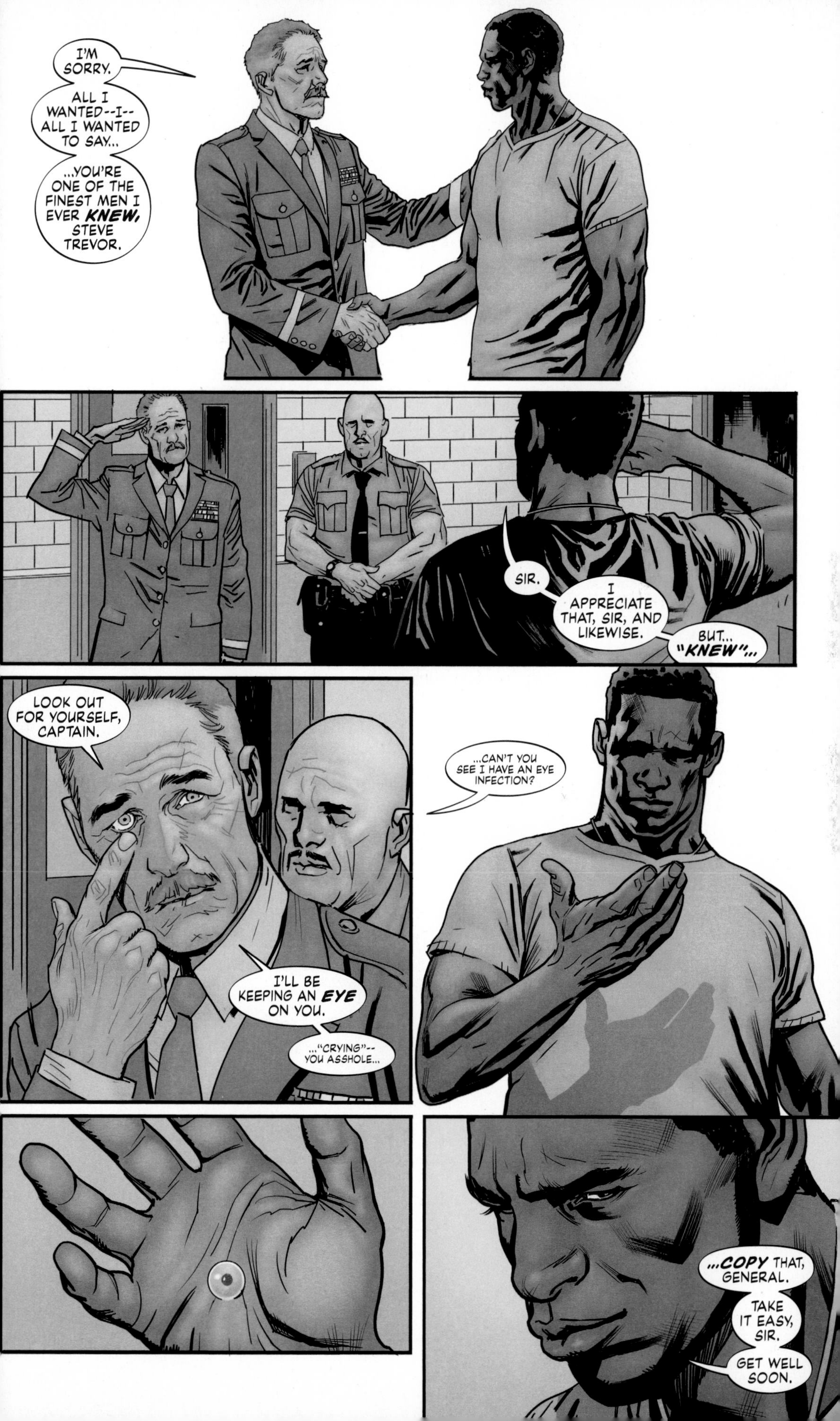
I'M SORRY.
ALL I WANTED--I-- ALL I WANTED TO SAY...
...YOU'RE ONE OF THE FINEST MEN I EVER KNEW, STEVE TREVOR.
SIR.
I APPRECIATE THAT, SIR, AND LIKEWISE.
BUT... "KNEW"...
LOOK OUT FOR YOURSELF, CAPTAIN.
...CAN'T YOU SEE I HAVE AN EYE INFECTION?
I'LL BE KEEPING AN EYE ON YOU.
..."CRYING"-- YOU ASSHOLE...
...COPY THAT, GENERAL.
TAKE IT EASY, SIR.
GET WELL SOON.

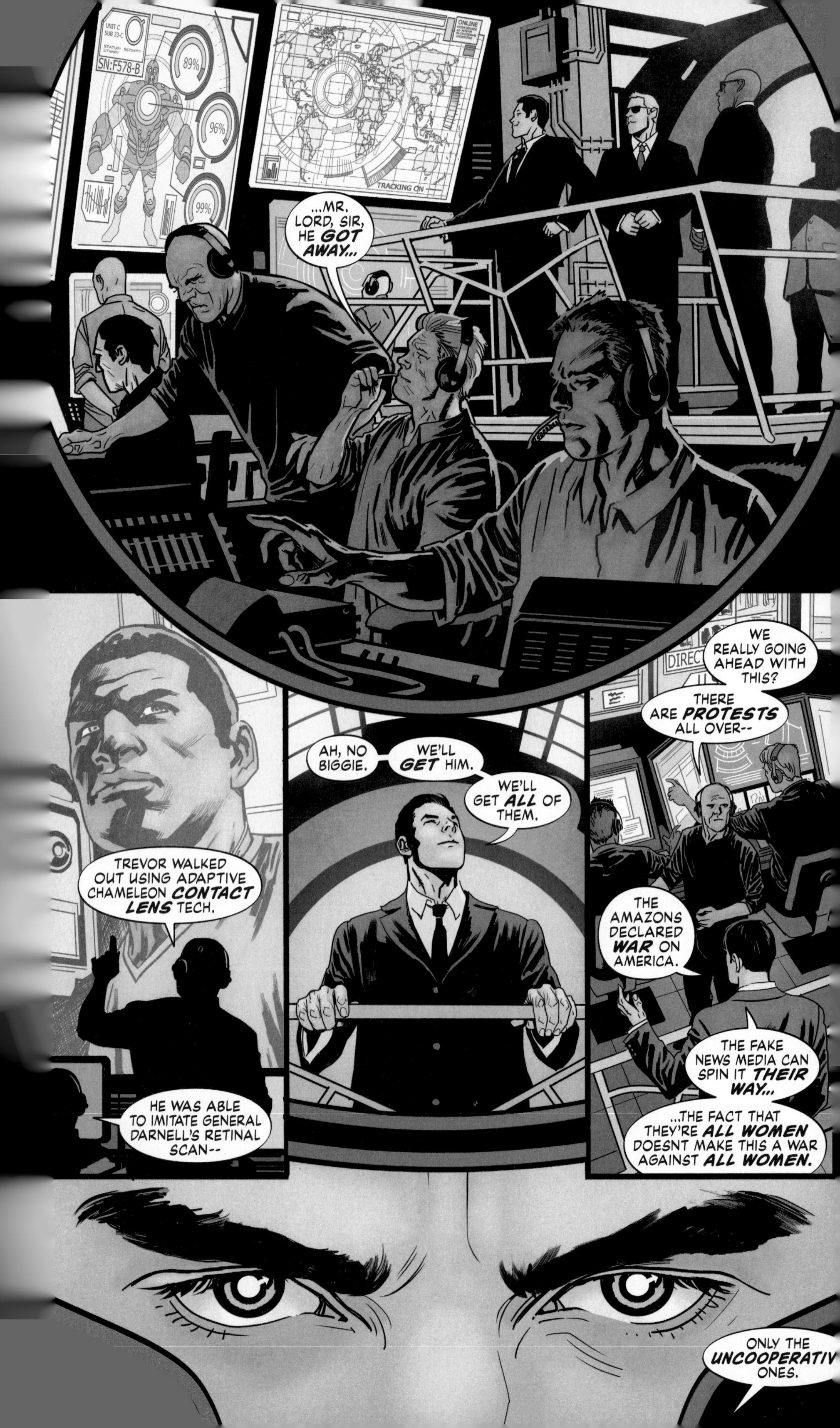
UNIT C
SUB 23-C
SN:F578-B
89%
96%
99%
ONLINE
TRACKING ON
...MR. LORD, SIR, HE GOT AWAY...
TREVOR WALKED OUT USING ADAPTIVE CHAMELEON CONTACT LENS TECH.
HE WAS ABLE TO IMITATE GENERAL DARNELL'S RETINAL SCAN--
AH, NO BIGGIE.
WE'LL GET HIM.
WE'LL GET ALL OF THEM.
WE REALLY GOING AHEAD WITH THIS?
THERE ARE PROTESTS ALL OVER--
THE AMAZONS DECLARED WAR ON AMERICA.
THE FAKE NEWS MEDIA CAN SPIN IT THEIR WAY...
...THE FACT THAT THEY'RE ALL WOMEN DOESN'T MAKE THIS A WAR AGAINST ALL WOMEN.
ONLY THE UNCOOPERATIV ONES.

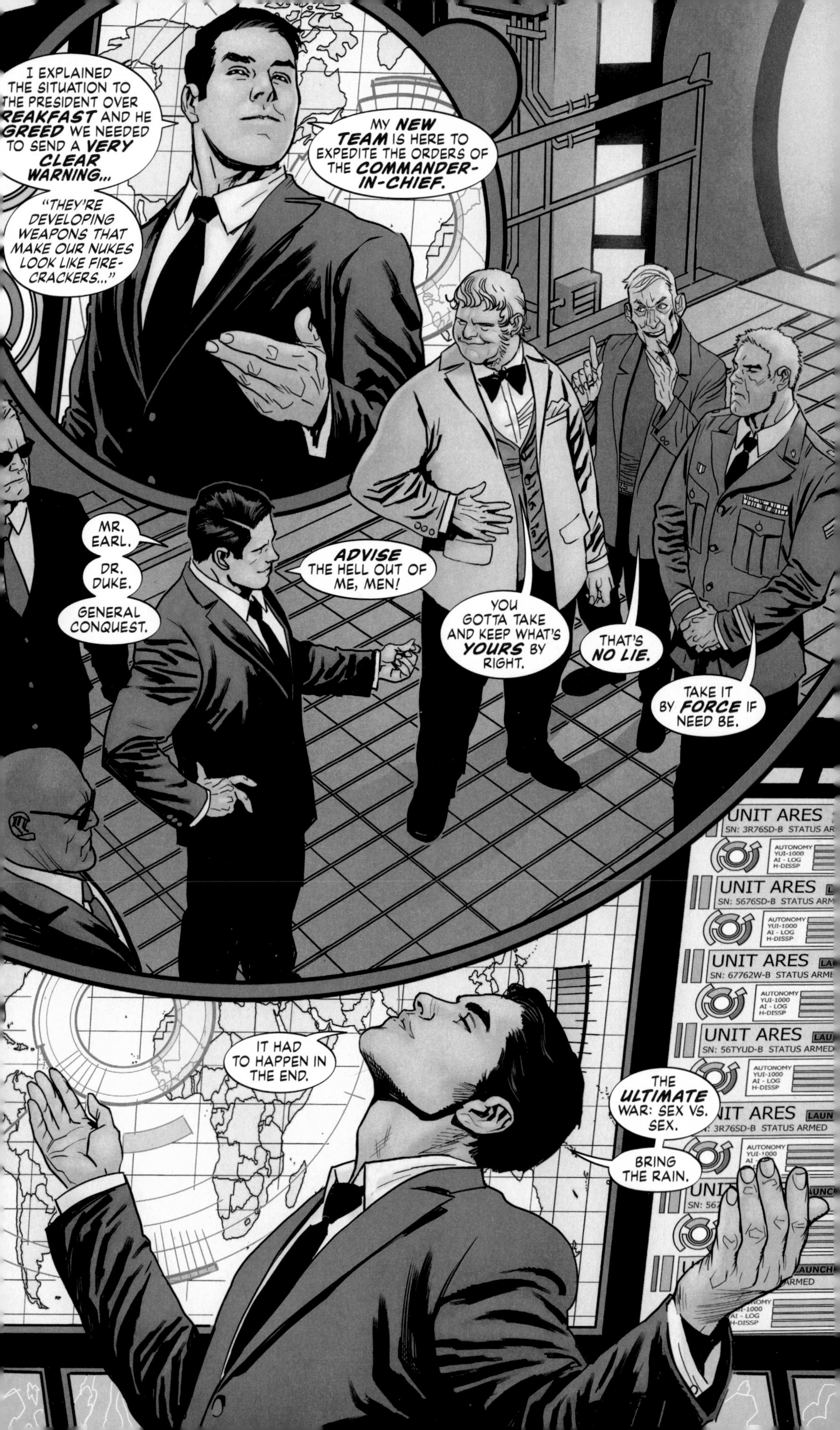
I EXPLAINED THE SITUATION TO THE PRESIDENT OVER REAKFAST AND HE GREED WE NEEDED TO SEND A VERY CLEAR WARNING...
"THEY'RE DEVELOPING WEAPONS THAT MAKE OUR NUKES LOOK LIKE FIRE-CRACKERS..."
MY NEW TEAM IS HERE TO EXPEDITE THE ORDERS OF THE COMMANDER-IN-CHIEF.
MR. EARL.
DR. DUKE.
GENERAL CONQUEST.
ADVISE THE HELL OUT OF ME, MEN!
YOU GOTTA TAKE AND KEEP WHAT'S YOURS BY RIGHT.
THAT'S NO LIE.
TAKE IT BY FORCE IF NEED BE.
IT HAD TO HAPPEN IN THE END.
THE ULTIMATE WAR: SEX VS. SEX.
BRING THE RAIN.

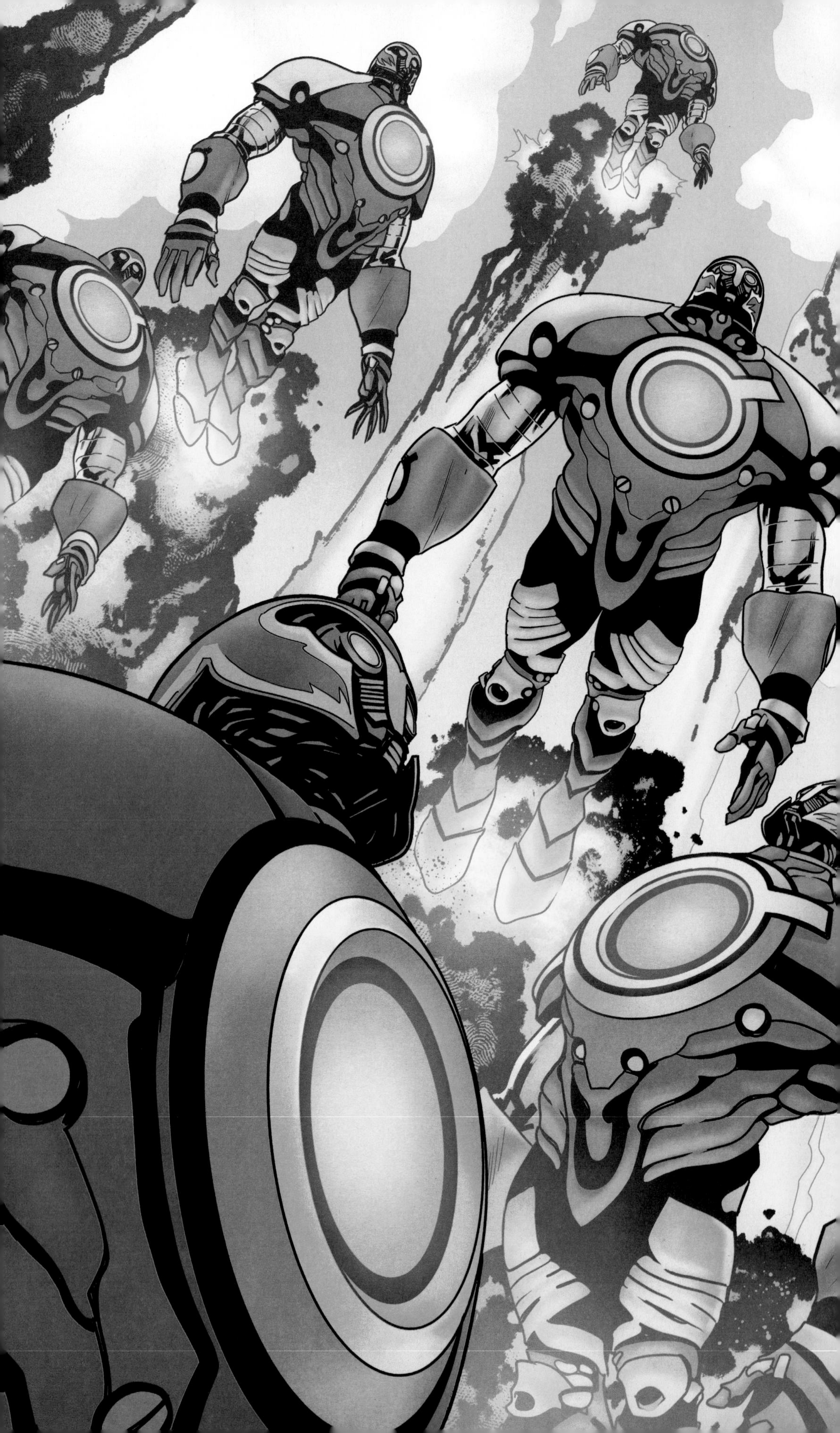

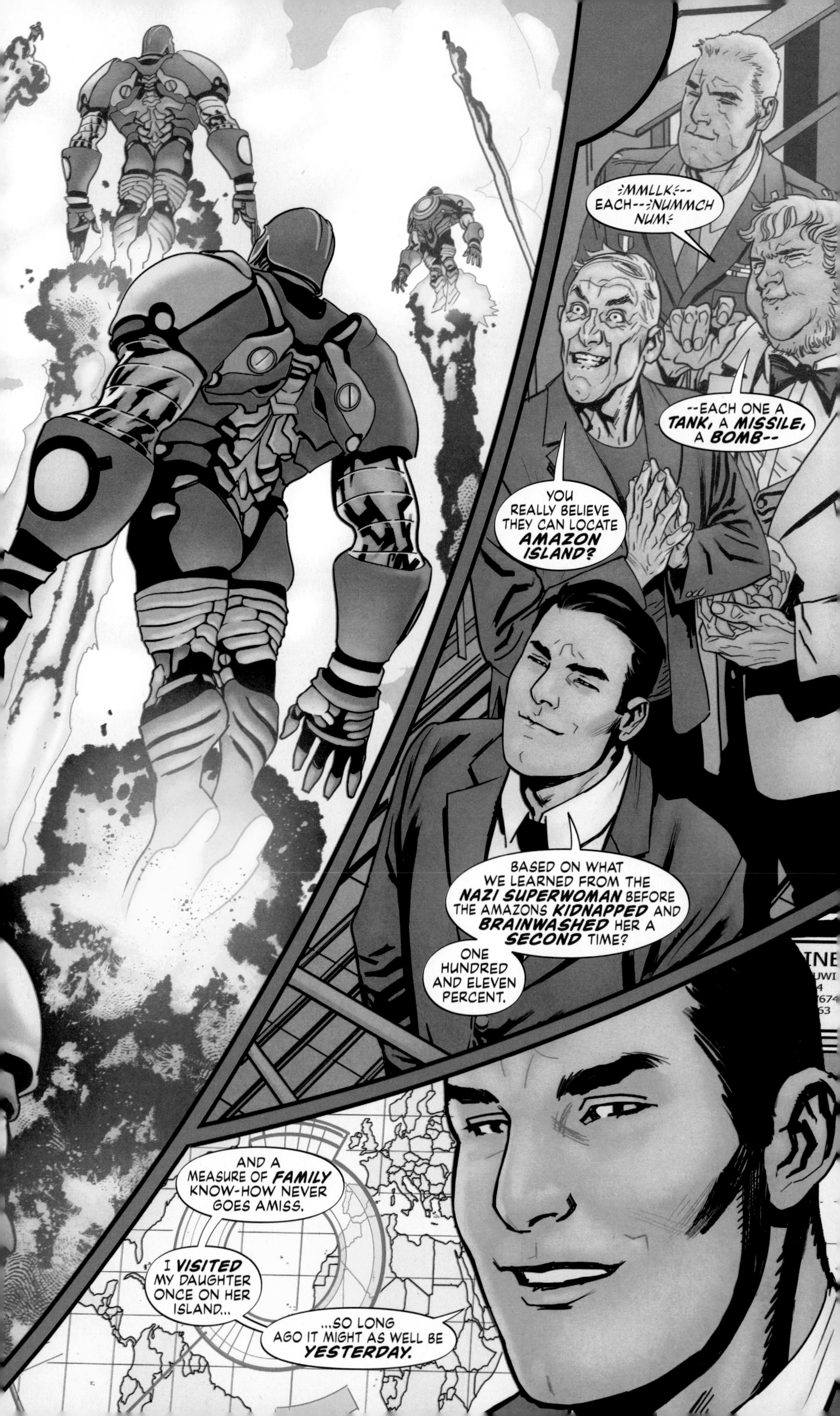

:MMLLK:-- EACH--:NUMMCH NUM:
--EACH ONE A TANK, A MISSILE, A BOMB--
YOU REALLY BELIEVE THEY CAN LOCATE AMAZON ISLAND?
BASED ON WHAT WE LEARNED FROM THE NAZI SUPERWOMAN BEFORE THE AMAZONS KIDNAPPED AND BRAINWASHED HER A SECOND TIME?
ONE HUNDRED AND ELEVEN PERCENT.
AND A MEASURE OF FAMILY KNOW-HOW NEVER GOES AMISS.
I VISITED MY DAUGHTER ONCE ON HER ISLAND...
...SO LONG AGO IT MIGHT AS WELL BE YESTERDAY.

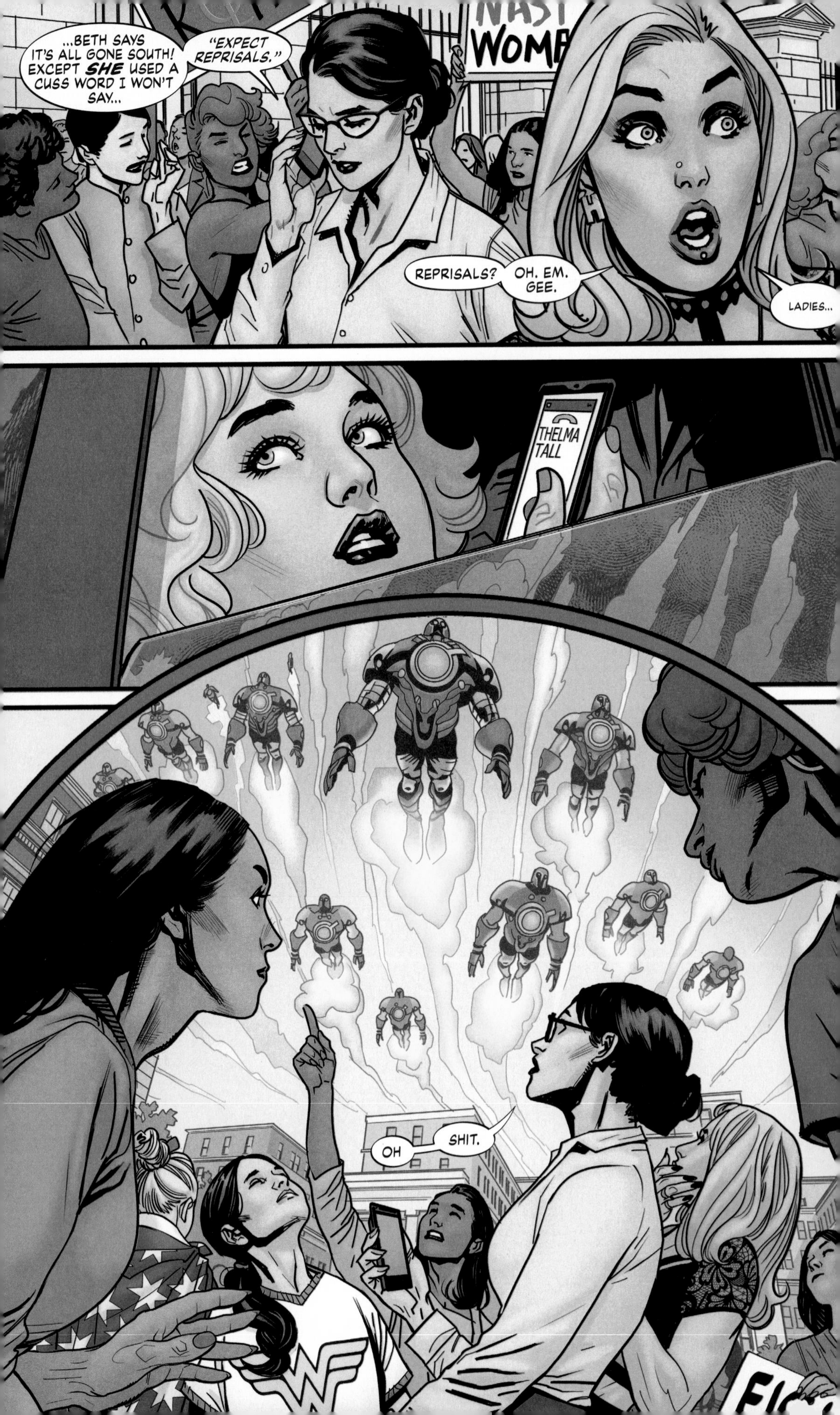
NAST
WOM
...BETH SAYS IT'S ALL GONE SOUTH! EXCEPT SHE USED A CUSS WORD I WON'T SAY...
"EXPECT REPRISALS."
REPRISALS?
OH. EM. GEE.
LADIES...
THELMA TALL
OH
SHIT.

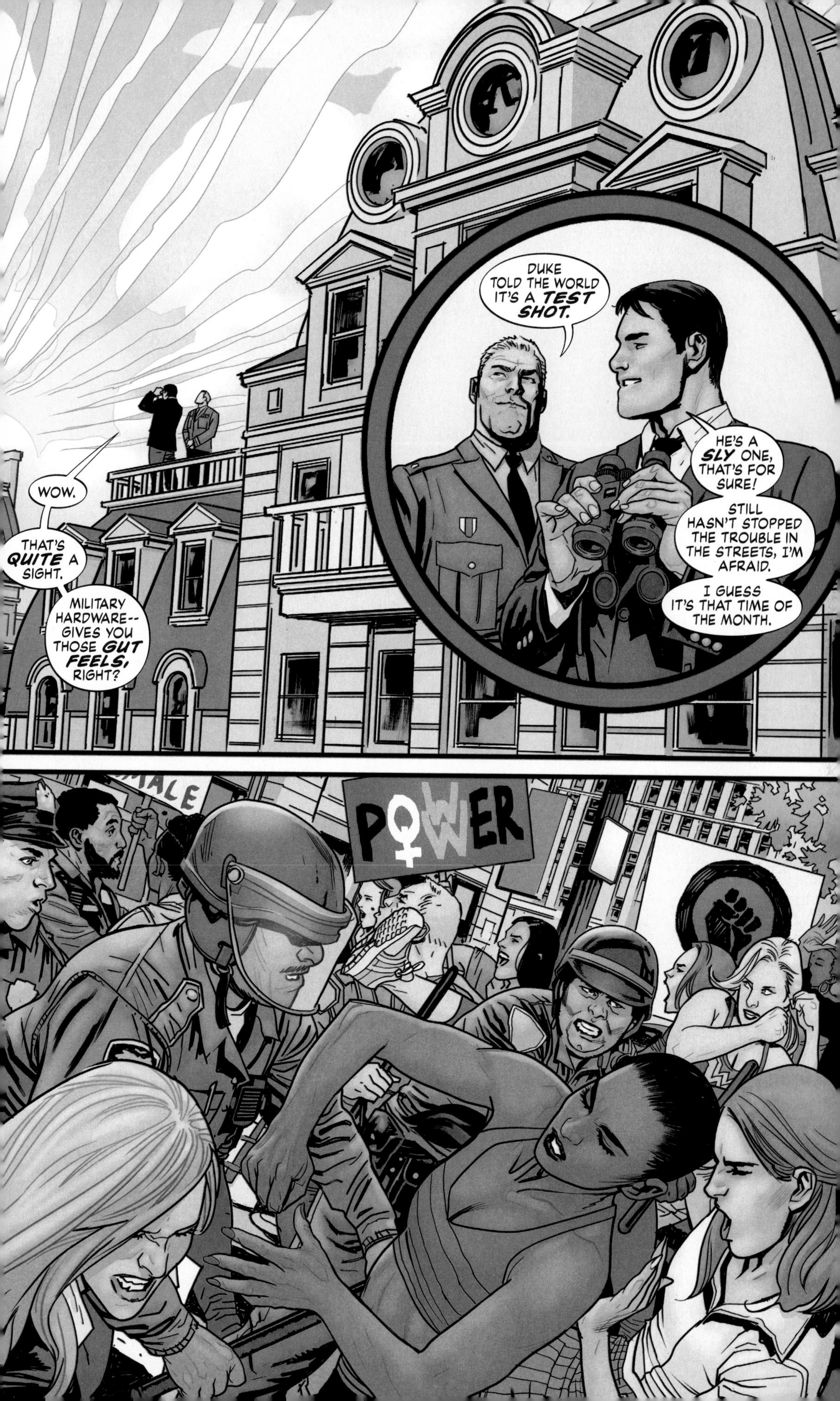

DUKE TOLD THE WORLD IT'S A TEST SHOT.
HE'S A SLY ONE, THAT'S FOR SURE!
STILL HASN'T STOPPED THE TROUBLE IN THE STREETS, I'M AFRAID.
I GUESS IT'S THAT TIME OF THE MONTH.
WOW.
THAT'S QUITE A SIGHT.
MILITARY HARDWARE--GIVES YOU THOSE GUT FEELS, RIGHT?
POWER

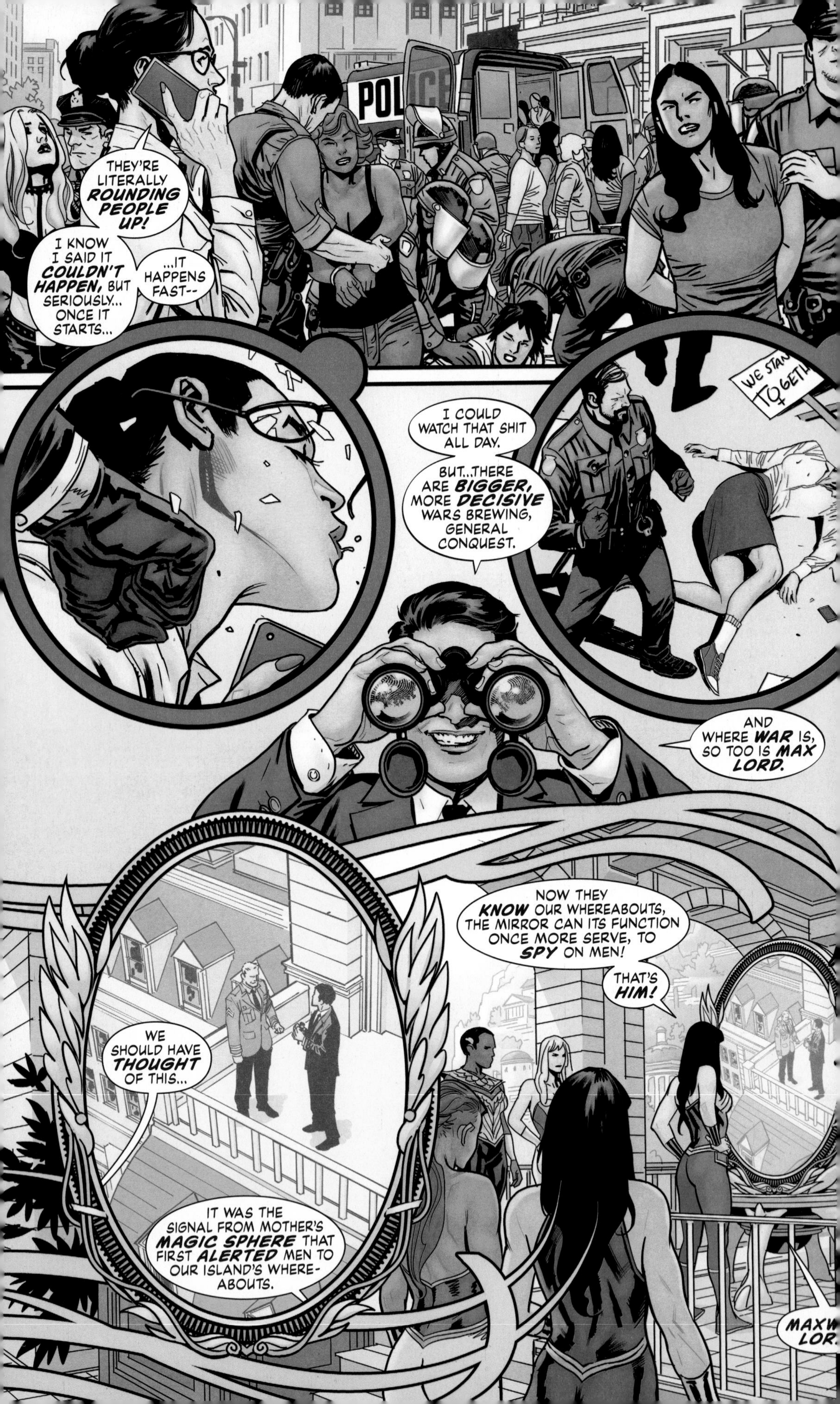

POLICE
THEY'RE LITERALLY ROUNDING PEOPLE UP!
I KNOW I SAID IT COULDN'T HAPPEN, BUT SERIOUSLY... ONCE IT STARTS...
...IT HAPPENS FAST--
I COULD WATCH THAT SHIT ALL DAY.
BUT...THERE ARE BIGGER, MORE DECISIVE WARS BREWING, GENERAL CONQUEST.
AND WHERE WAR IS, SO TOO IS MAX LORD.
NOW THEY KNOW OUR WHEREABOUTS, THE MIRROR CAN ITS FUNCTION ONCE MORE SERVE, TO SPY ON MEN!
THAT'S HIM!
WE SHOULD HAVE THOUGHT OF THIS...
IT WAS THE SIGNAL FROM MOTHER'S MAGIC SPHERE THAT FIRST ALERTED MEN TO OUR ISLAND'S WHERE-ABOUTS.

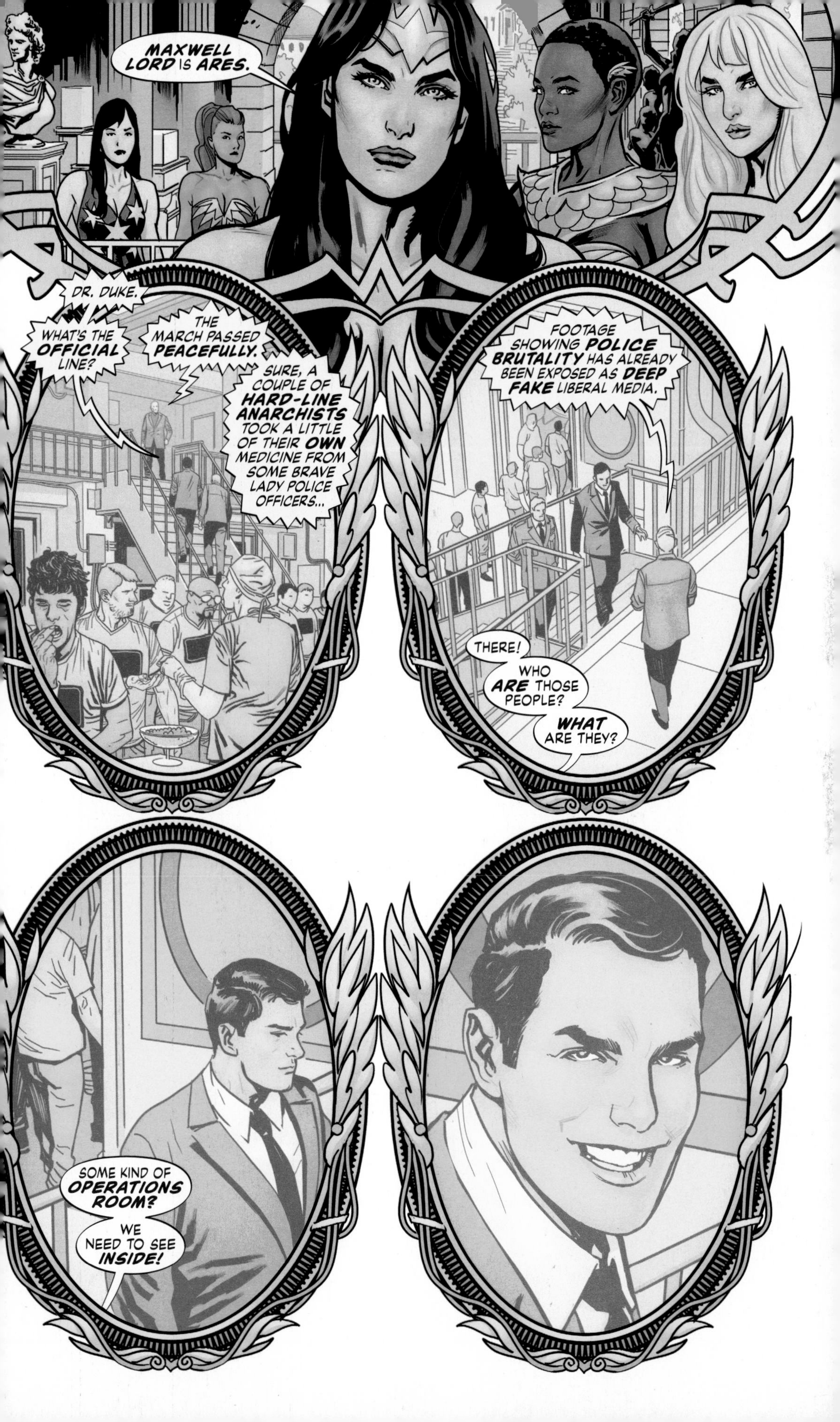
MAXWELL LORD IS ARES.
DR. DUKE.
WHAT'S THE OFFICIAL LINE?
THE MARCH PASSED PEACEFULLY.
SURE, A COUPLE OF HARD-LINE ANARCHISTS TOOK A LITTLE OF THEIR OWN MEDICINE FROM SOME BRAVE LADY POLICE OFFICERS...
FOOTAGE SHOWING POLICE BRUTALITY HAS ALREADY BEEN EXPOSED AS DEEP FAKE LIBERAL MEDIA.
THERE!
WHO ARE THOSE PEOPLE?
WHAT ARE THEY?
SOME KIND OF OPERATIONS ROOM?
WE NEED TO SEE INSIDE!

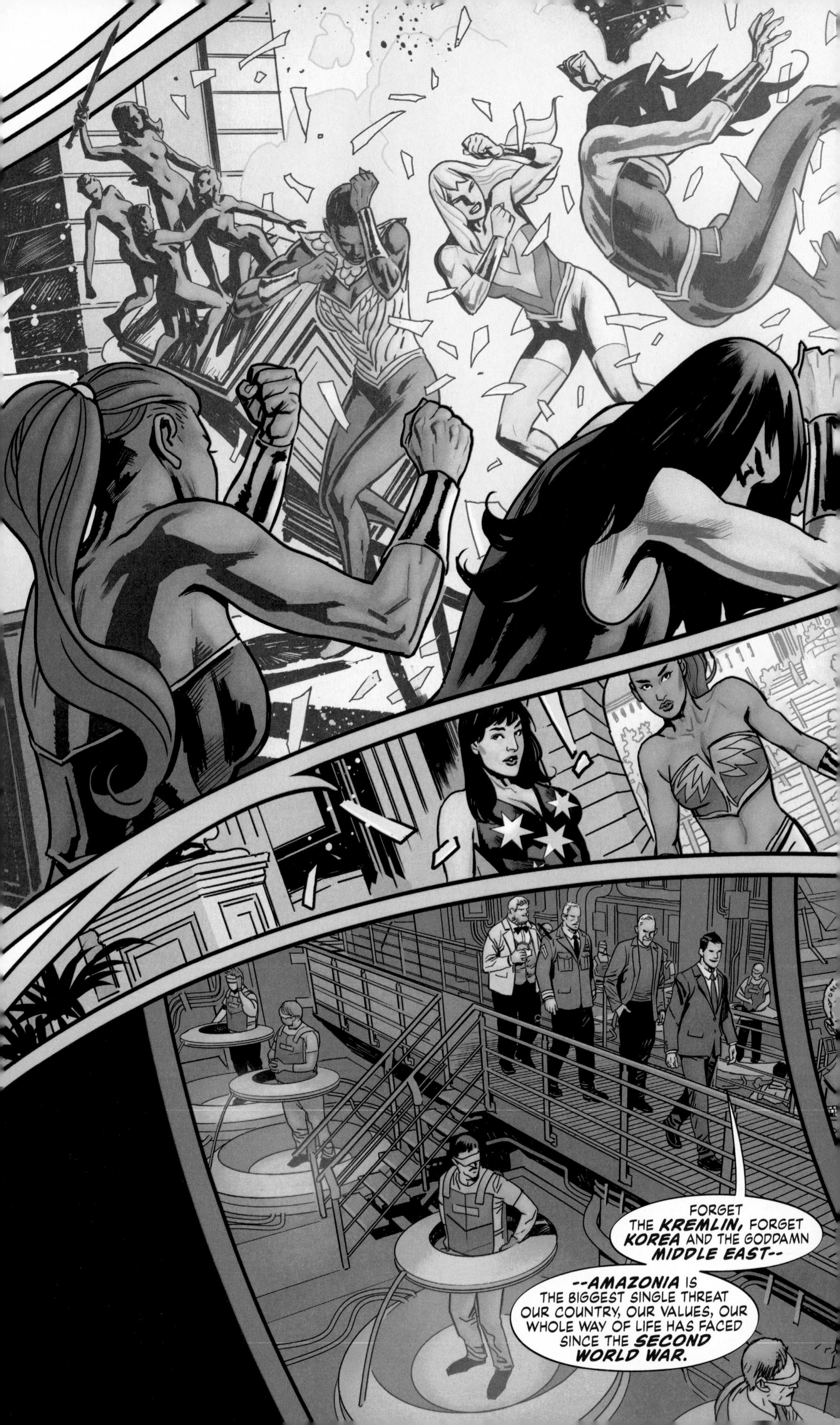
FORGET THE KREMLIN, FORGET KOREA AND THE GODDAMN MIDDLE EAST--
--AMAZONIA IS THE BIGGEST SINGLE THREAT OUR COUNTRY, OUR VALUES, OUR WHOLE WAY OF LIFE HAS FACED SINCE THE SECOND WORLD WAR.

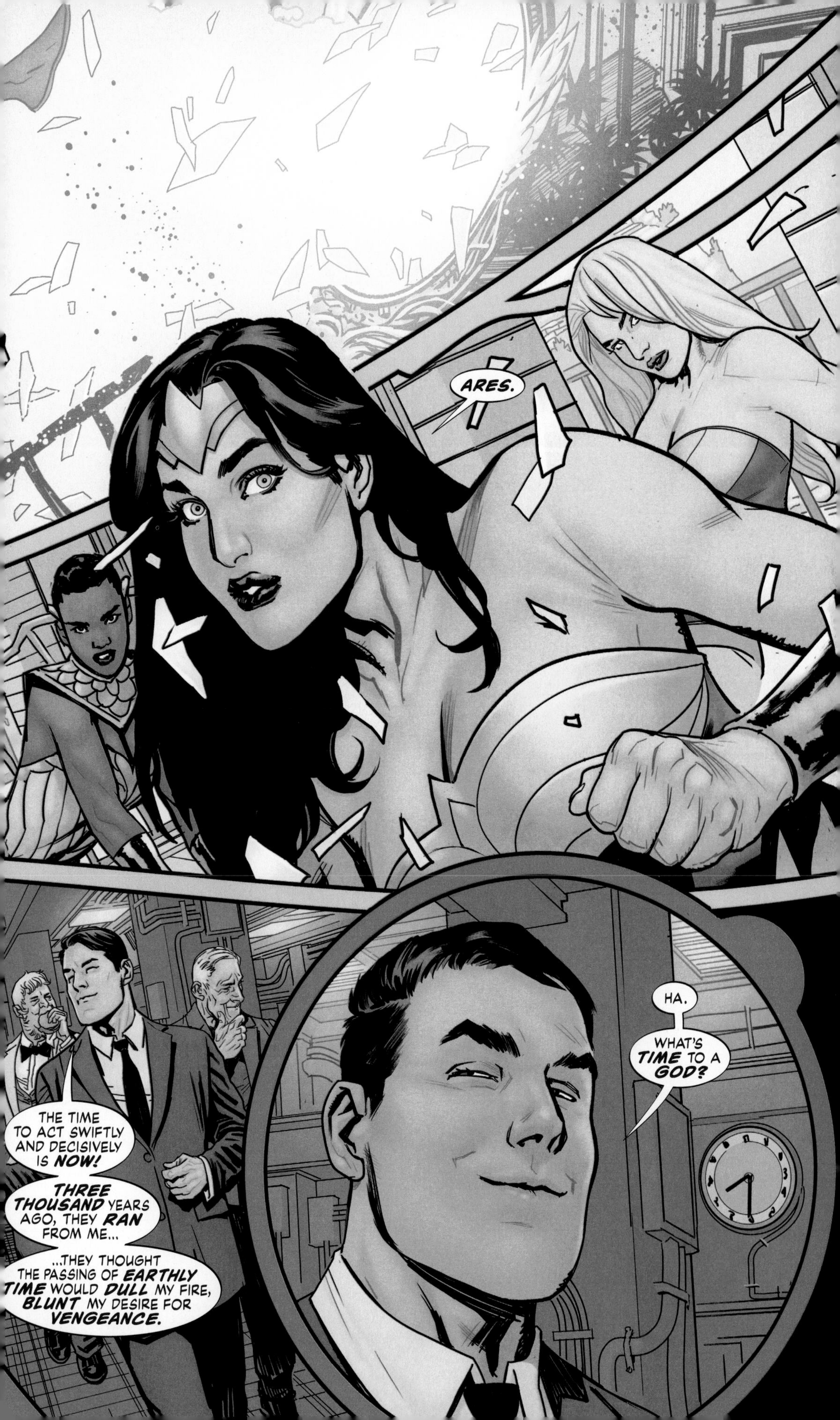

ARES.
THE TIME TO ACT SWIFTLY AND DECISIVELY IS NOW!
THREE THOUSAND YEARS AGO, THEY RAN FROM ME...
...THEY THOUGHT THE PASSING OF EARTHLY TIME WOULD DULL MY FIRE, BLUNT MY DESIRE FOR VENGEANCE.
HA.
WHAT'S TIME TO A GOD?

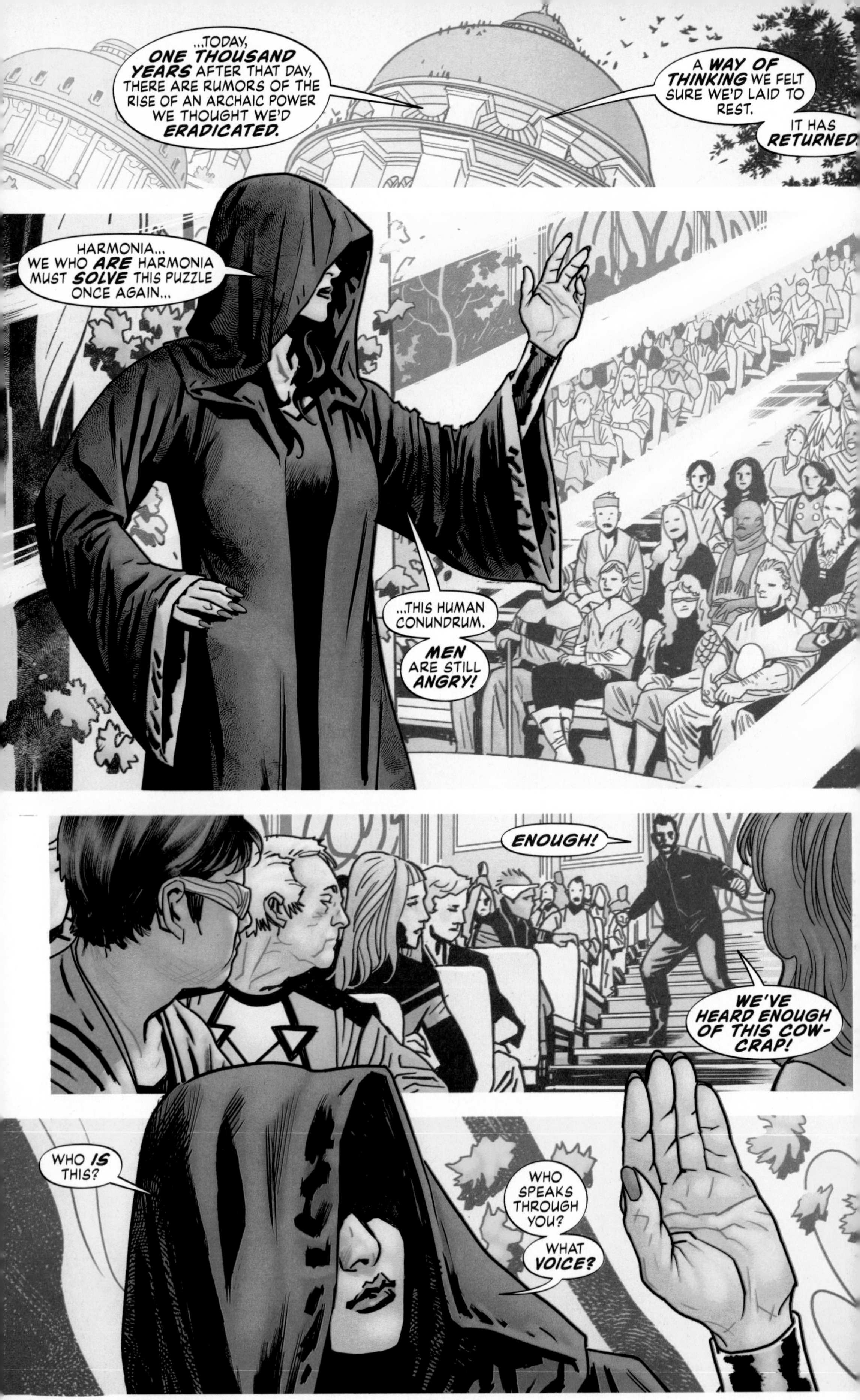
...TODAY, ONE THOUSAND YEARS AFTER THAT DAY, THERE ARE RUMORS OF THE RISE OF AN ARCHAIC POWER WE THOUGHT WE'D ERADICATED.
A WAY OF THINKING WE FELT SURE WE'D LAID TO REST.
IT HAS RETURNED.
HARMONIA... WE WHO ARE HARMONIA MUST SOLVE THIS PUZZLE ONCE AGAIN...
...THIS HUMAN CONUNDRUM.
MEN ARE STILL ANGRY!
ENOUGH!
WE'VE HEARD ENOUGH OF THIS COW-CRAP!
WHO IS THIS?
WHO SPEAKS THROUGH YOU?
WHAT VOICE?

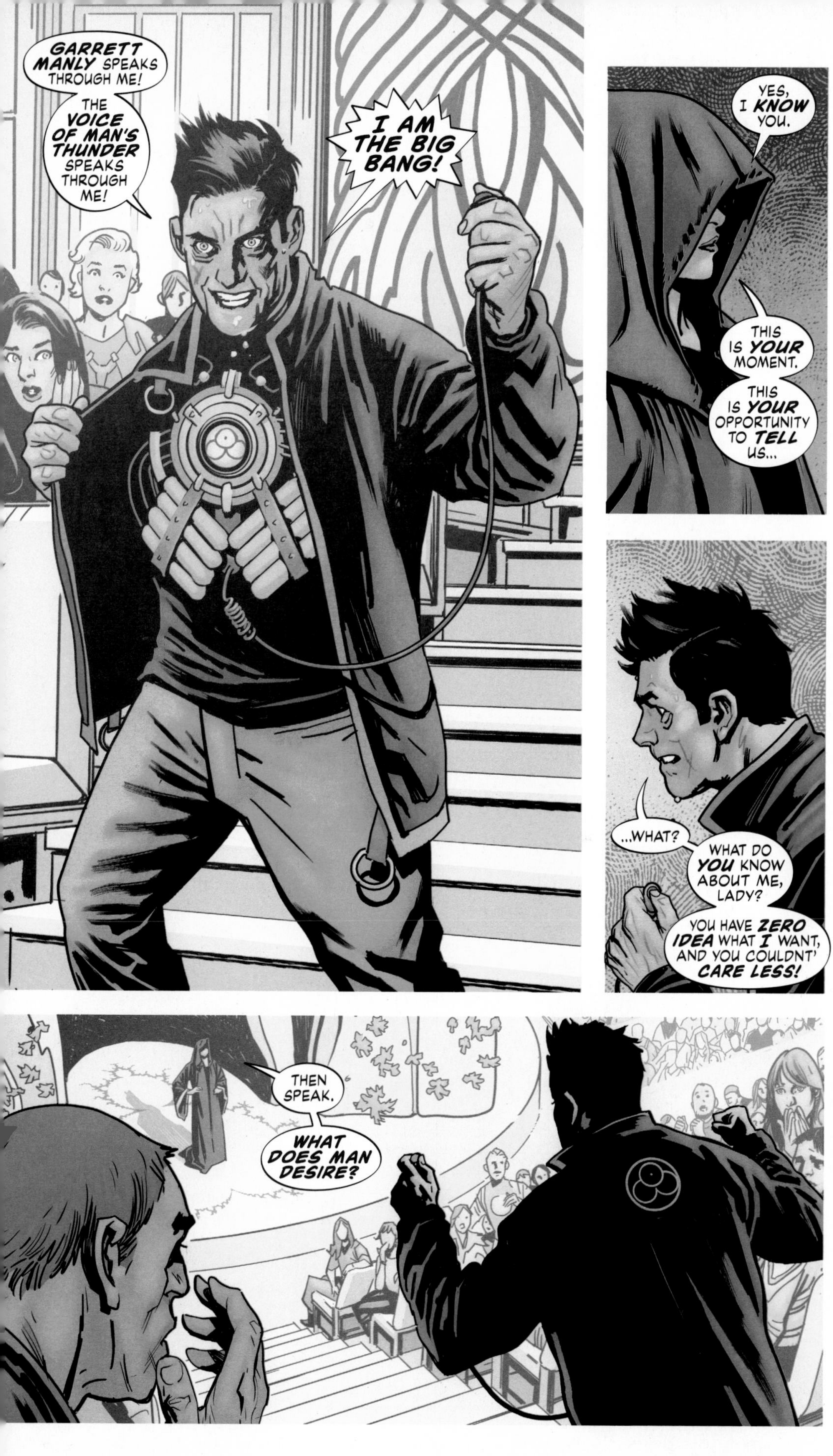
GARRETT MANLY SPEAKS THROUGH ME!
THE VOICE OF MAN'S THUNDER SPEAKS THROUGH ME!
I AM THE BIG BANG!
YES, I KNOW YOU.
THIS IS YOUR MOMENT.
THIS IS YOUR OPPORTUNITY TO TELL US...
...WHAT?
WHAT DO YOU KNOW ABOUT ME, LADY?
YOU HAVE ZERO IDEA WHAT I WANT, AND YOU COULDNT' CARE LESS!
THEN SPEAK.
WHAT DOES MAN DESIRE?

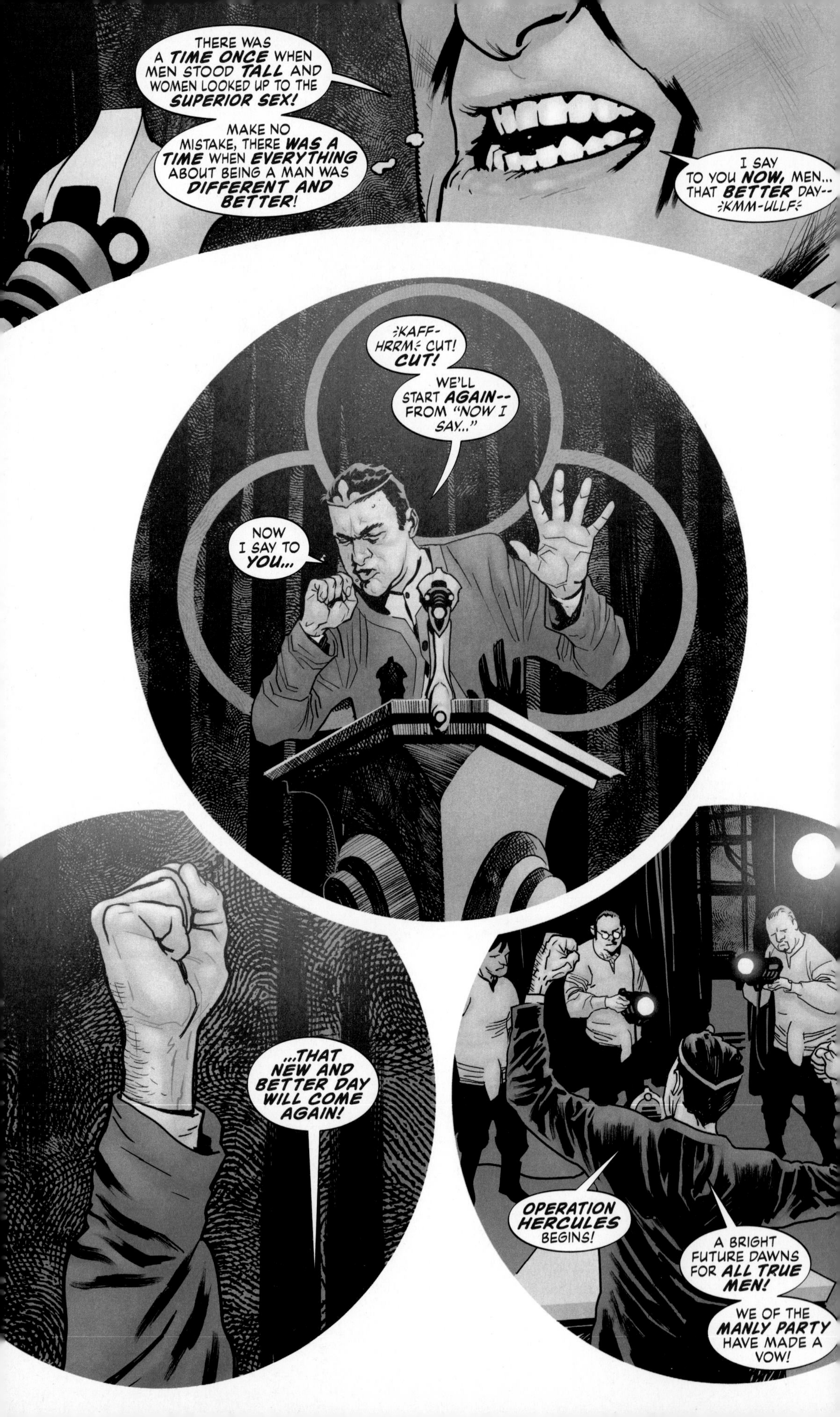
THERE WAS A TIME ONCE WHEN MEN STOOD TALL AND WOMEN LOOKED UP TO THE SUPERIOR SEX!
MAKE NO MISTAKE, THERE WAS A TIME WHEN EVERYTHING ABOUT BEING A MAN WAS DIFFERENT AND BETTER!
I SAY TO YOU NOW, MEN... THAT BETTER DAY-- ≈KMM-ULLF≈
≈KAFF-HRRM≈ CUT! CUT!
WE'LL START AGAIN-- FROM "NOW I SAY..."
NOW I SAY TO YOU...
...THAT NEW AND BETTER DAY WILL COME AGAIN!
OPERATION HERCULES BEGINS!
A BRIGHT FUTURE DAWNS FOR ALL TRUE MEN!
WE OF THE MANLY PARTY HAVE MADE A VOW!

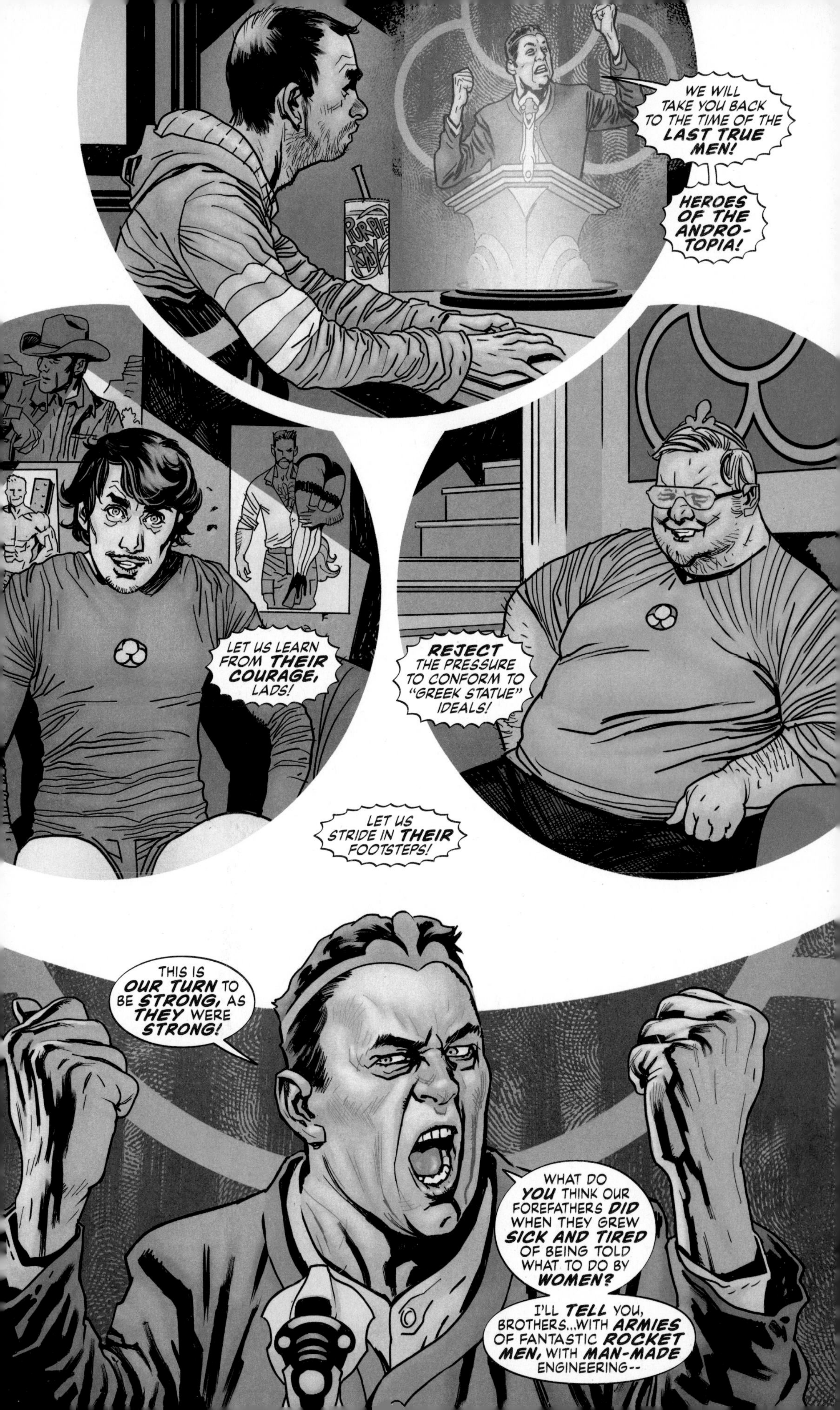

WE WILL TAKE YOU BACK TO THE TIME OF THE LAST TRUE MEN!
HEROES OF THE ANDRO-TOPIA!
LET US LEARN FROM THEIR COURAGE, LADS!
REJECT THE PRESSURE TO CONFORM TO "GREEK STATUE" IDEALS!
LET US STRIDE IN THEIR FOOTSTEPS!
THIS IS OUR TURN TO BE STRONG, AS THEY WERE STRONG!
WHAT DO YOU THINK OUR FOREFATHERS DID WHEN THEY GREW SICK AND TIRED OF BEING TOLD WHAT TO DO BY WOMEN?
I'LL TELL YOU, BROTHERS...WITH ARMIES OF FANTASTIC ROCKET MEN, WITH MAN-MADE ENGINEERING--

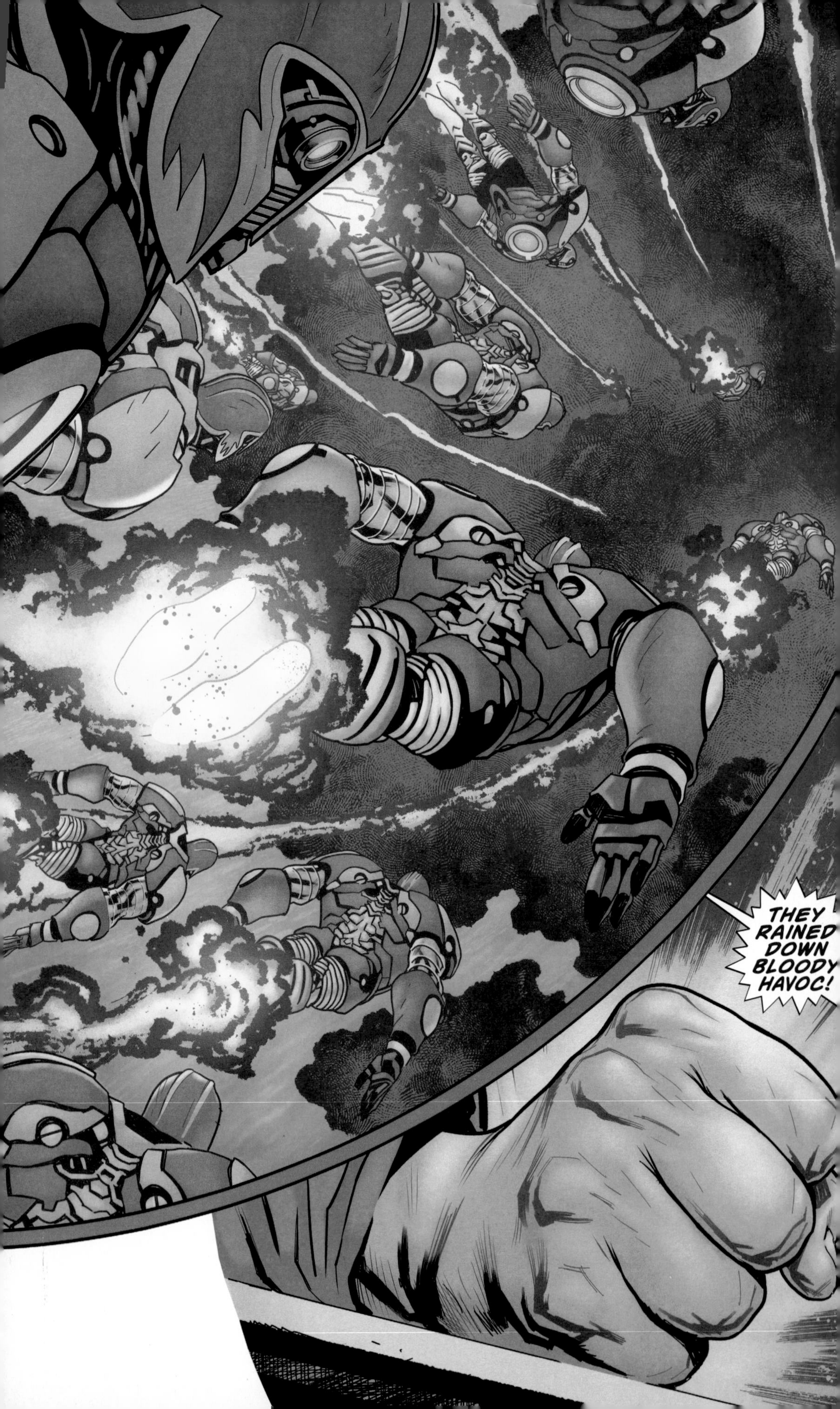
THEY RAINED DOWN BLOODY HAVOC!

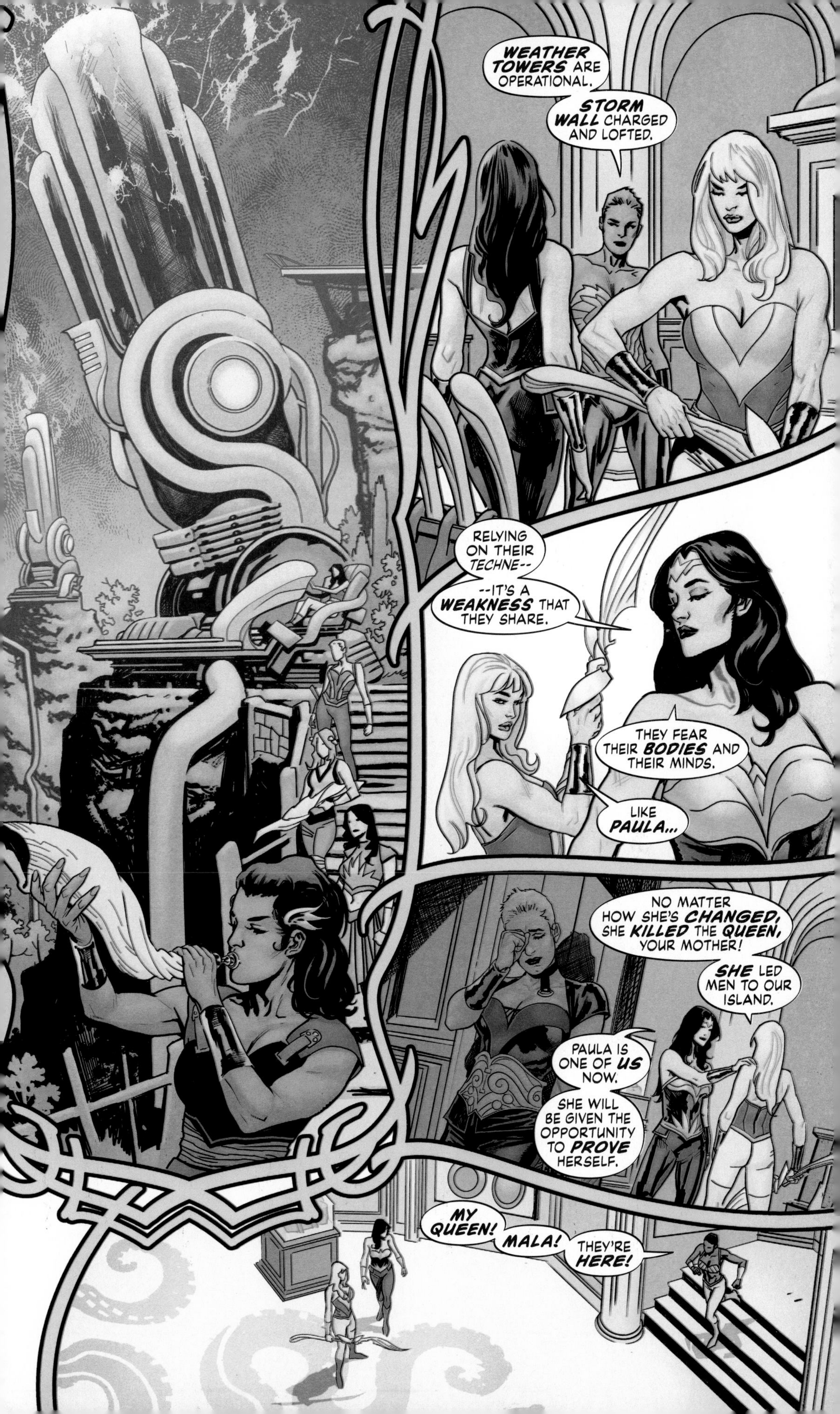
WEATHER TOWERS ARE OPERATIONAL.
STORM WALL CHARGED AND LOFTED.
RELYING ON THEIR TECHNE--
--IT'S A WEAKNESS THAT THEY SHARE.
THEY FEAR THEIR BODIES AND THEIR MINDS.
LIKE PAULA...
NO MATTER HOW SHE'S CHANGED, SHE KILLED THE QUEEN, YOUR MOTHER!
SHE LED MEN TO OUR ISLAND.
PAULA IS ONE OF US NOW.
SHE WILL BE GIVEN THE OPPORTUNITY TO PROVE HERSELF.
MY QUEEN!
MALA!
THEY'RE HERE!

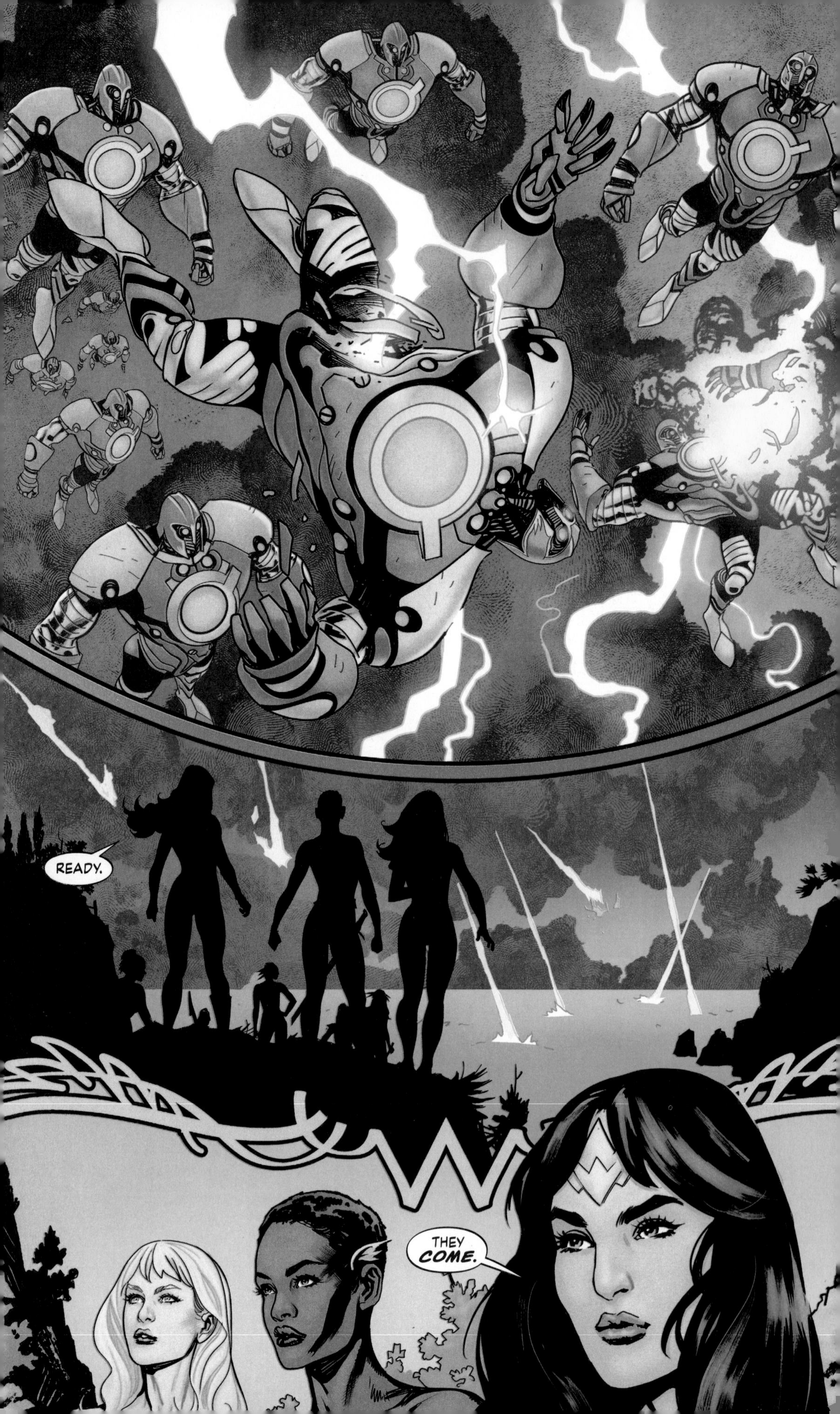
READY.
THEY COME.

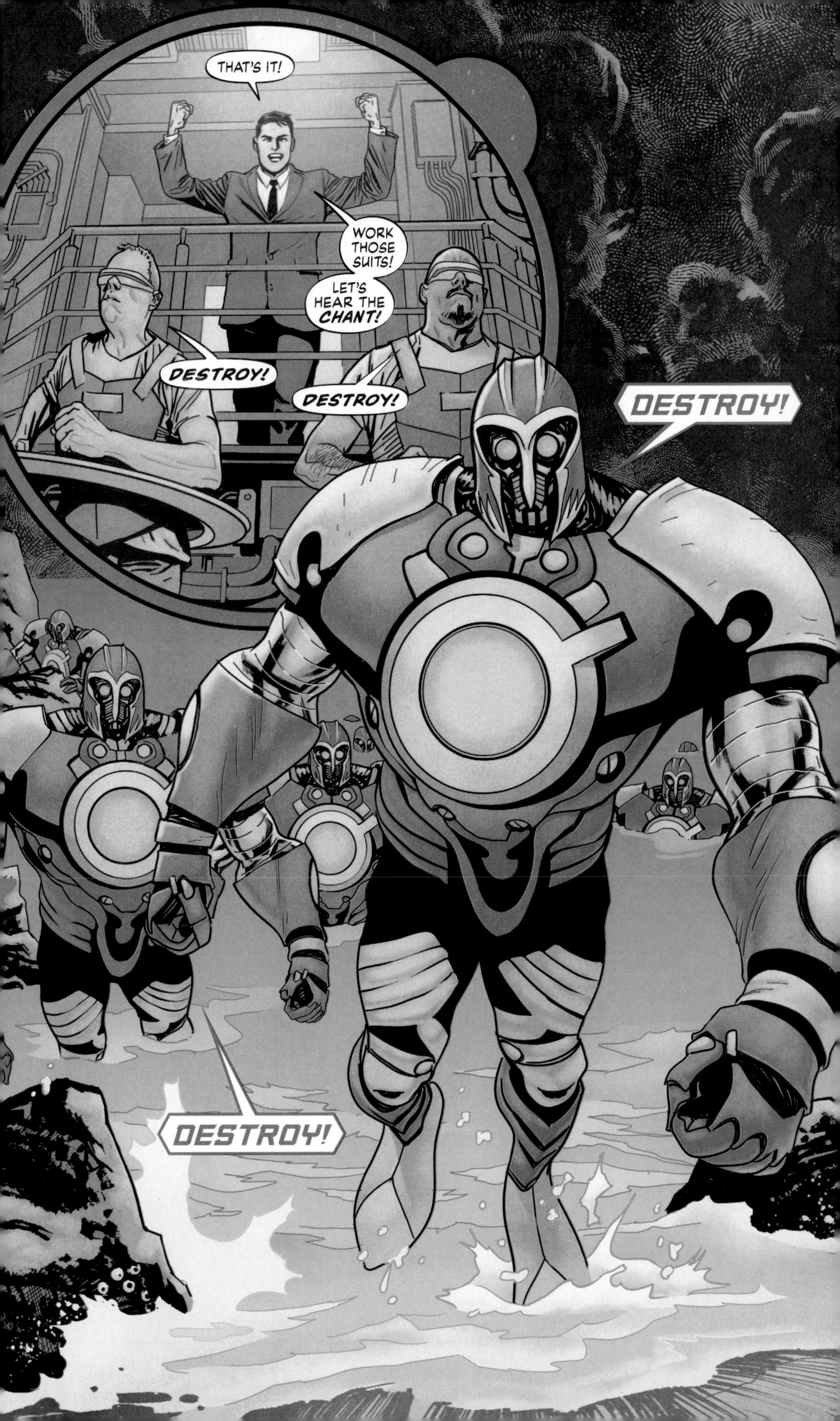
THAT'S IT!
WORK THOSE SUITS!
LET'S HEAR THE CHANT!
DESTROY!
DESTROY!
DESTROY!
DESTROY!

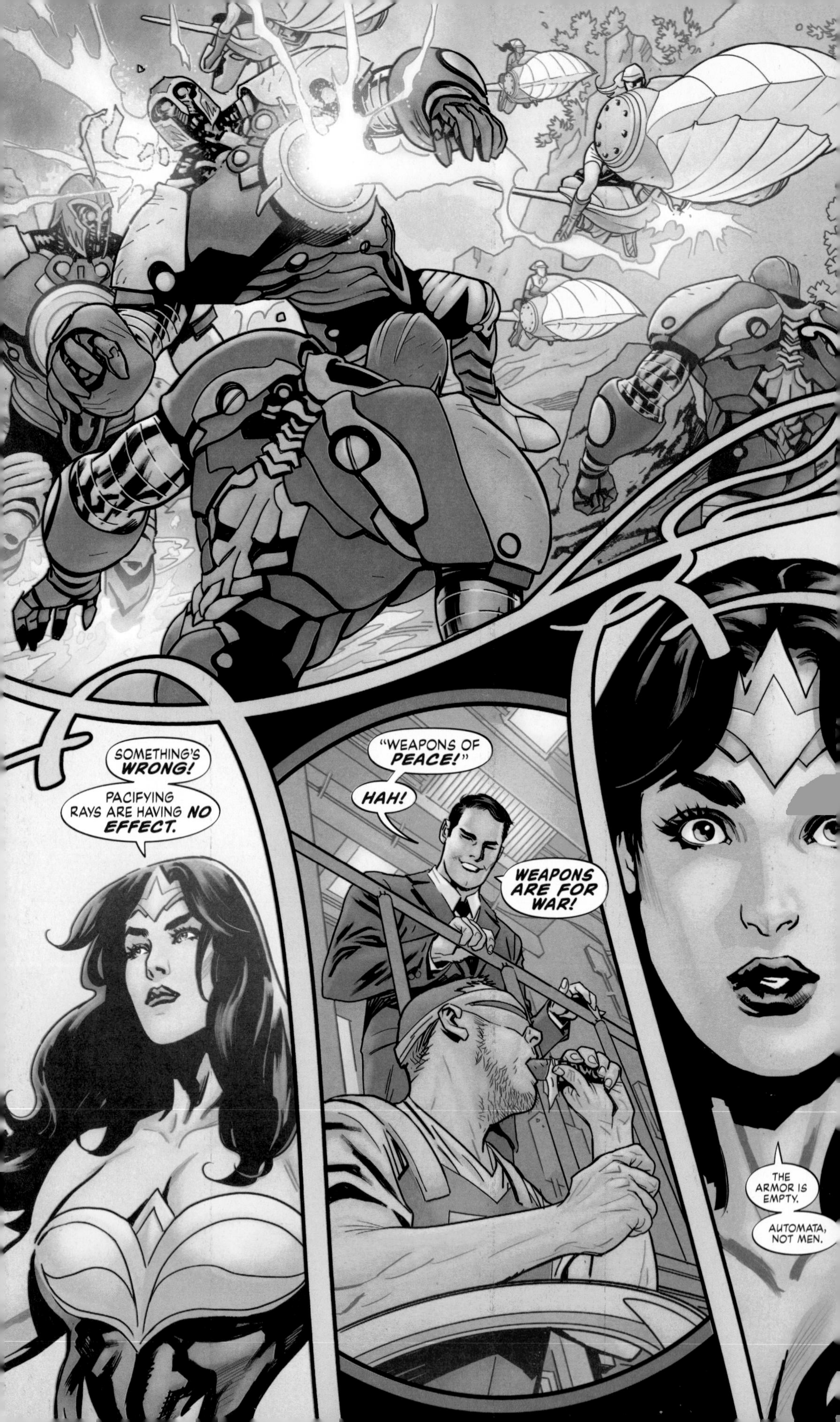
SOMETHING'S WRONG!
PACIFYING RAYS ARE HAVING NO EFFECT.
"WEAPONS OF PEACE!"
HAH!
WEAPONS ARE FOR WAR!
THE ARMOR IS EMPTY.
AUTOMATA, NOT MEN.

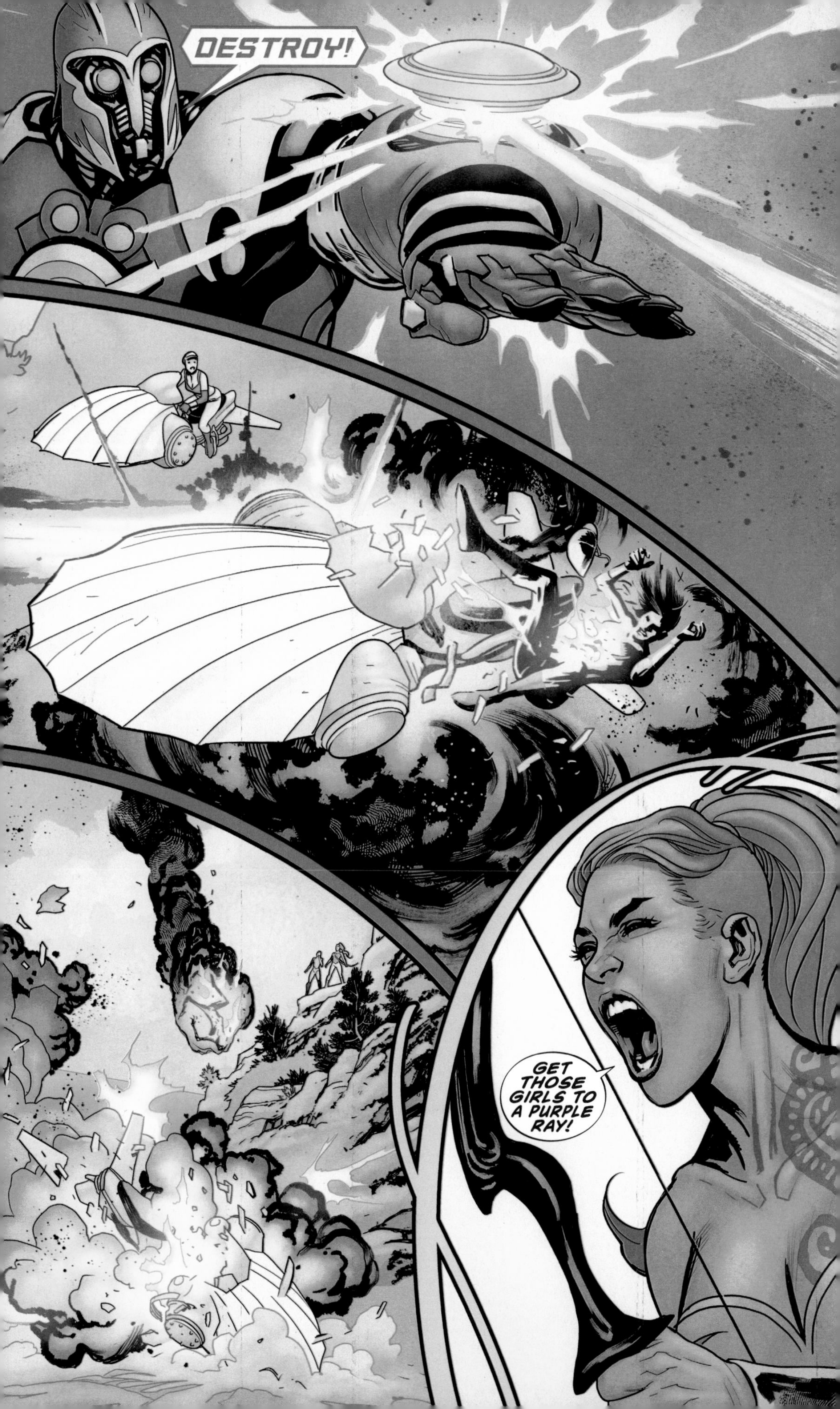
DESTROY!
GET THOSE GIRLS TO A PURPLE RAY!

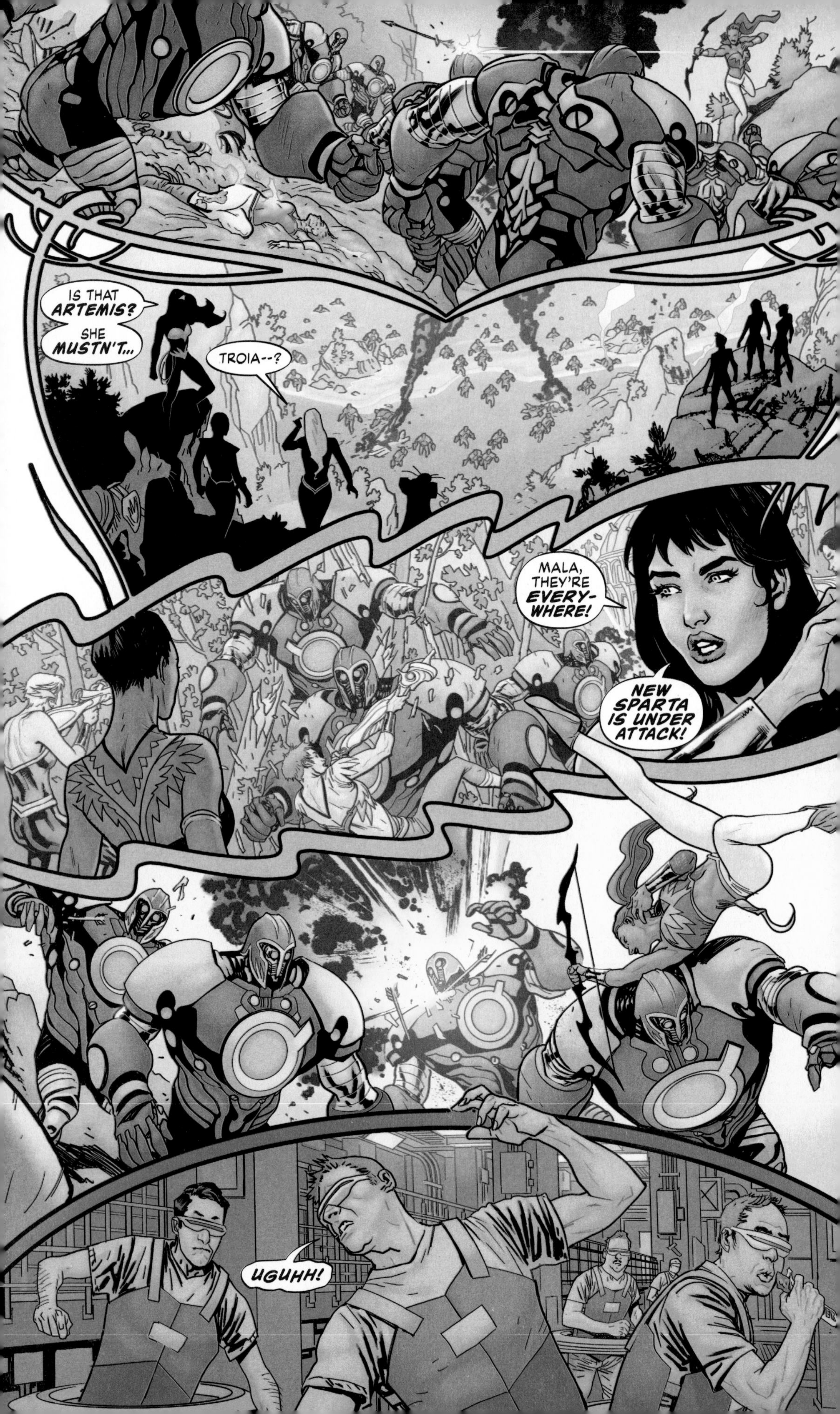
IS THAT ARTEMIS? SHE MUSTN'T...
TROIA--?
MALA, THEY'RE EVERYWHERE!
NEW SPARTA IS UNDER ATTACK!
UGUHH!

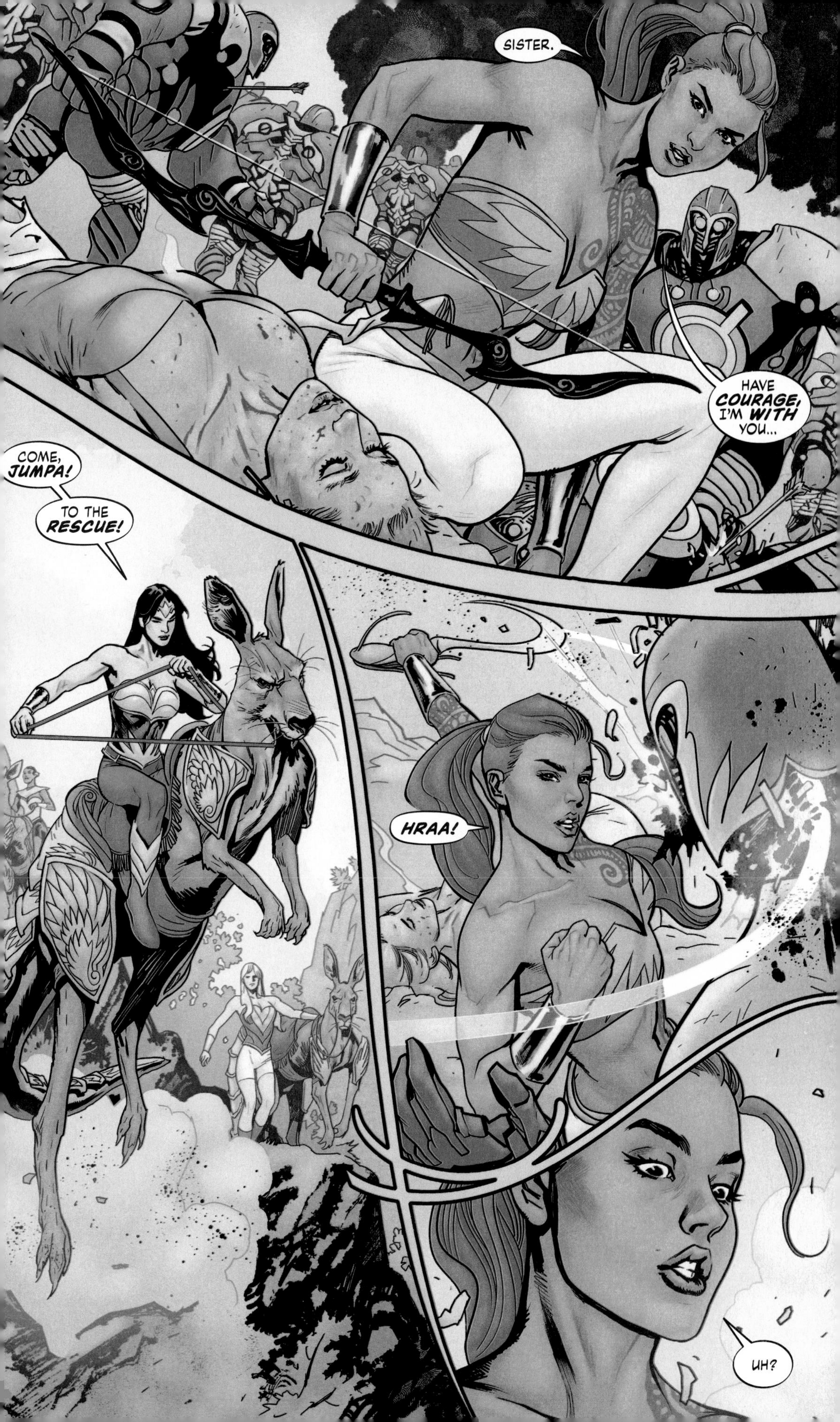
SISTER.
HAVE COURAGE, I'M WITH YOU...
COME, JUMPA!
TO THE RESCUE!
HRAA!
UH?

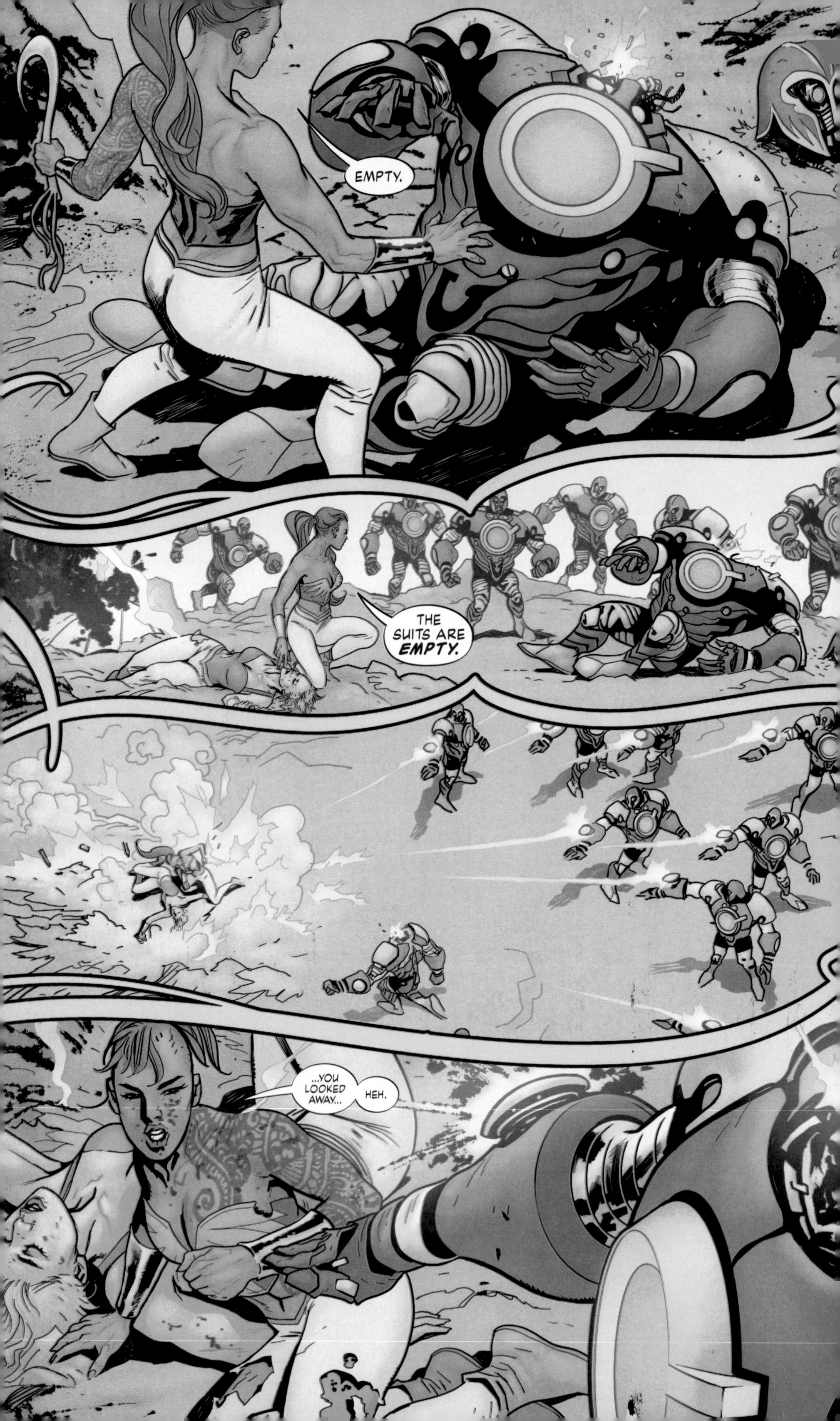
EMPTY.
THE SUITS ARE EMPTY.
...YOU LOOKED AWAY...
HEH.

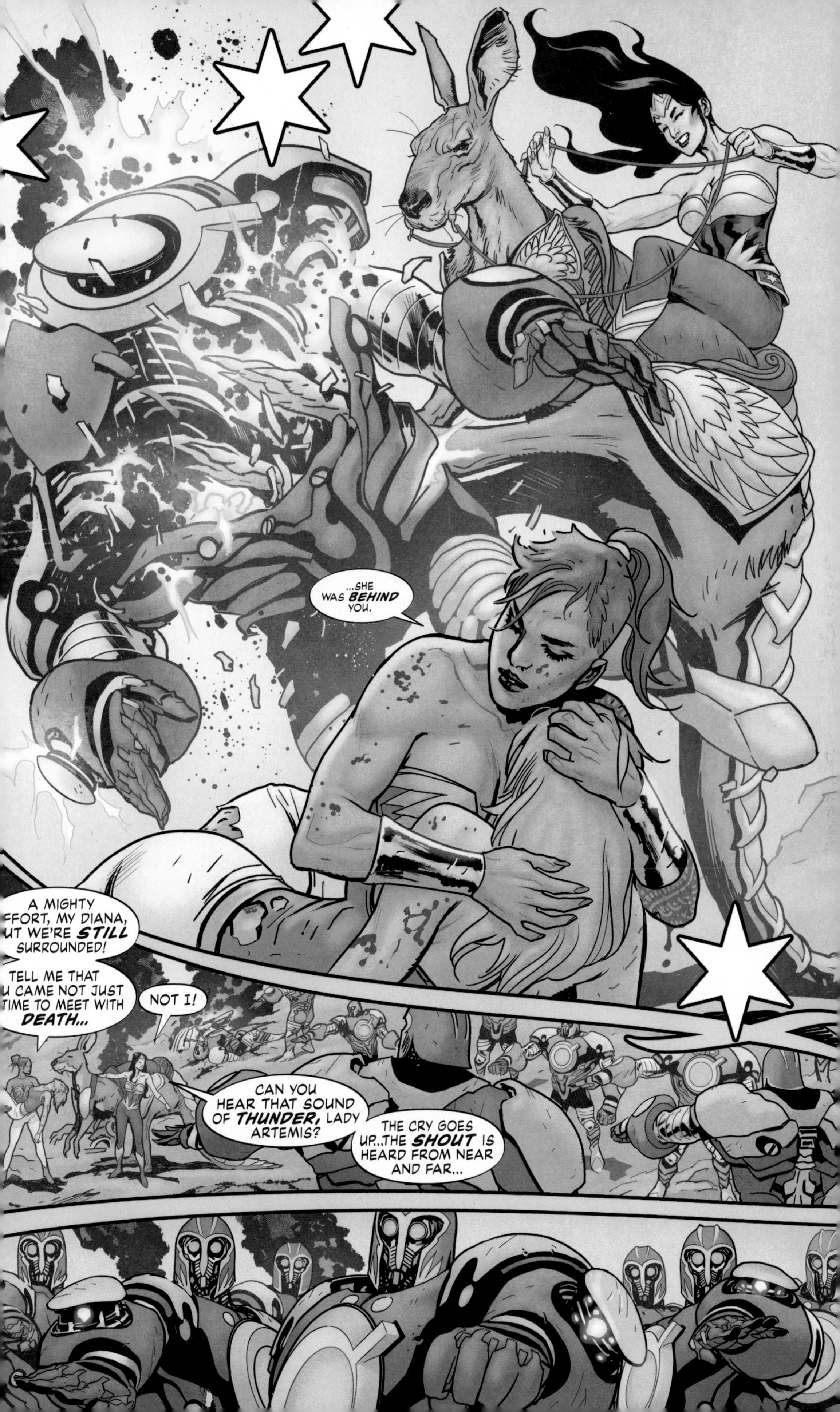
...SHE WAS BEHIND YOU.
A MIGHTY FFORT, MY DIANA, UT WE'RE STILL SURROUNDED!
TELL ME THAT U CAME NOT JUST TIME TO MEET WITH DEATH...
NOT I!
CAN YOU HEAR THAT SOUND OF THUNDER, LADY ARTEMIS?
THE CRY GOES UP...THE SHOUT IS HEARD FROM NEAR AND FAR...

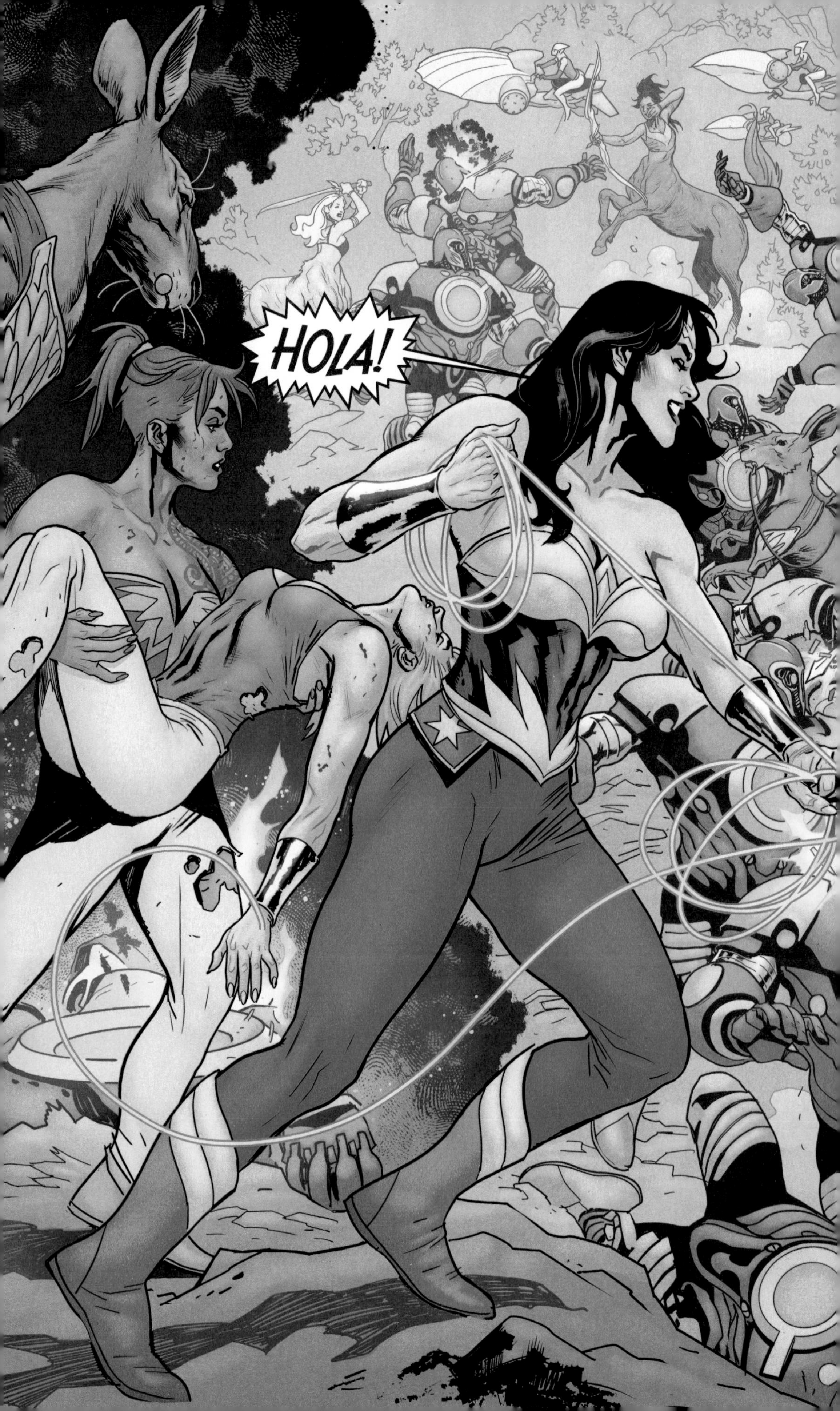
HOLA!

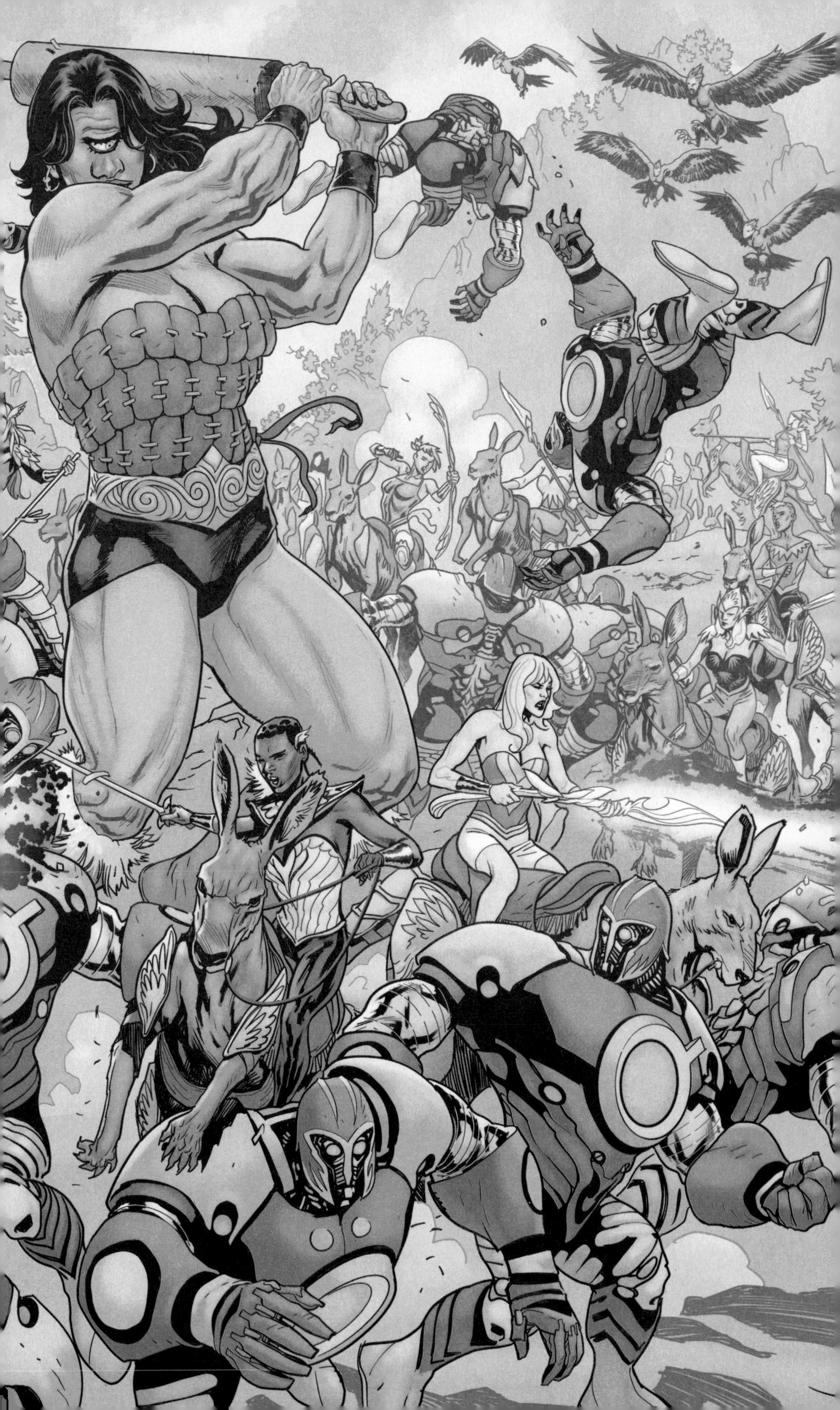

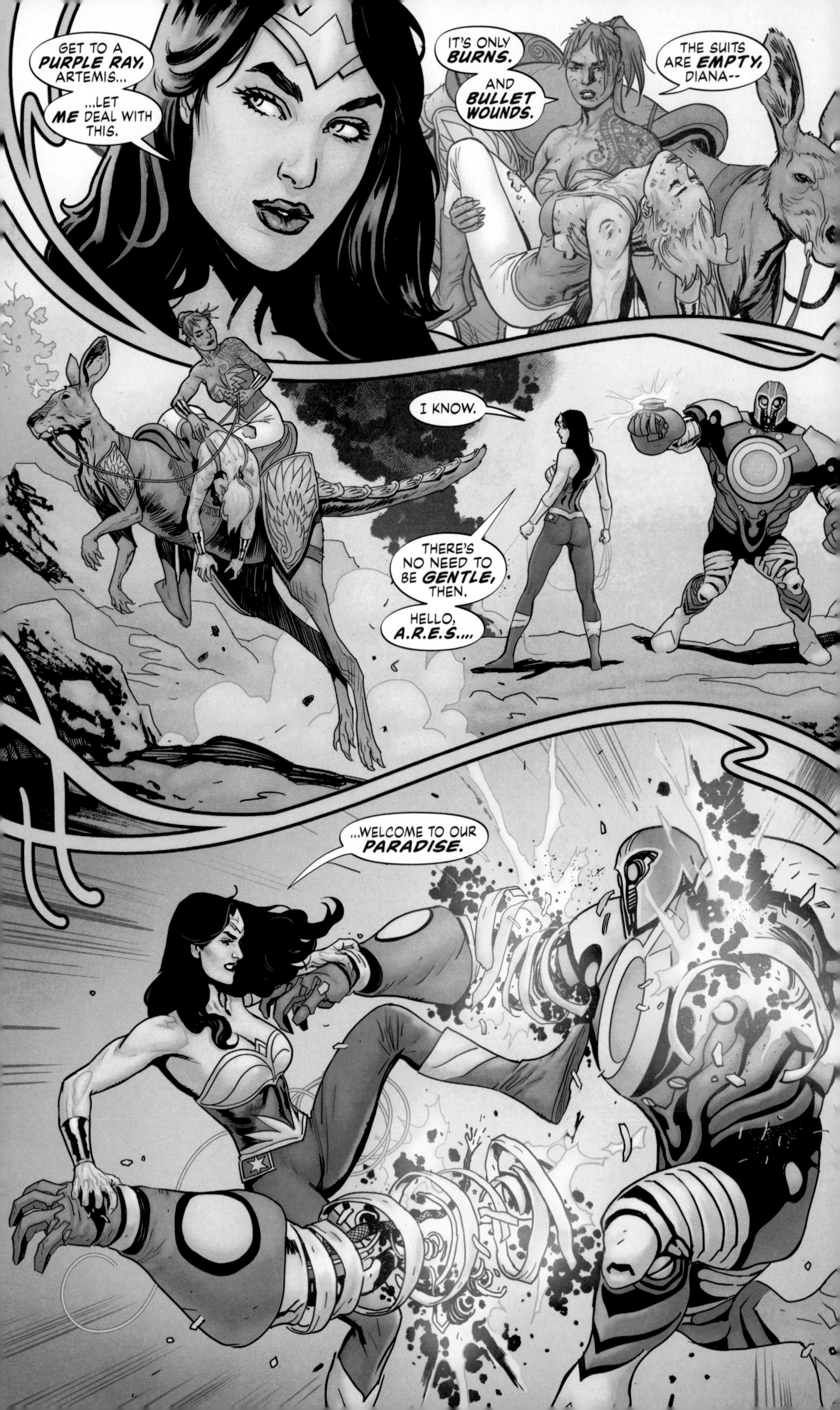
GET TO A PURPLE RAY, ARTEMIS...
...LET ME DEAL WITH THIS.
IT'S ONLY BURNS.
AND BULLET WOUNDS.
THE SUITS ARE EMPTY, DIANA--
I KNOW.
THERE'S NO NEED TO BE GENTLE, THEN.
HELLO, A.R.E.S....
...WELCOME TO OUR PARADISE.

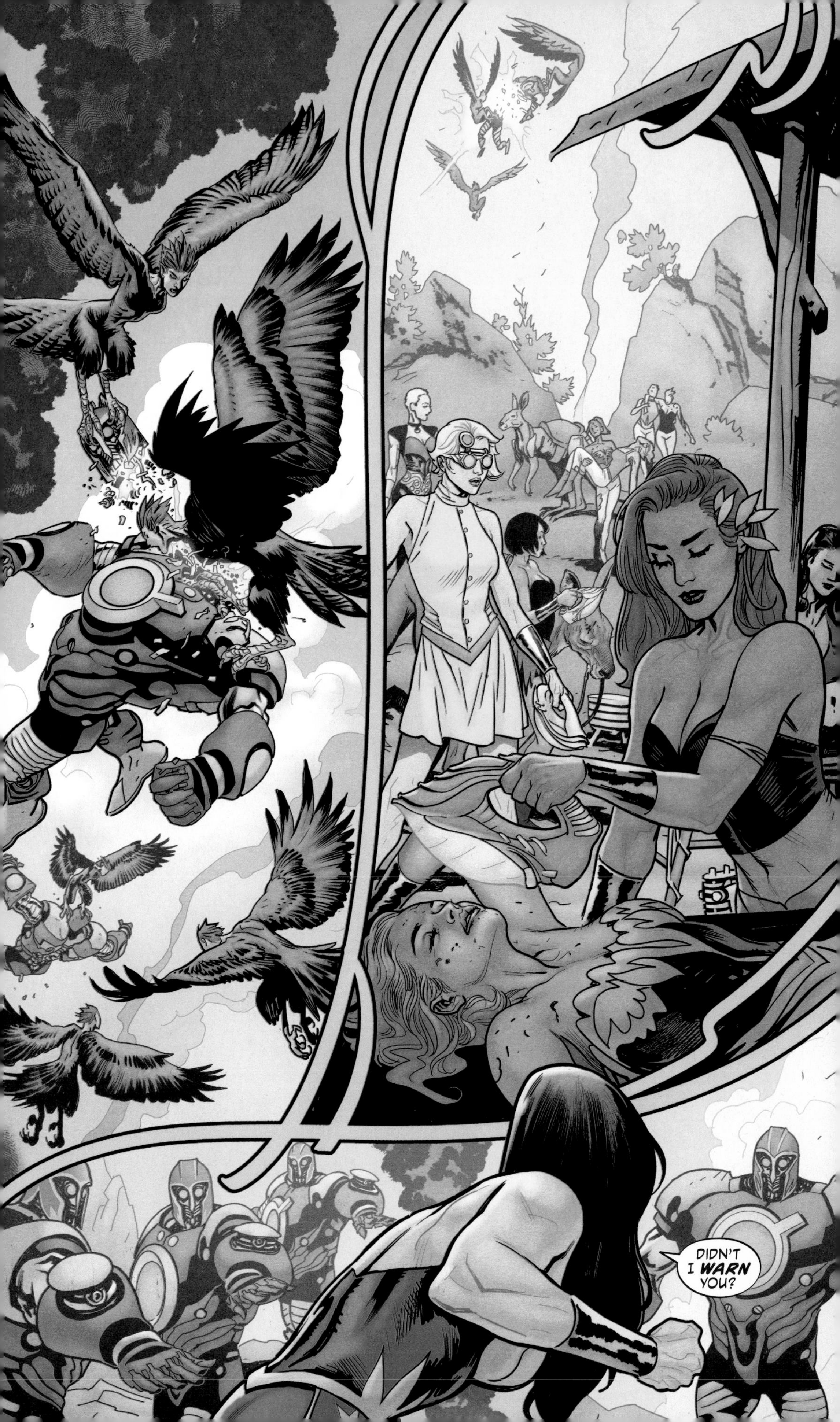
DIDN'T I WARN YOU?

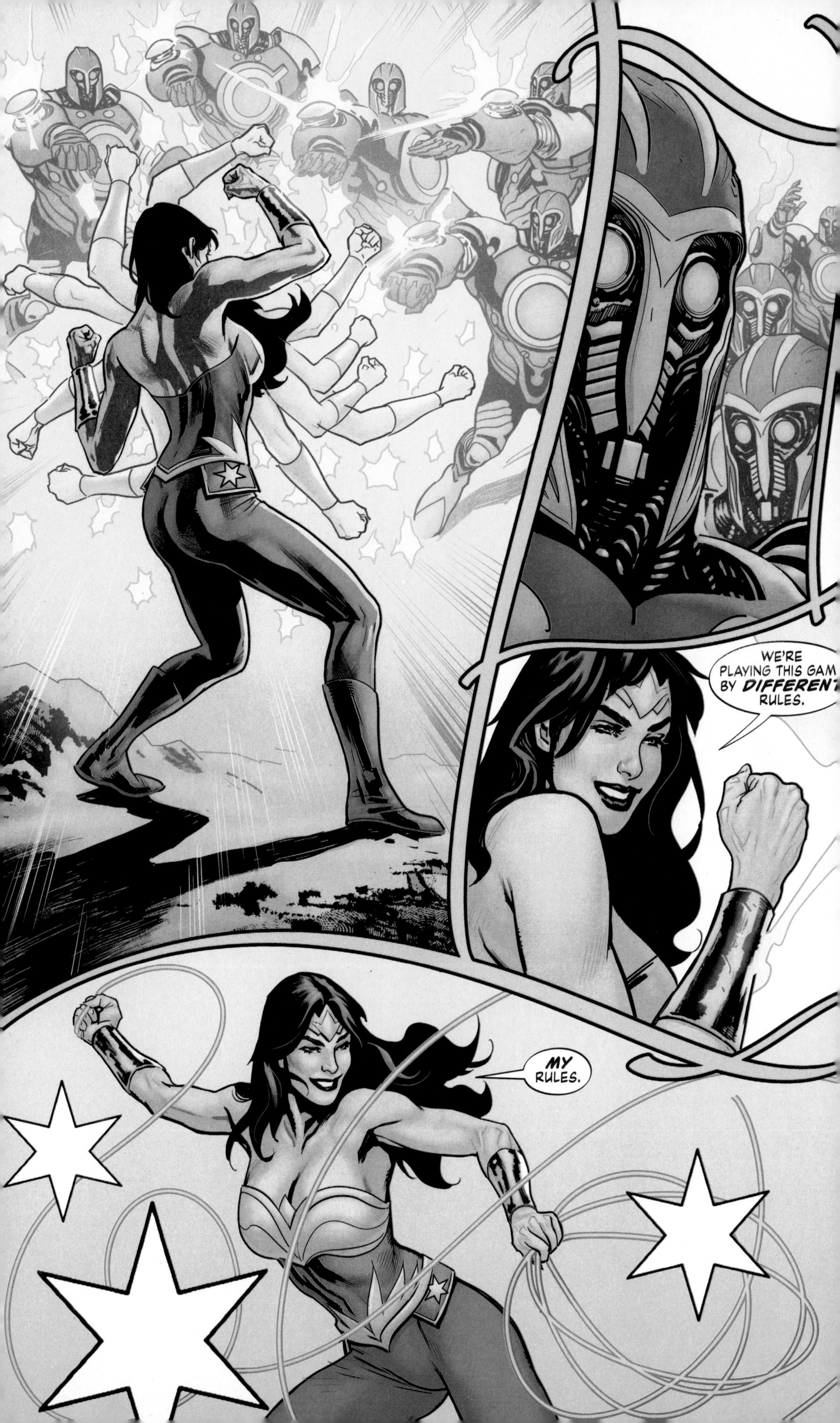
WE'RE PLAYING THIS GAM BY DIFFERENT RULES.
MY RULES.

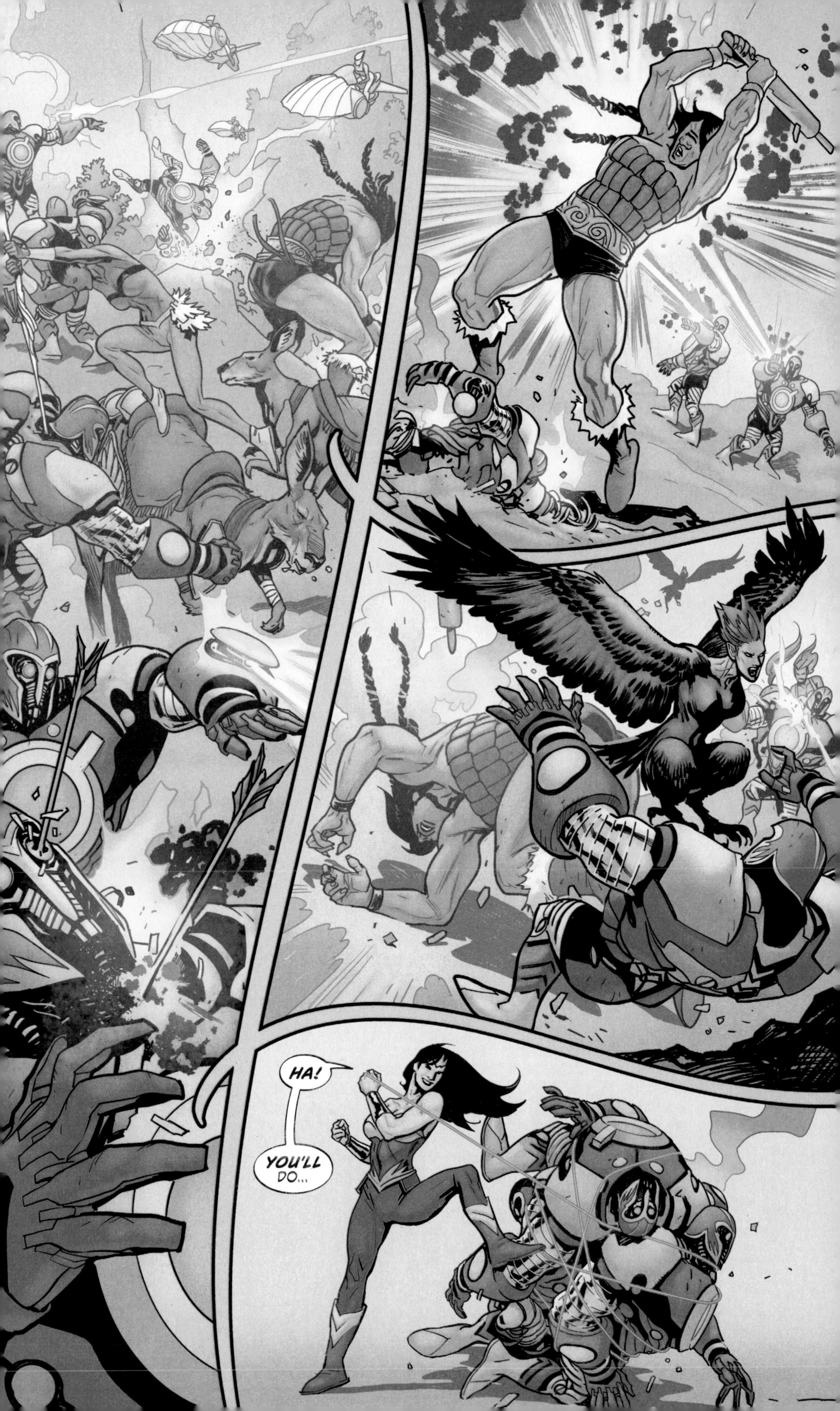
HA!
YOU'LL DO...

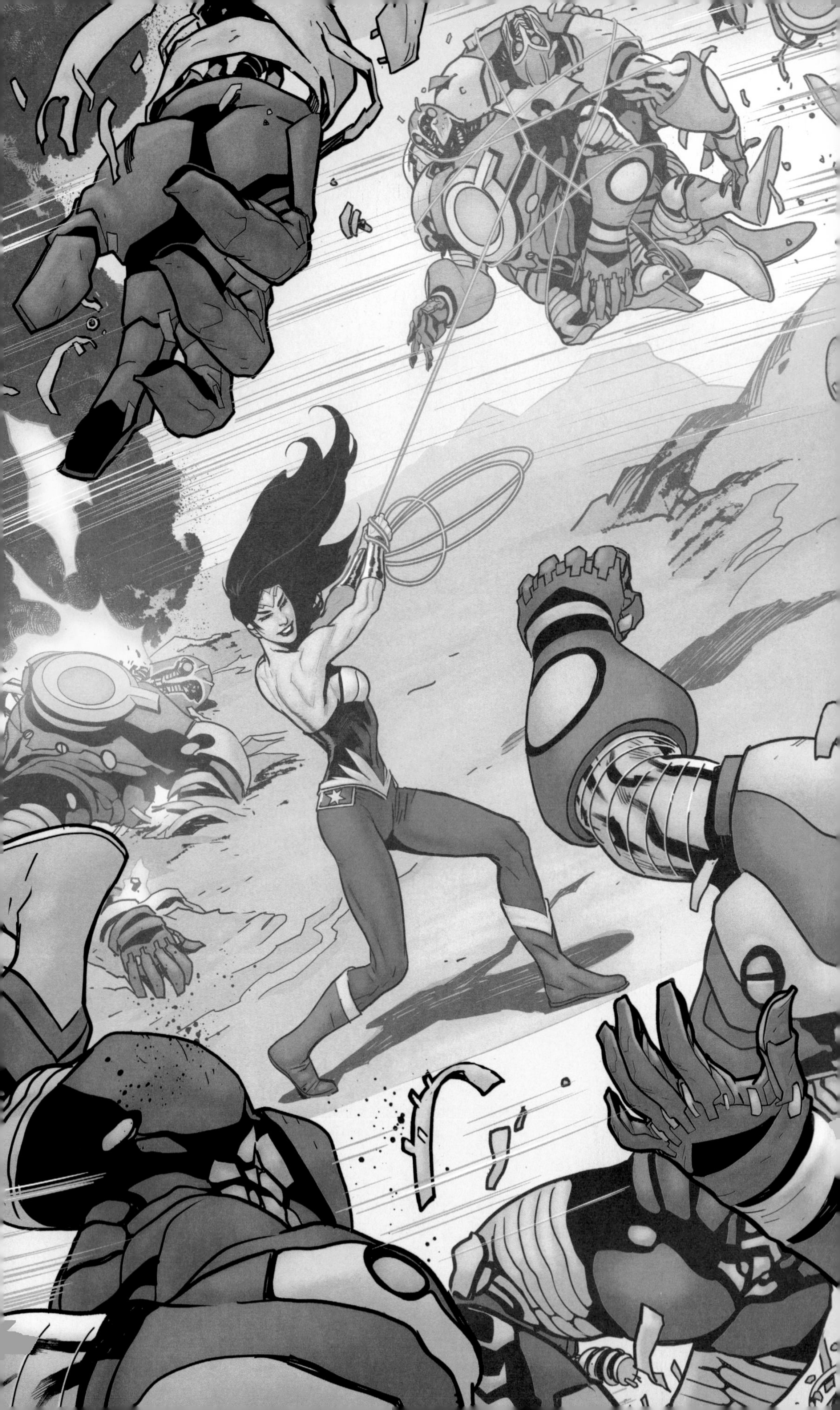

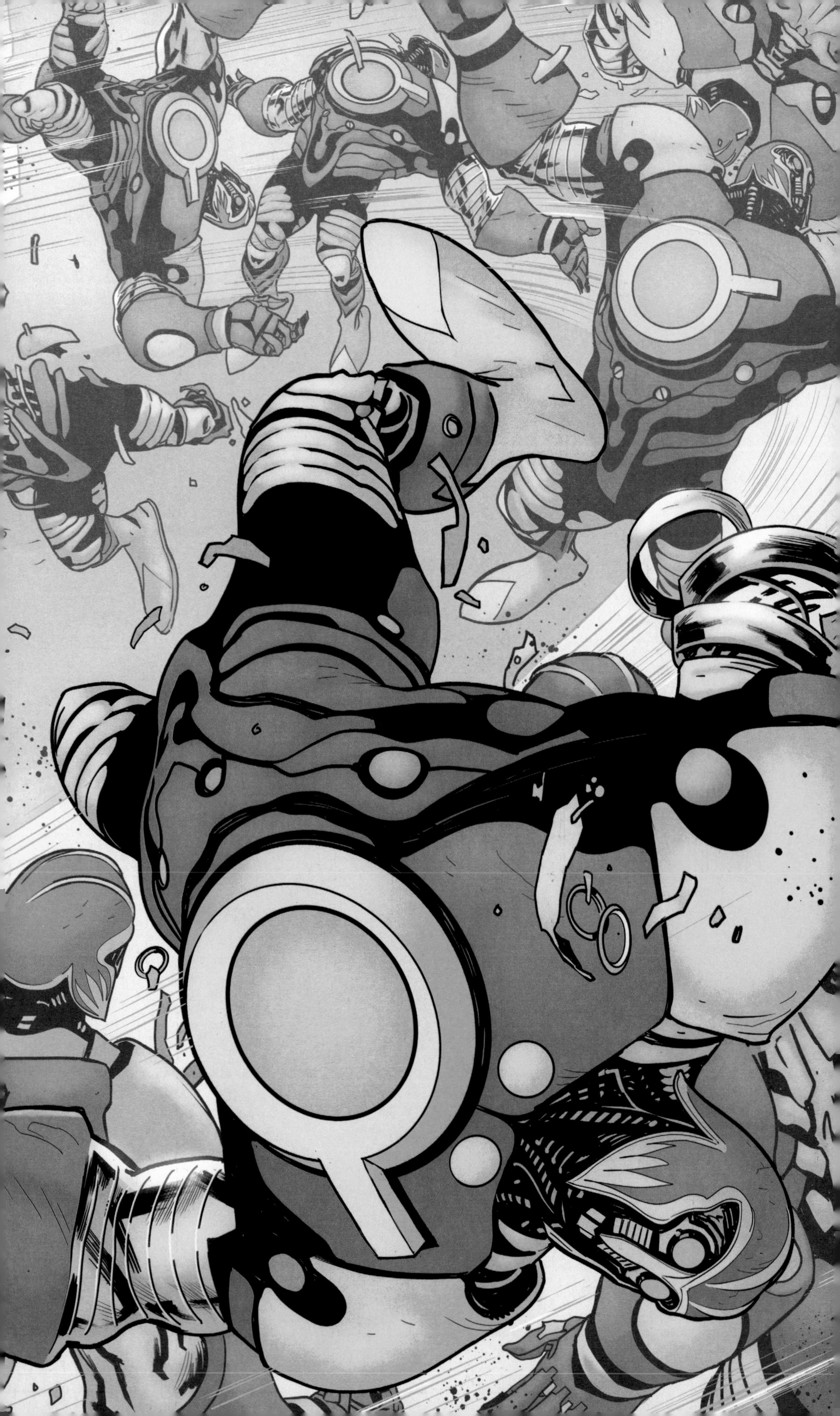

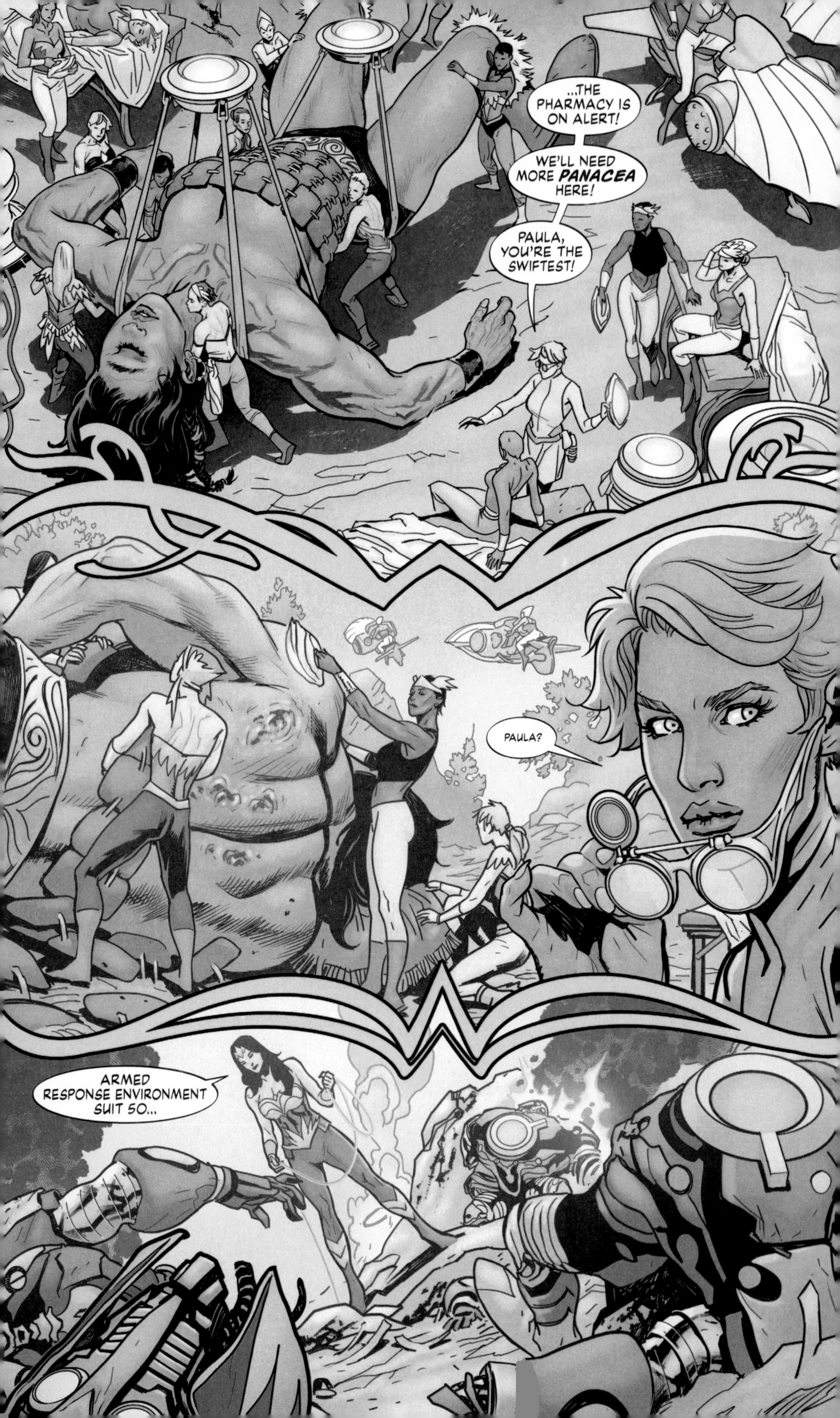
...THE PHARMACY IS ON ALERT!
WE'LL NEED MORE ***PANACEA*** HERE!
PAULA, YOU'RE THE SWIFTEST!
PAULA?
ARMED RESPONSE ENVIRONMENT SUIT 50...

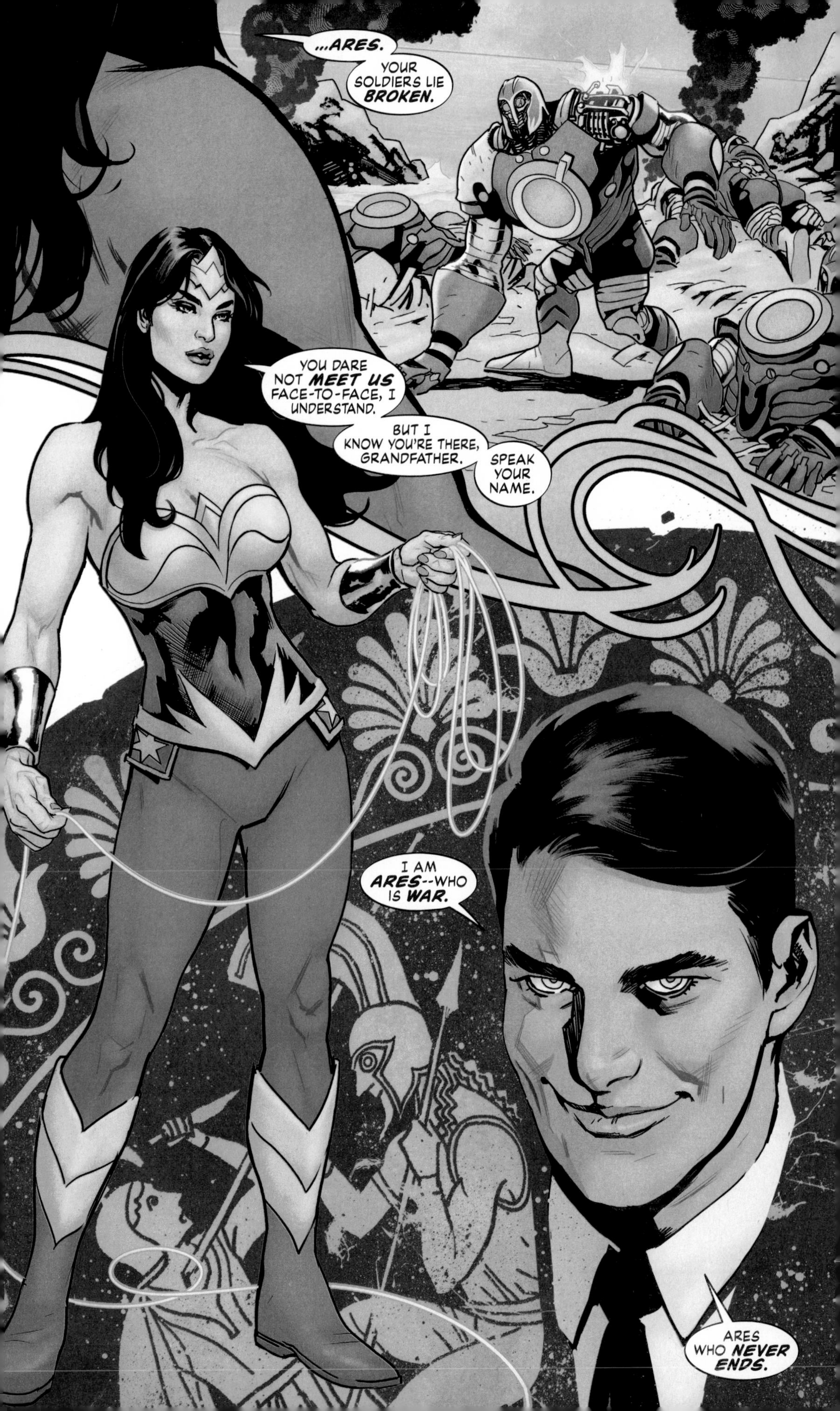
...ARES.
YOUR SOLDIERS LIE BROKEN.
YOU DARE NOT MEET US FACE-TO-FACE, I UNDERSTAND.
BUT I KNOW YOU'RE THERE, GRANDFATHER.
SPEAK YOUR NAME.
I AM ARES--WHO IS WAR.
ARES WHO NEVER ENDS.

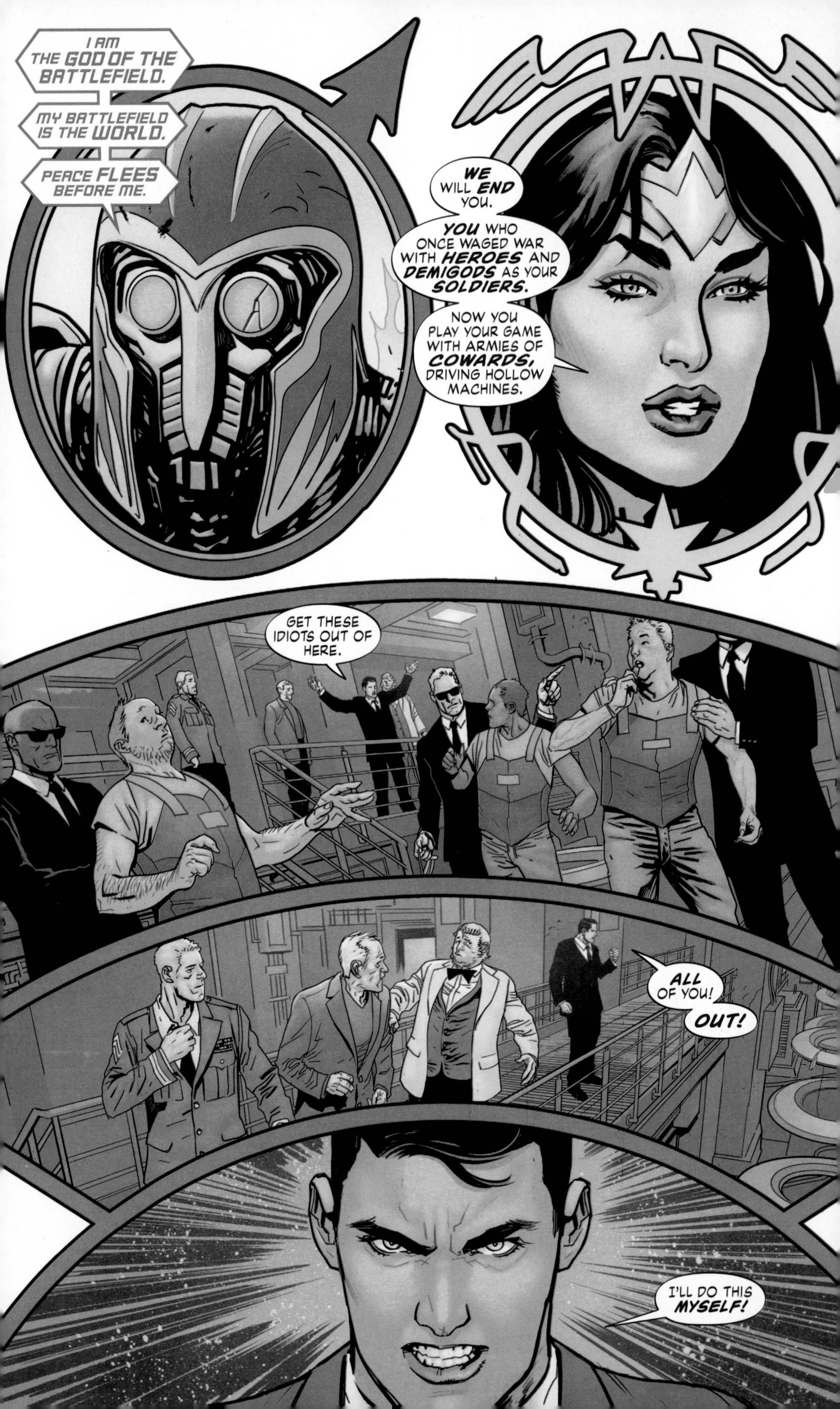
I AM THE GOD OF THE BATTLEFIELD.
MY BATTLEFIELD IS THE WORLD.
PEACE FLEES BEFORE ME.
WE WILL END YOU.
YOU WHO ONCE WAGED WAR WITH HEROES AND DEMIGODS AS YOUR SOLDIERS.
NOW YOU PLAY YOUR GAME WITH ARMIES OF COWARDS, DRIVING HOLLOW MACHINES.
GET THESE IDIOTS OUT OF HERE.
ALL OF YOU!
OUT!
I'LL DO THIS MYSELF!

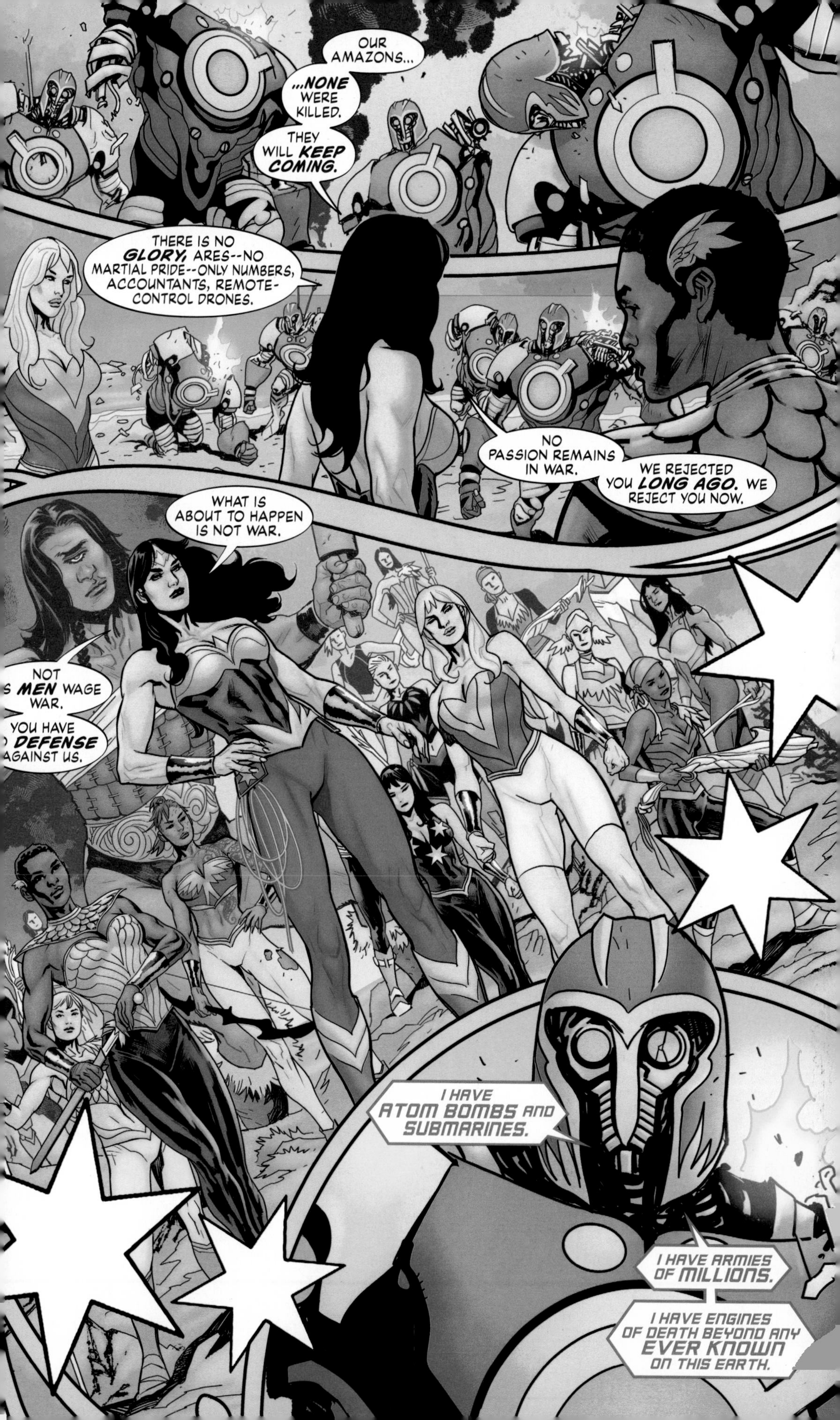
OUR AMAZONS...
...NONE WERE KILLED.
THEY WILL KEEP COMING.
THERE IS NO GLORY, ARES--NO MARTIAL PRIDE--ONLY NUMBERS, ACCOUNTANTS, REMOTE-CONTROL DRONES.
NO PASSION REMAINS IN WAR.
WE REJECTED YOU LONG AGO. WE REJECT YOU NOW.
WHAT IS ABOUT TO HAPPEN IS NOT WAR.
NOT
MEN WAGE WAR.
YOU HAVE
DEFENSE AGAINST US.
I HAVE ATOM BOMBS AND SUBMARINES.
I HAVE ARMIES OF MILLIONS.
I HAVE ENGINES OF DEATH BEYOND ANY EVER KNOWN ON THIS EARTH.

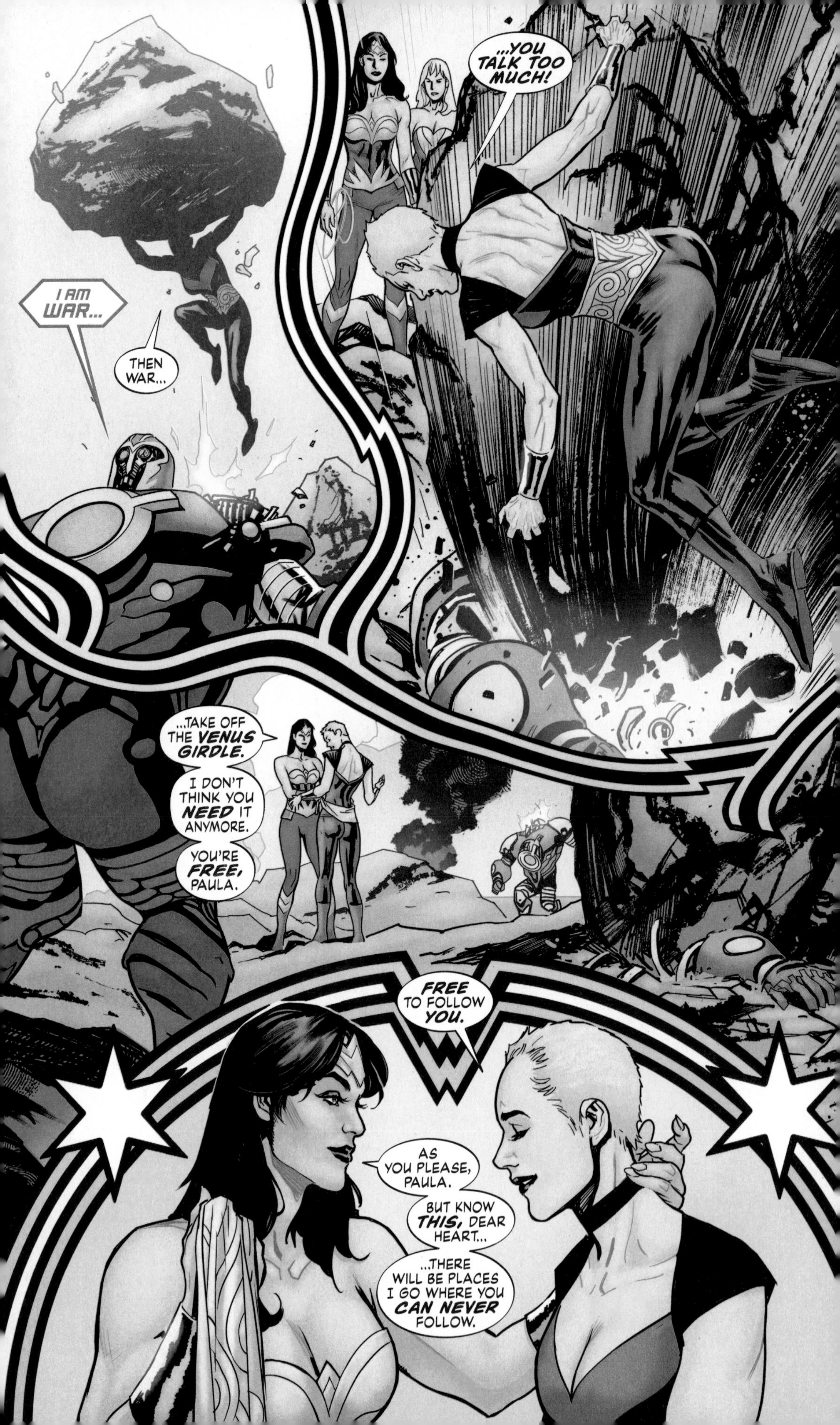
...YOU TALK TOO MUCH!
I AM WAR...
THEN WAR...
...TAKE OFF THE VENUS GIRDLE.
I DON'T THINK YOU NEED IT ANYMORE.
YOU'RE FREE, PAULA.
FREE TO FOLLOW YOU.
AS YOU PLEASE, PAULA.
BUT KNOW THIS, DEAR HEART...
...THERE WILL BE PLACES I GO WHERE YOU CAN NEVER FOLLOW.

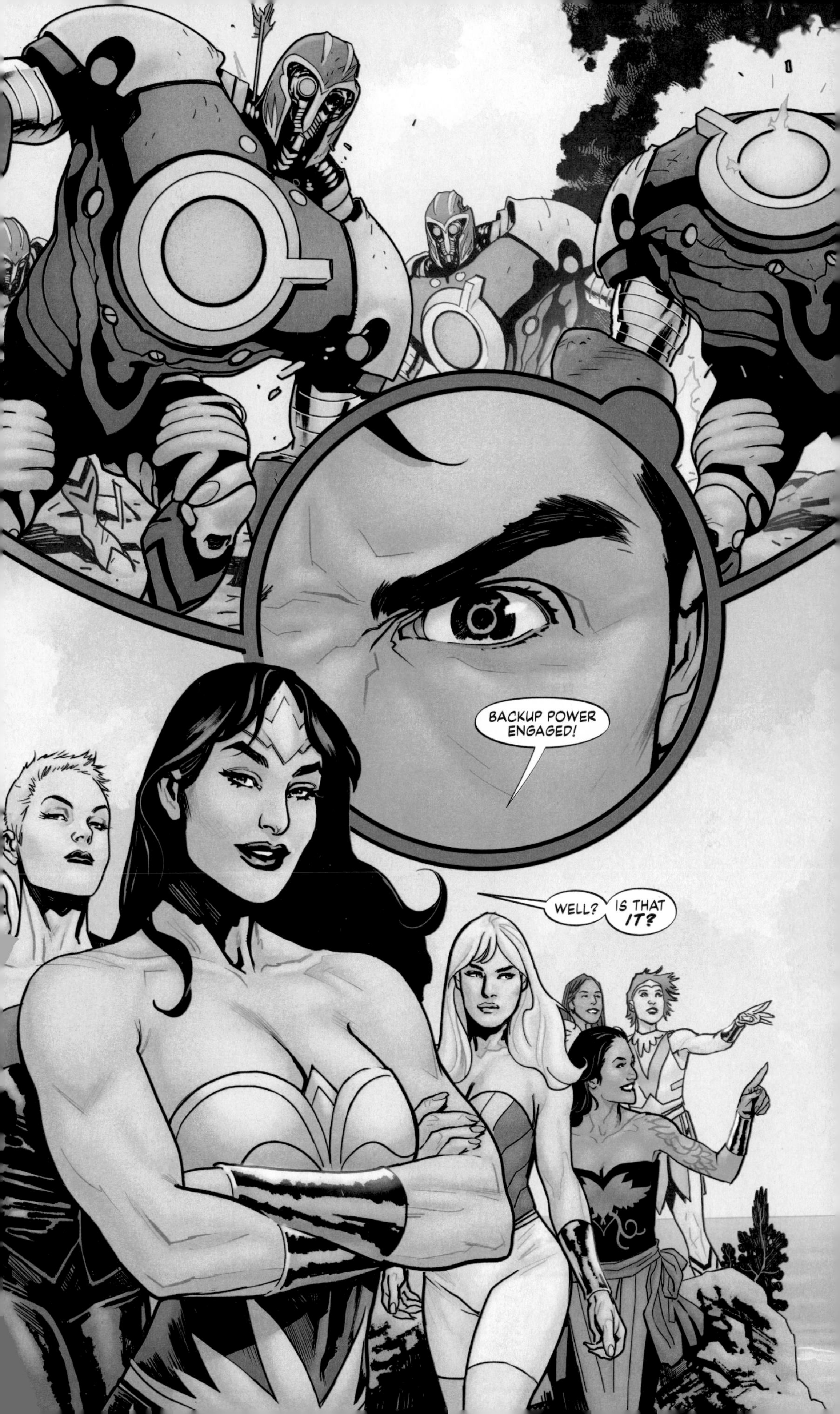
BACKUP POWER ENGAGED!
WELL?
IS THAT *IT?*

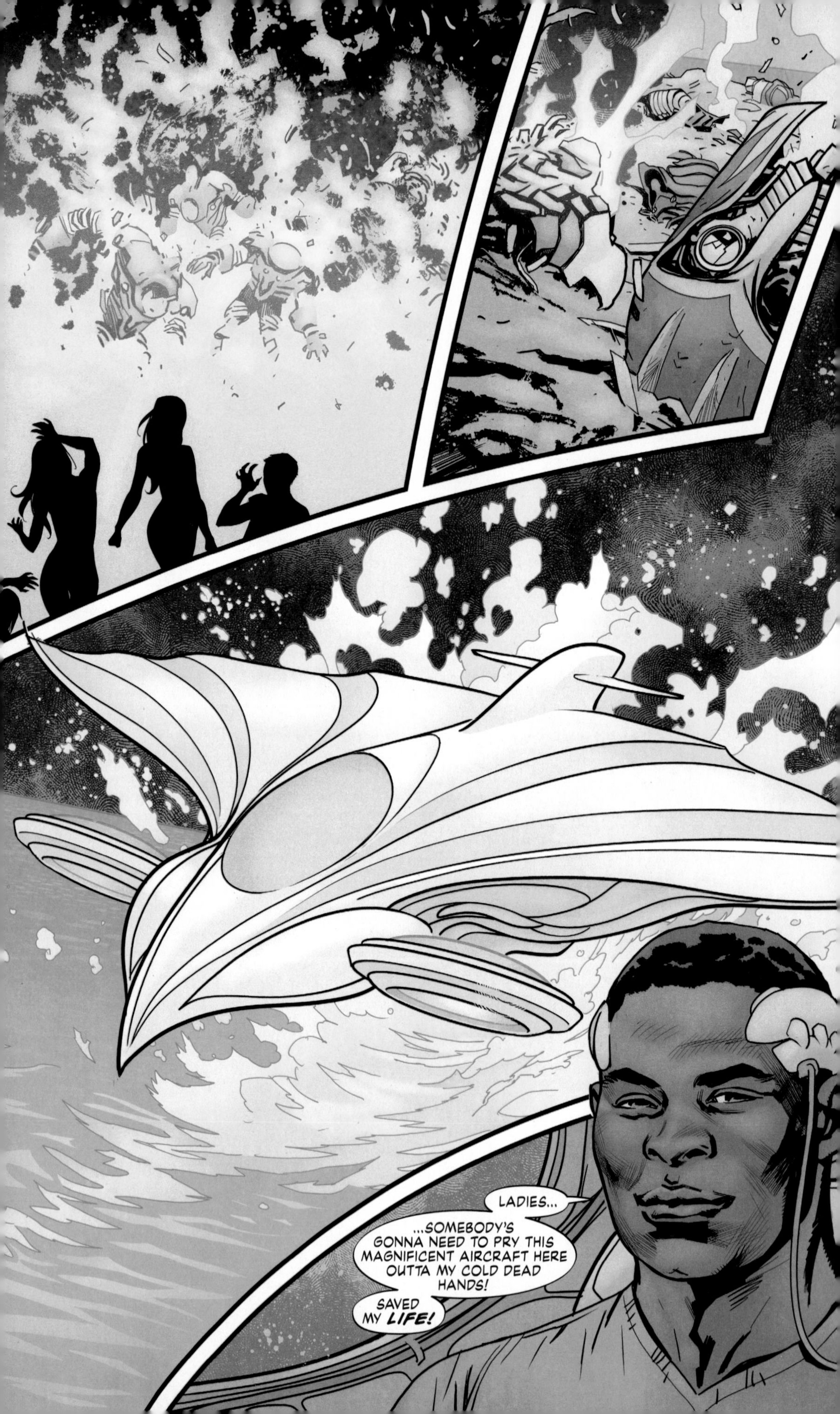
LADIES...
...SOMEBODY'S GONNA NEED TO PRY THIS MAGNIFICENT AIRCRAFT HERE OUTTA MY COLD DEAD HANDS!
SAVED MY LIFE!

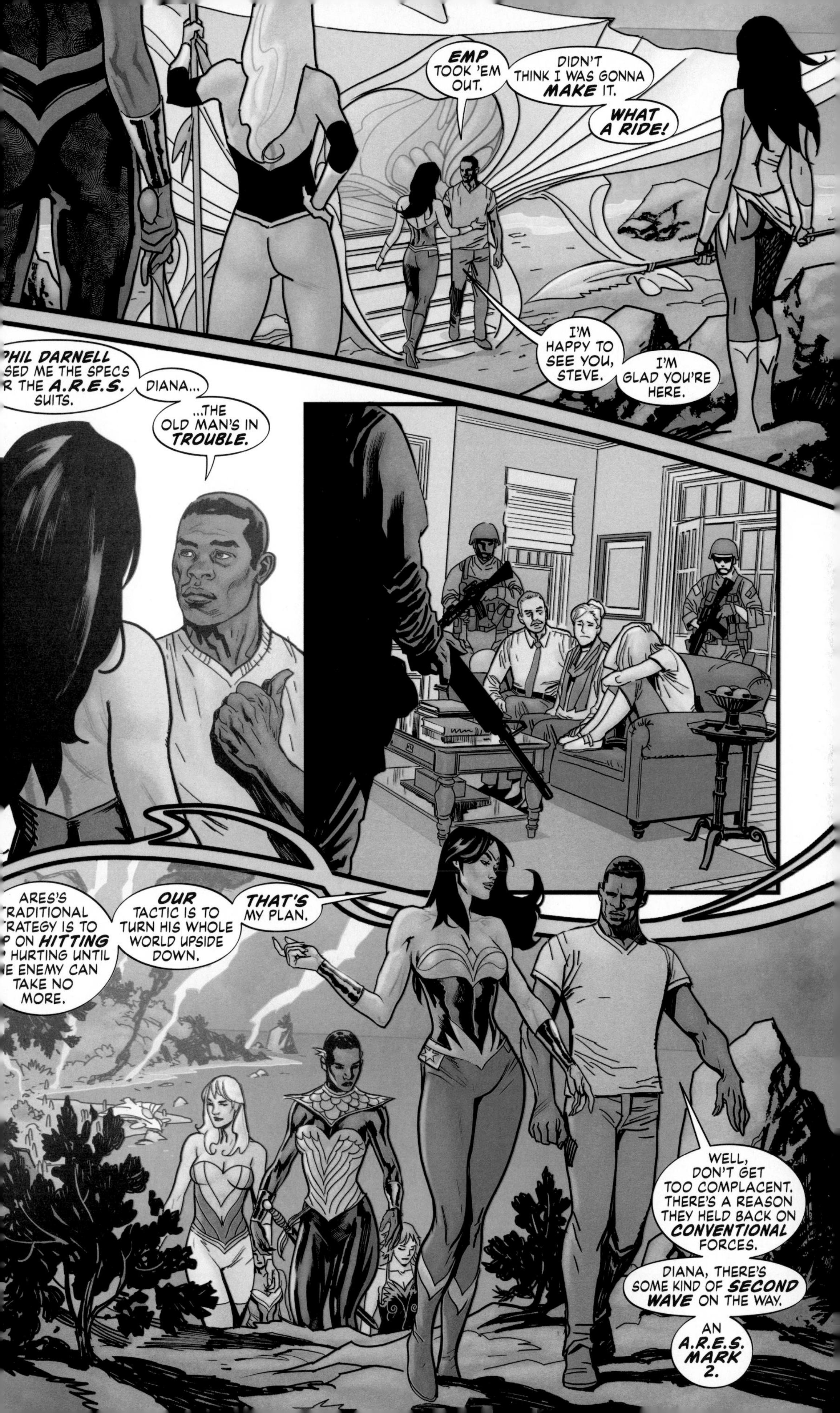
EMP TOOK 'EM OUT.
DIDN'T THINK I WAS GONNA MAKE IT.
WHAT A RIDE!
I'M HAPPY TO SEE YOU, STEVE.
I'M GLAD YOU'RE HERE.
PHIL DARNELL SED ME THE SPECS R THE A.R.E.S. SUITS.
DIANA...
...THE OLD MAN'S IN TROUBLE.
ARES'S TRADITIONAL TRATEGY IS TO P ON HITTING HURTING UNTIL E ENEMY CAN TAKE NO MORE.
OUR TACTIC IS TO TURN HIS WHOLE WORLD UPSIDE DOWN.
THAT'S MY PLAN.
WELL, DON'T GET TOO COMPLACENT. THERE'S A REASON THEY HELD BACK ON CONVENTIONAL FORCES.
DIANA, THERE'S SOME KIND OF SECOND WAVE ON THE WAY.
AN A.R.E.S. MARK 2.

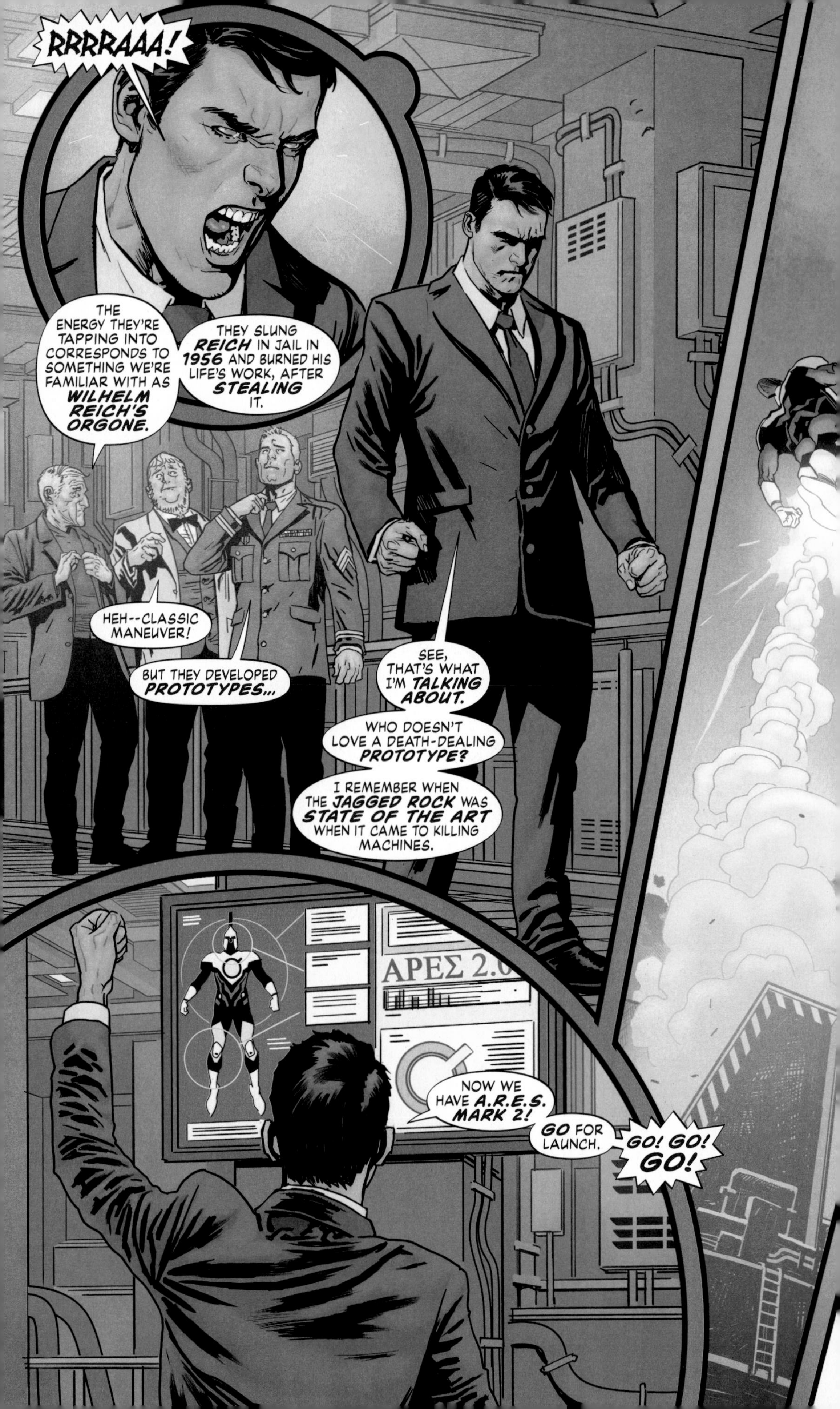

RRRRAAA!
THE ENERGY THEY'RE TAPPING INTO CORRESPONDS TO SOMETHING WE'RE FAMILIAR WITH AS WILHELM REICH'S ORGONE.
THEY SLUNG REICH IN JAIL IN 1956 AND BURNED HIS LIFE'S WORK, AFTER STEALING IT.
HEH--CLASSIC MANEUVER!
BUT THEY DEVELOPED PROTOTYPES...
SEE, THAT'S WHAT I'M TALKING ABOUT.
WHO DOESN'T LOVE A DEATH-DEALING PROTOTYPE?
I REMEMBER WHEN THE JAGGED ROCK WAS STATE OF THE ART WHEN IT CAME TO KILLING MACHINES.
ΑΡΕΣ 2.0
NOW WE HAVE A.R.E.S. MARK 2!
GO FOR LAUNCH.
GO! GO! GO!

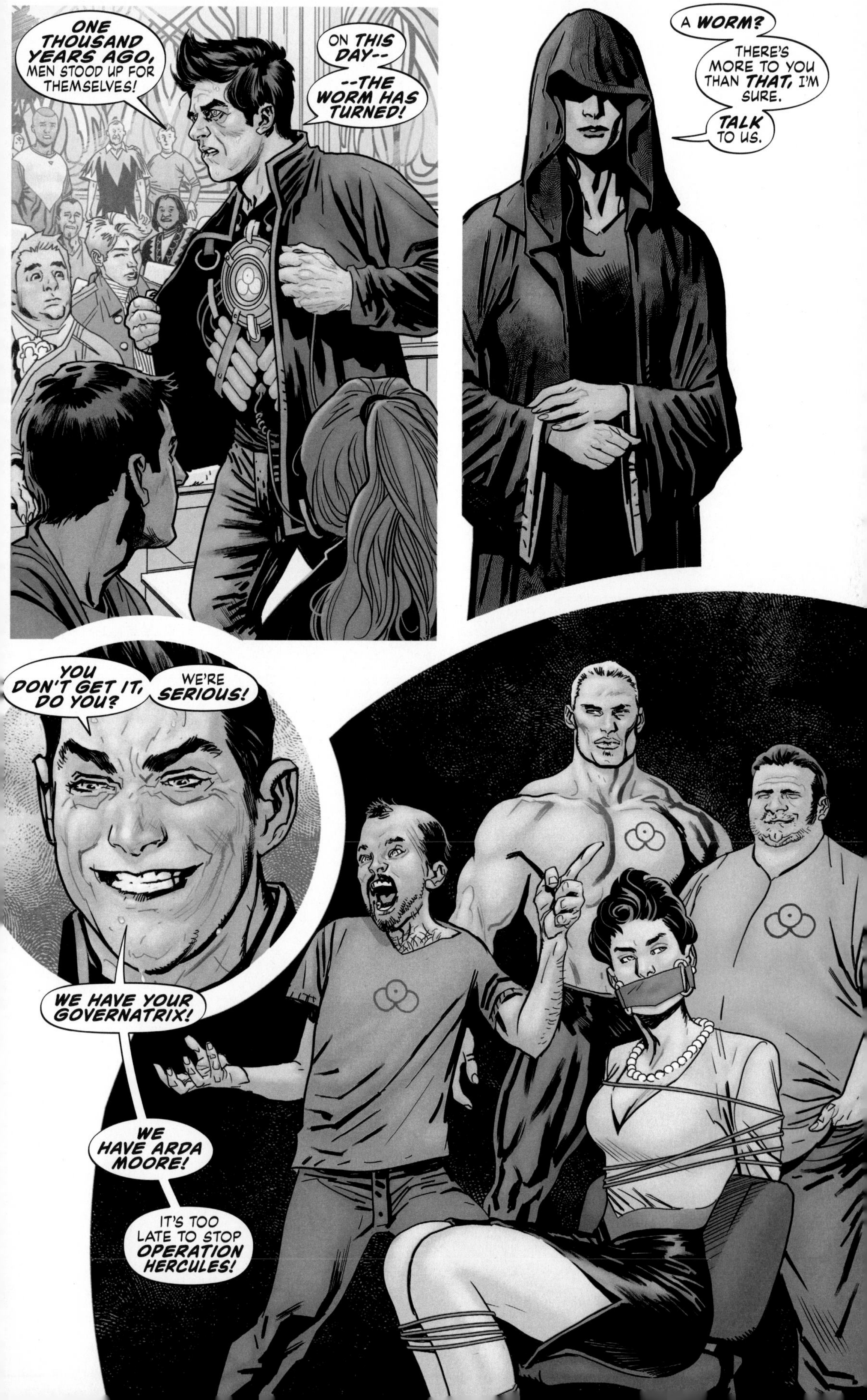
ONE THOUSAND YEARS AGO, MEN STOOD UP FOR THEMSELVES!
ON THIS DAY--
--THE WORM HAS TURNED!
A WORM?
THERE'S MORE TO YOU THAN THAT, I'M SURE.
TALK TO US.
YOU DON'T GET IT, DO YOU?
WE'RE SERIOUS!
WE HAVE YOUR GOVERNATRIX!
WE HAVE ARDA MOORE!
IT'S TOO LATE TO STOP OPERATION HERCULES!

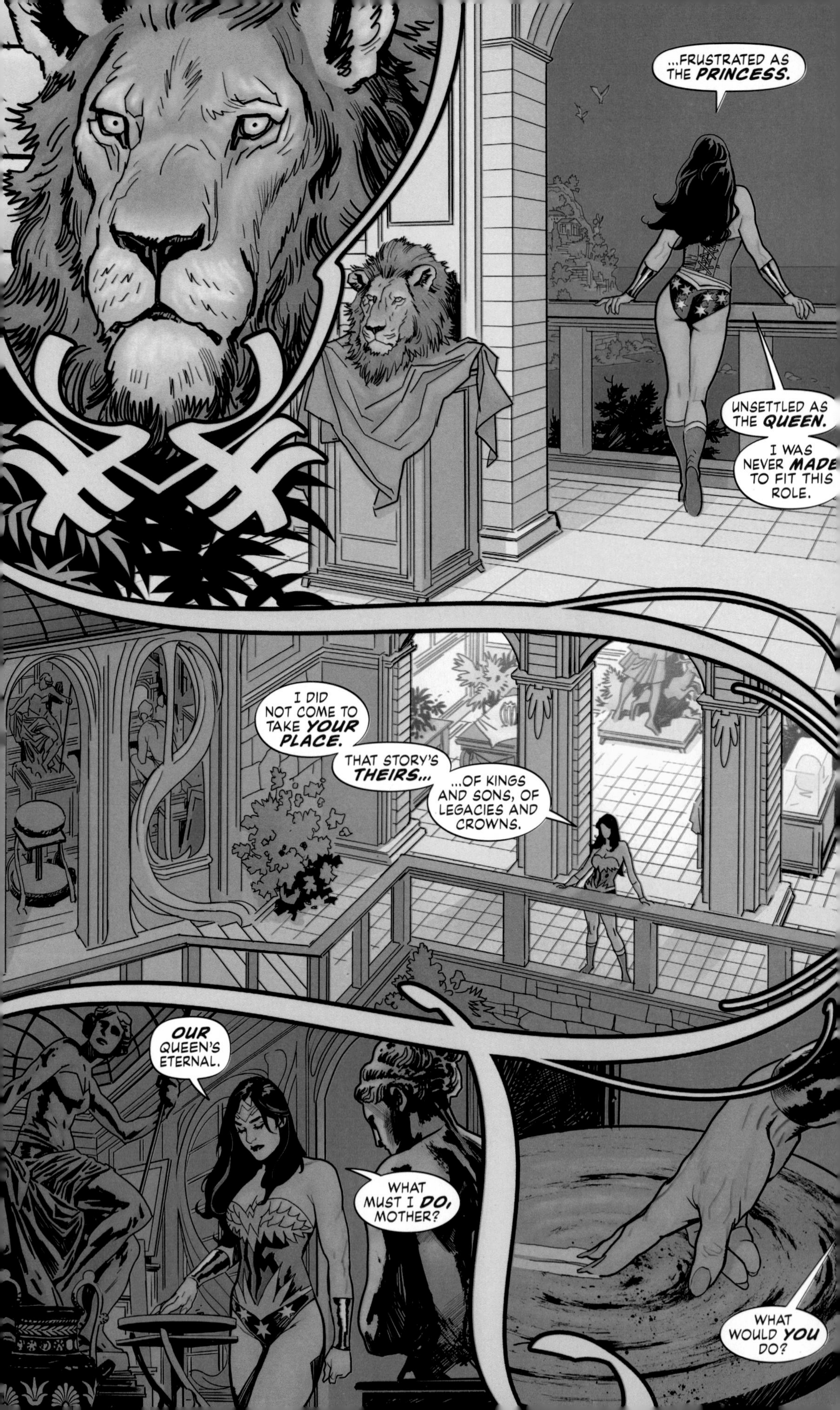
...FRUSTRATED AS THE PRINCESS.
UNSETTLED AS THE QUEEN.
I WAS NEVER MADE TO FIT THIS ROLE.
I DID NOT COME TO TAKE YOUR PLACE.
THAT STORY'S THEIRS...
...OF KINGS AND SONS, OF LEGACIES AND CROWNS.
OUR QUEEN'S ETERNAL.
WHAT MUST I DO, MOTHER?
WHAT WOULD YOU DO?

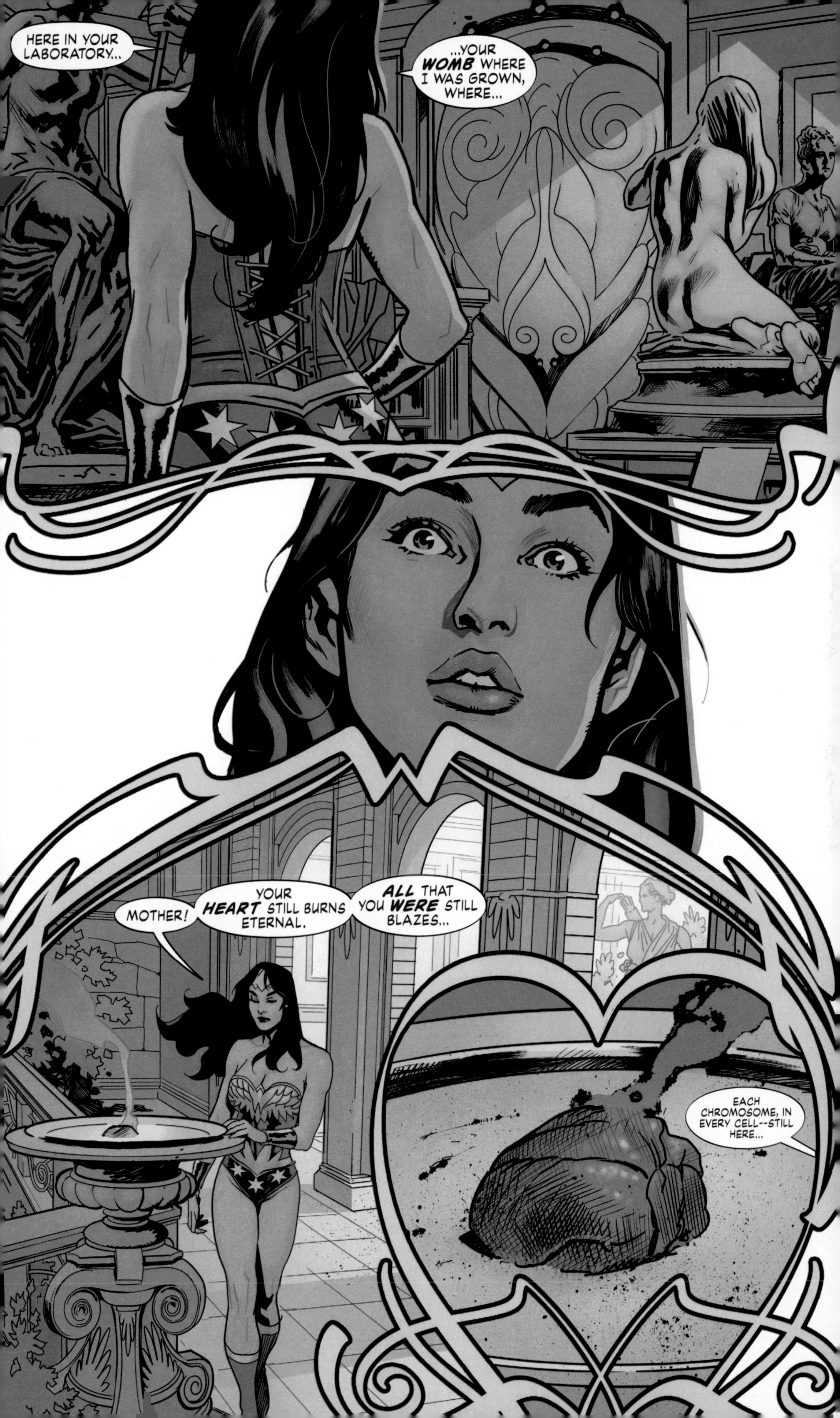
HERE IN YOUR LABORATORY...
...YOUR WOMB WHERE I WAS GROWN, WHERE...
MOTHER!
YOUR HEART STILL BURNS ETERNAL.
ALL THAT YOU WERE STILL BLAZES...
EACH CHROMOSOME, IN EVERY CELL--STILL HERE...

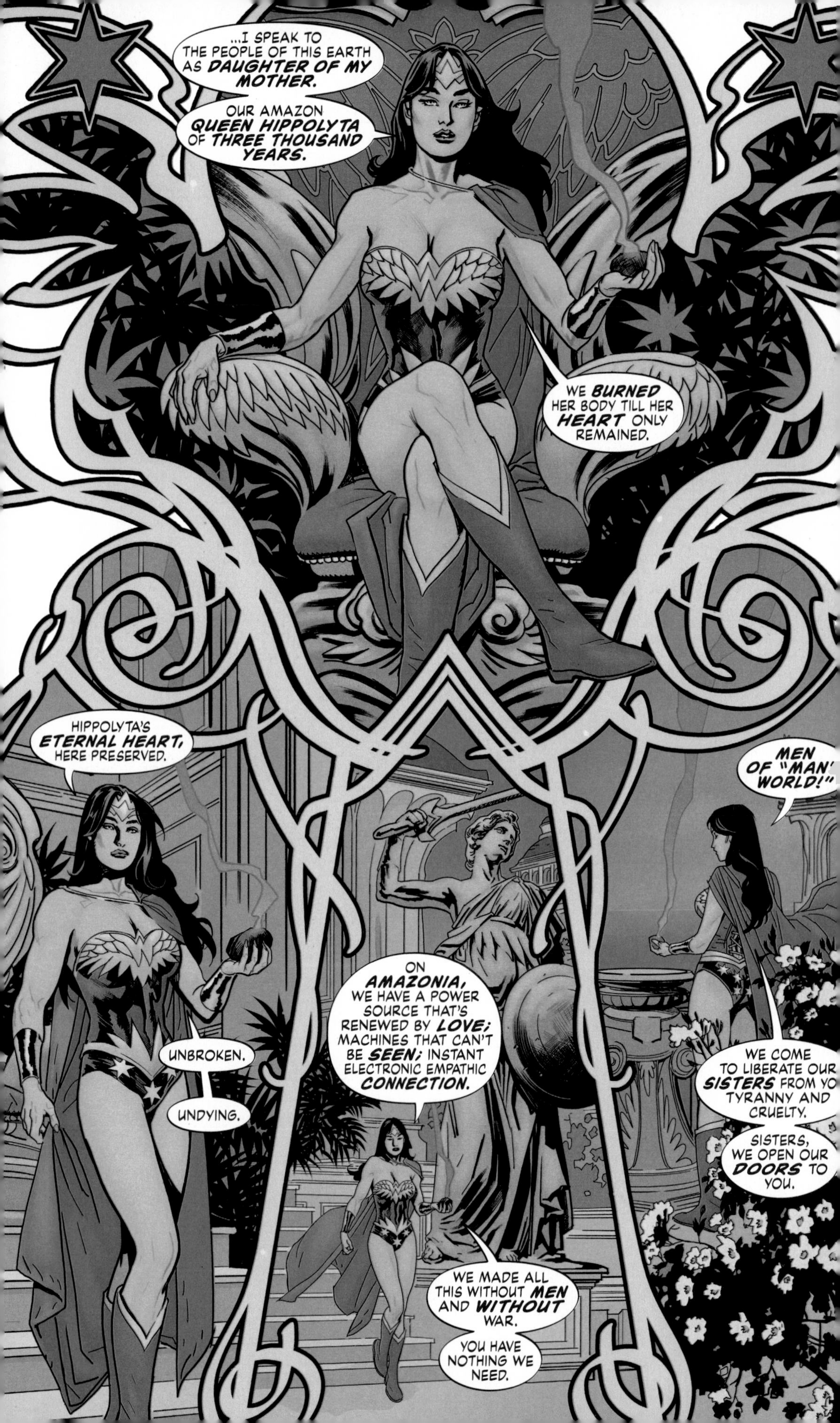

...I SPEAK TO THE PEOPLE OF THIS EARTH AS DAUGHTER OF MY MOTHER.
OUR AMAZON QUEEN HIPPOLYTA OF THREE THOUSAND YEARS.
WE BURNED HER BODY TILL HER HEART ONLY REMAINED.
HIPPOLYTA'S ETERNAL HEART, HERE PRESERVED.
UNBROKEN.
UNDYING.
ON AMAZONIA, WE HAVE A POWER SOURCE THAT'S RENEWED BY LOVE; MACHINES THAT CAN'T BE SEEN; INSTANT ELECTRONIC EMPATHIC CONNECTION.
WE MADE ALL THIS WITHOUT MEN AND WITHOUT WAR.
YOU HAVE NOTHING WE NEED.
MEN OF "MAN' WORLD!"
WE COME TO LIBERATE OUR SISTERS FROM YO TYRANNY AND CRUELTY.
SISTERS, WE OPEN OUR DOORS TO YOU.

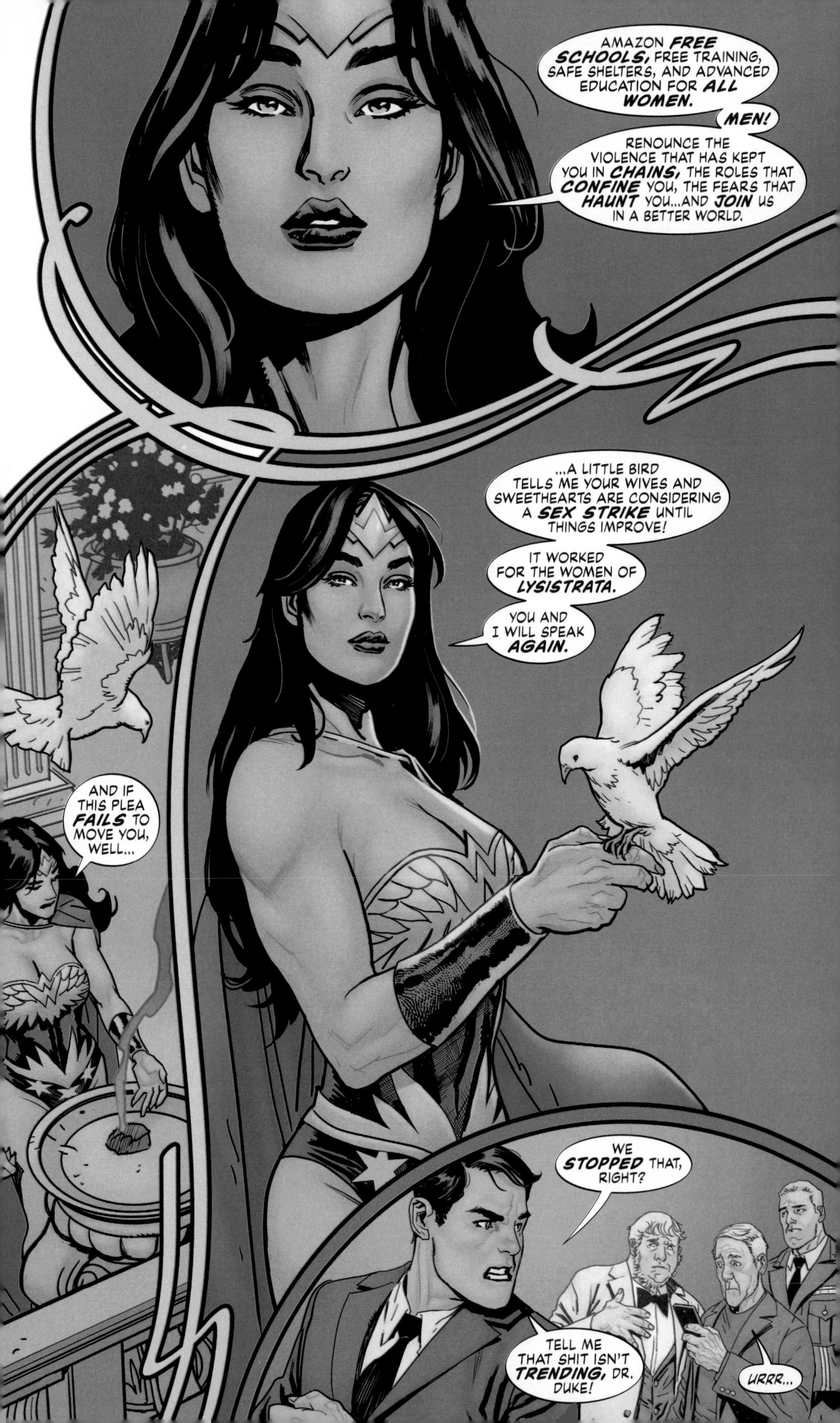
AMAZON FREE SCHOOLS, FREE TRAINING, SAFE SHELTERS, AND ADVANCED EDUCATION FOR ALL WOMEN.
MEN!
RENOUNCE THE VIOLENCE THAT HAS KEPT YOU IN CHAINS, THE ROLES THAT CONFINE YOU, THE FEARS THAT HAUNT YOU...AND JOIN US IN A BETTER WORLD.
...A LITTLE BIRD TELLS ME YOUR WIVES AND SWEETHEARTS ARE CONSIDERING A SEX STRIKE UNTIL THINGS IMPROVE!
IT WORKED FOR THE WOMEN OF LYSISTRATA.
YOU AND I WILL SPEAK AGAIN.
AND IF THIS PLEA FAILS TO MOVE YOU, WELL...
WE STOPPED THAT, RIGHT?
TELL ME THAT SHIT ISN'T TRENDING, DR. DUKE!
URRR...

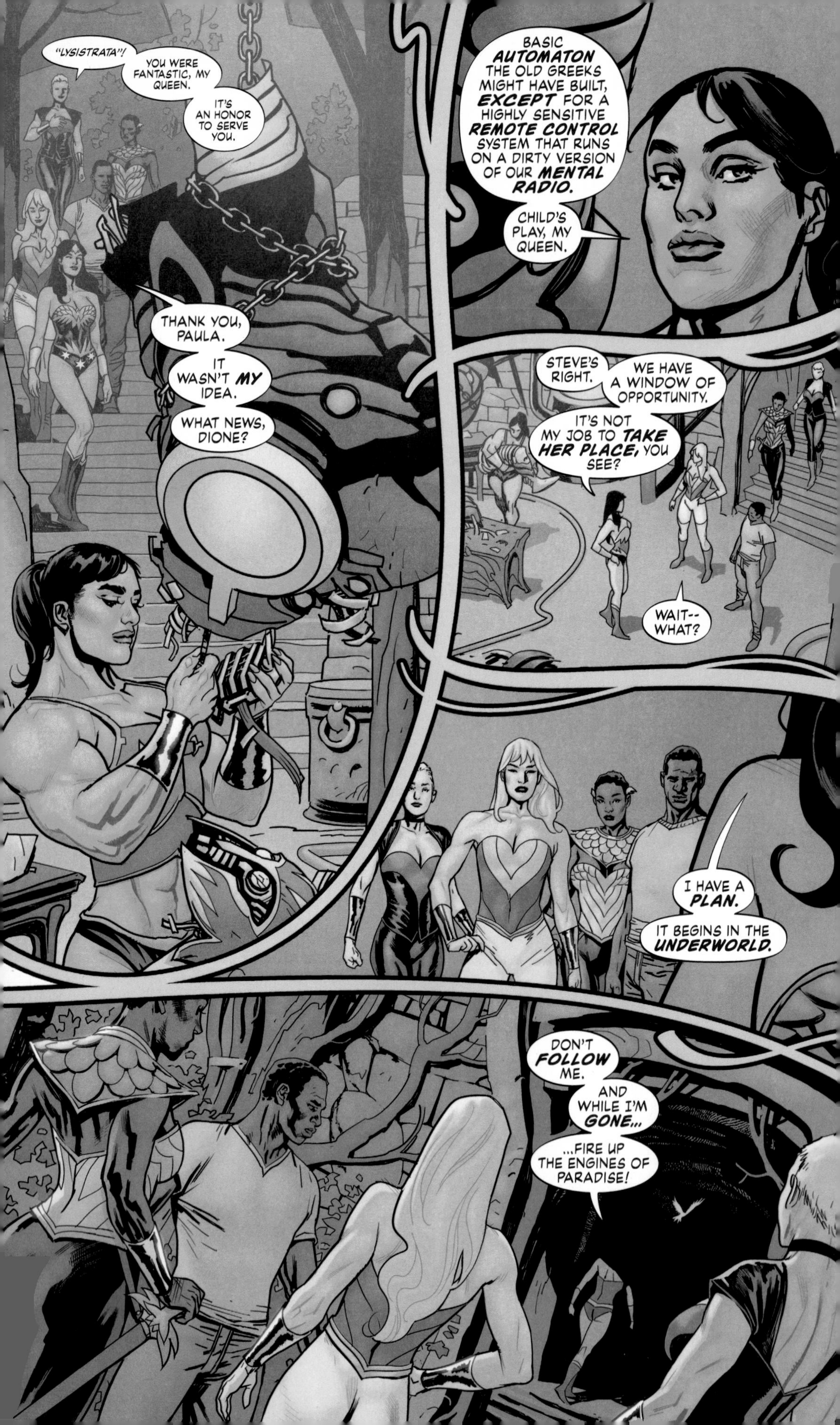
"LYSISTRATA"!
YOU WERE FANTASTIC, MY QUEEN.
IT'S AN HONOR TO SERVE YOU.
THANK YOU, PAULA.
IT WASN'T MY IDEA.
WHAT NEWS, DIONE?
BASIC AUTOMATON THE OLD GREEKS MIGHT HAVE BUILT, EXCEPT FOR A HIGHLY SENSITIVE REMOTE CONTROL SYSTEM THAT RUNS ON A DIRTY VERSION OF OUR MENTAL RADIO.
CHILD'S PLAY, MY QUEEN.
STEVE'S RIGHT.
WE HAVE A WINDOW OF OPPORTUNITY.
IT'S NOT MY JOB TO TAKE HER PLACE, YOU SEE?
WAIT-- WHAT?
I HAVE A PLAN.
IT BEGINS IN THE UNDERWORLD.
DON'T FOLLOW ME.
AND WHILE I'M GONE...
...FIRE UP THE ENGINES OF PARADISE!

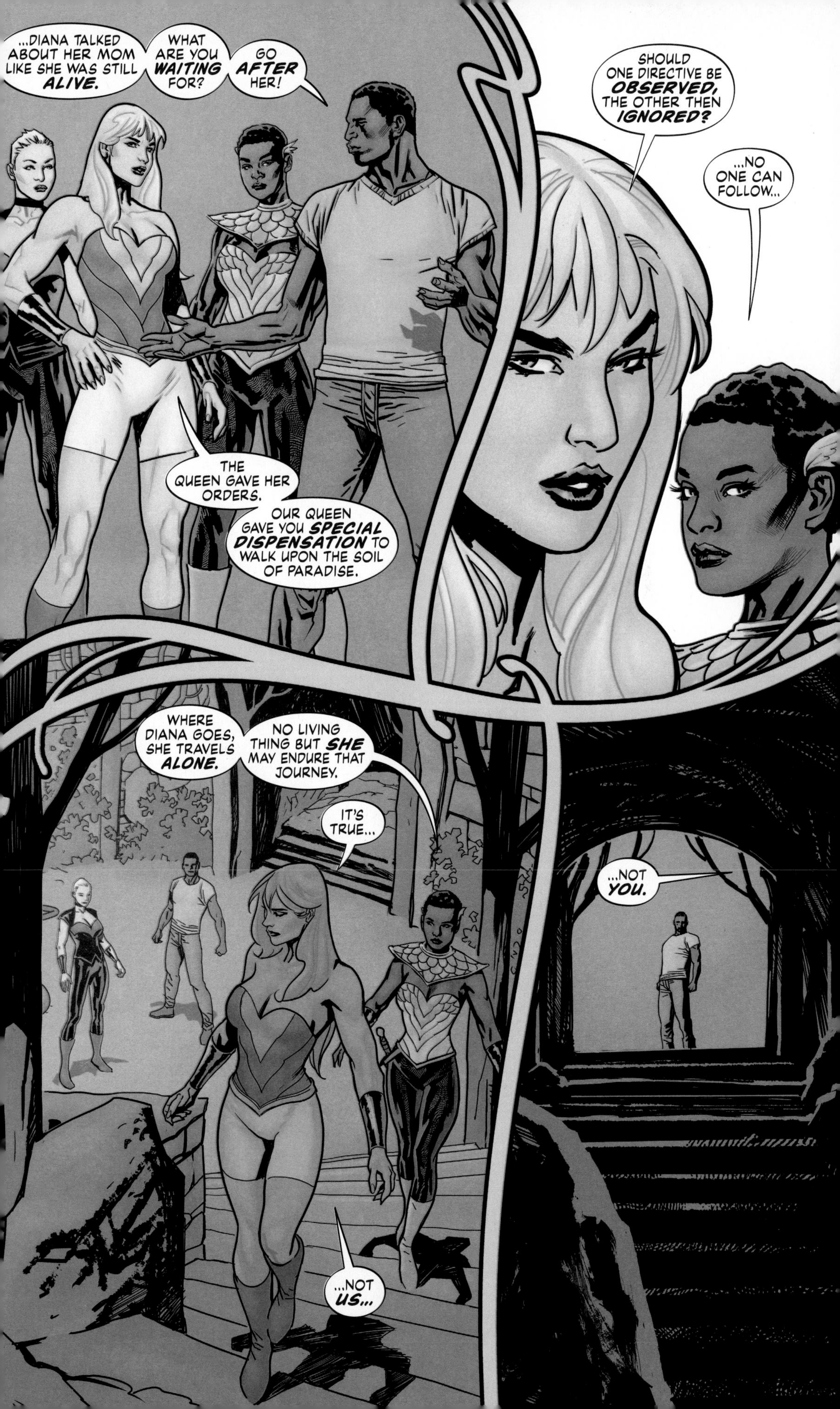

...DIANA TALKED ABOUT HER MOM LIKE SHE WAS STILL ALIVE.
WHAT ARE YOU WAITING FOR?
GO AFTER HER!
THE QUEEN GAVE HER ORDERS.
OUR QUEEN GAVE YOU SPECIAL DISPENSATION TO WALK UPON THE SOIL OF PARADISE.
SHOULD ONE DIRECTIVE BE OBSERVED, THE OTHER THEN IGNORED?
...NO ONE CAN FOLLOW...
WHERE DIANA GOES, SHE TRAVELS ALONE.
NO LIVING THING BUT SHE MAY ENDURE THAT JOURNEY.
IT'S TRUE...
...NOT US...
...NOT YOU.

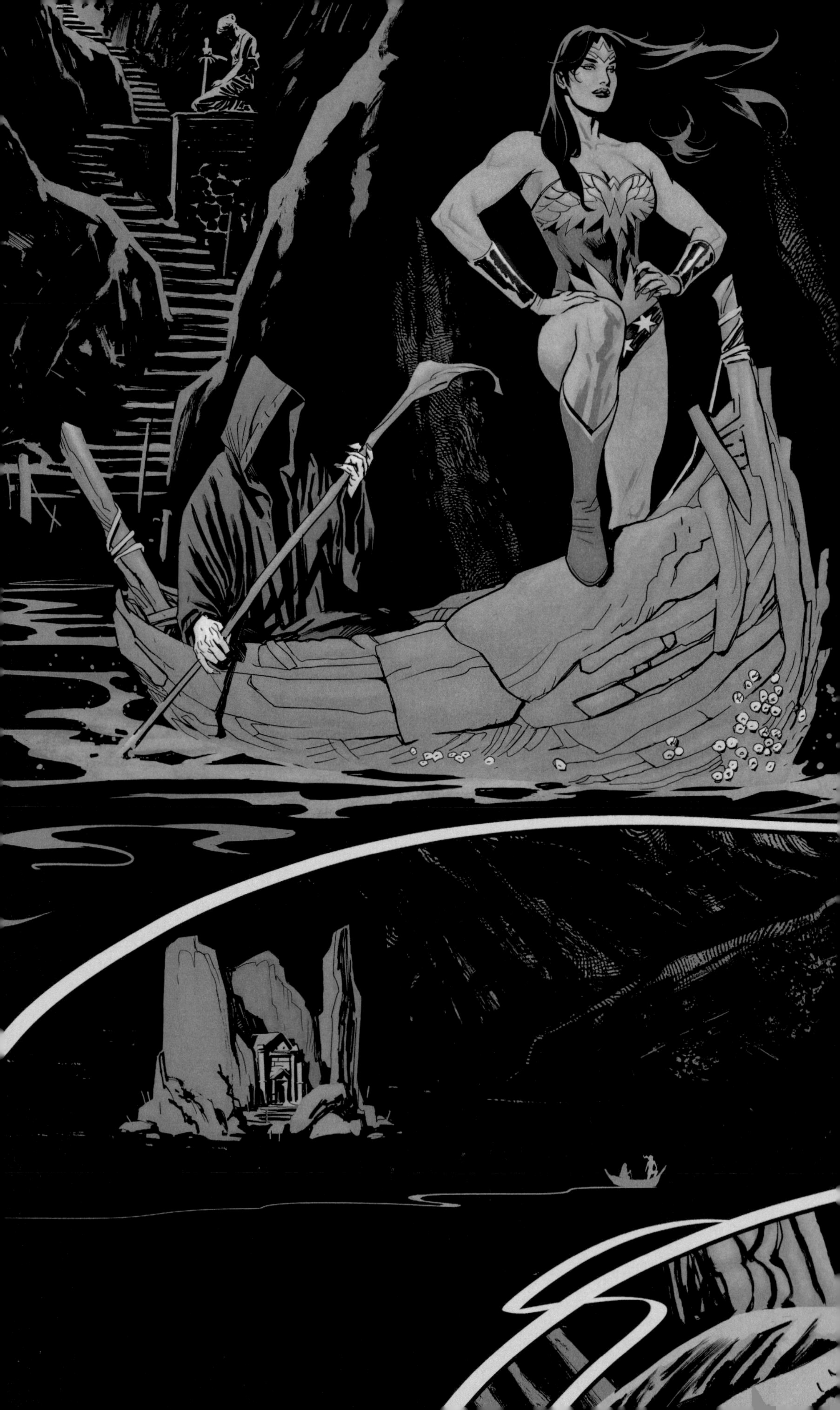

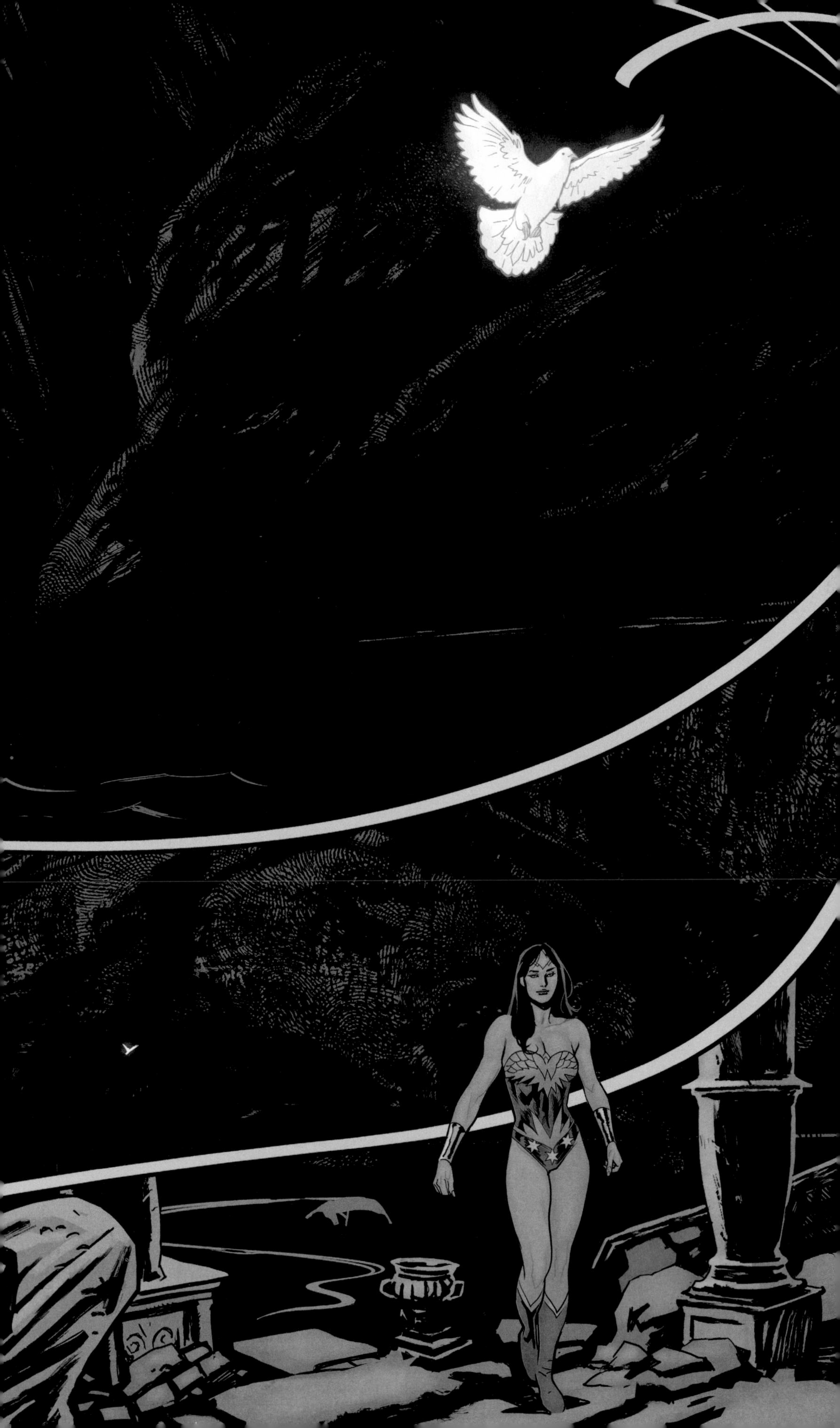

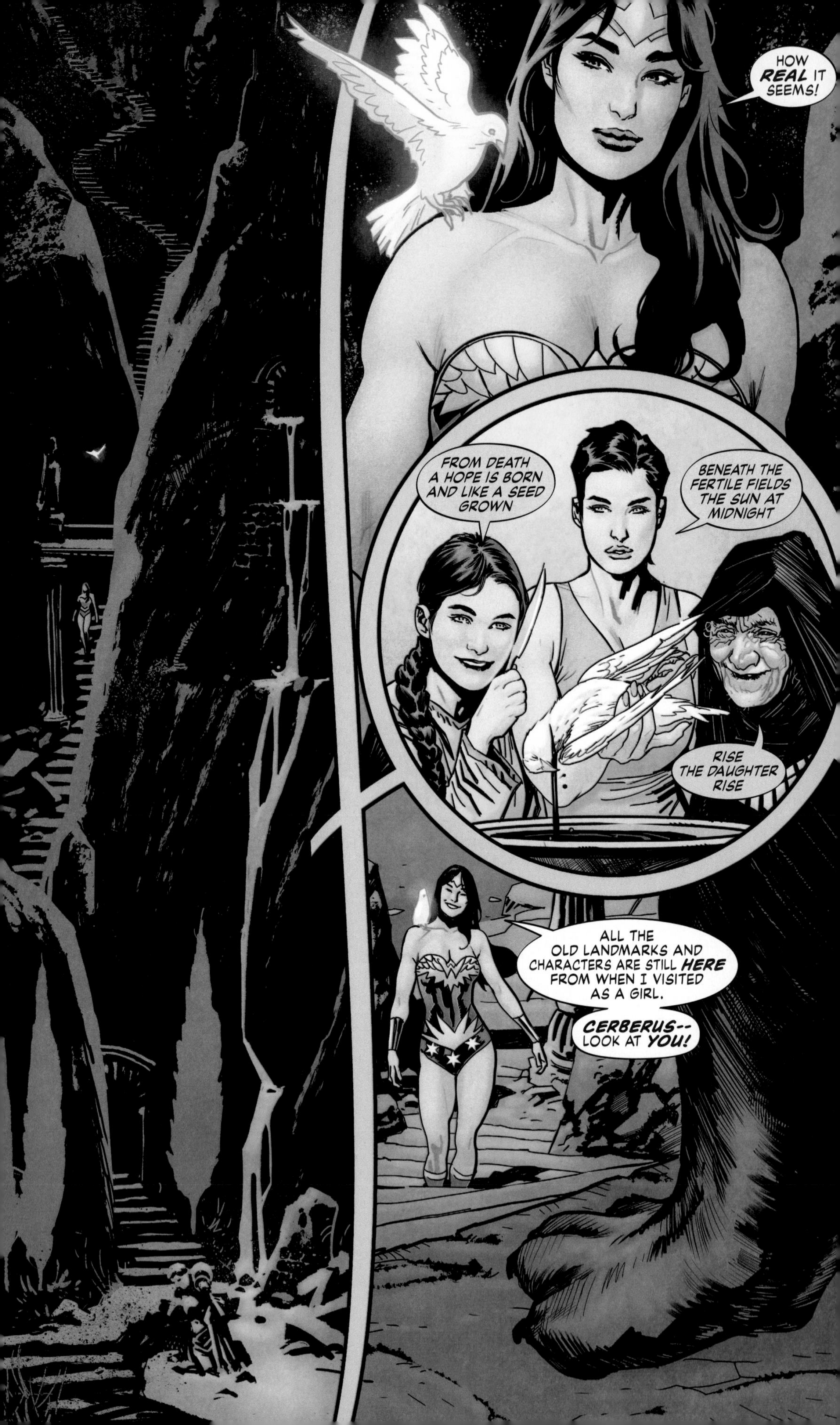

HOW REAL IT SEEMS!
FROM DEATH A HOPE IS BORN AND LIKE A SEED GROWN
BENEATH THE FERTILE FIELDS THE SUN AT MIDNIGHT
RISE THE DAUGHTER RISE
ALL THE OLD LANDMARKS AND CHARACTERS ARE STILL HERE FROM WHEN I VISITED AS A GIRL.
CERBERUS-- LOOK AT YOU!

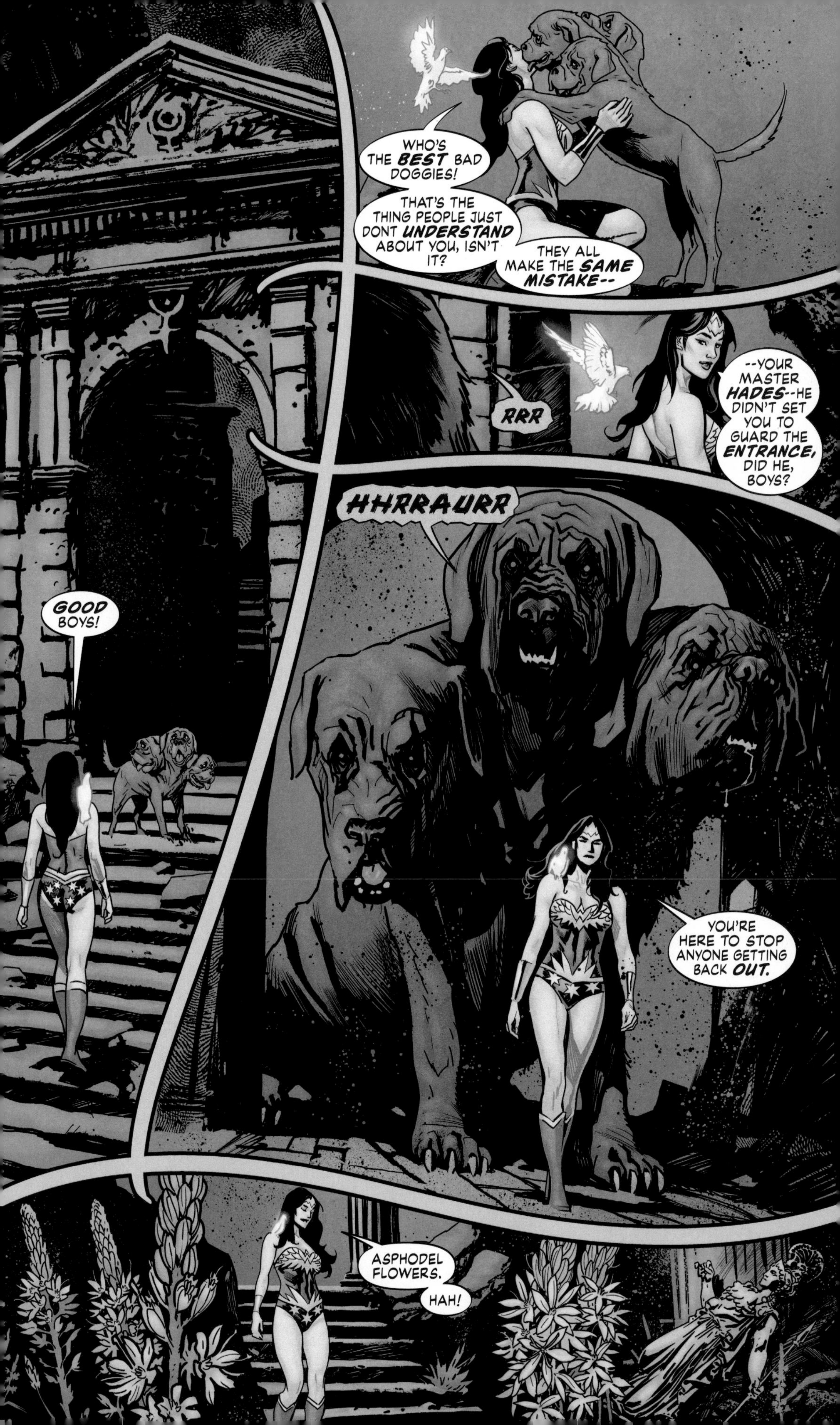
WHO'S THE BEST BAD DOGGIES!
THAT'S THE THING PEOPLE JUST DONT UNDERSTAND ABOUT YOU, ISN'T IT?
THEY ALL MAKE THE SAME MISTAKE--
RRR
--YOUR MASTER HADES--HE DIDN'T SET YOU TO GUARD THE ENTRANCE, DID HE, BOYS?
GOOD BOYS!
HHRRAURR
YOU'RE HERE TO STOP ANYONE GETTING BACK OUT.
ASPHODEL FLOWERS.
HAH!

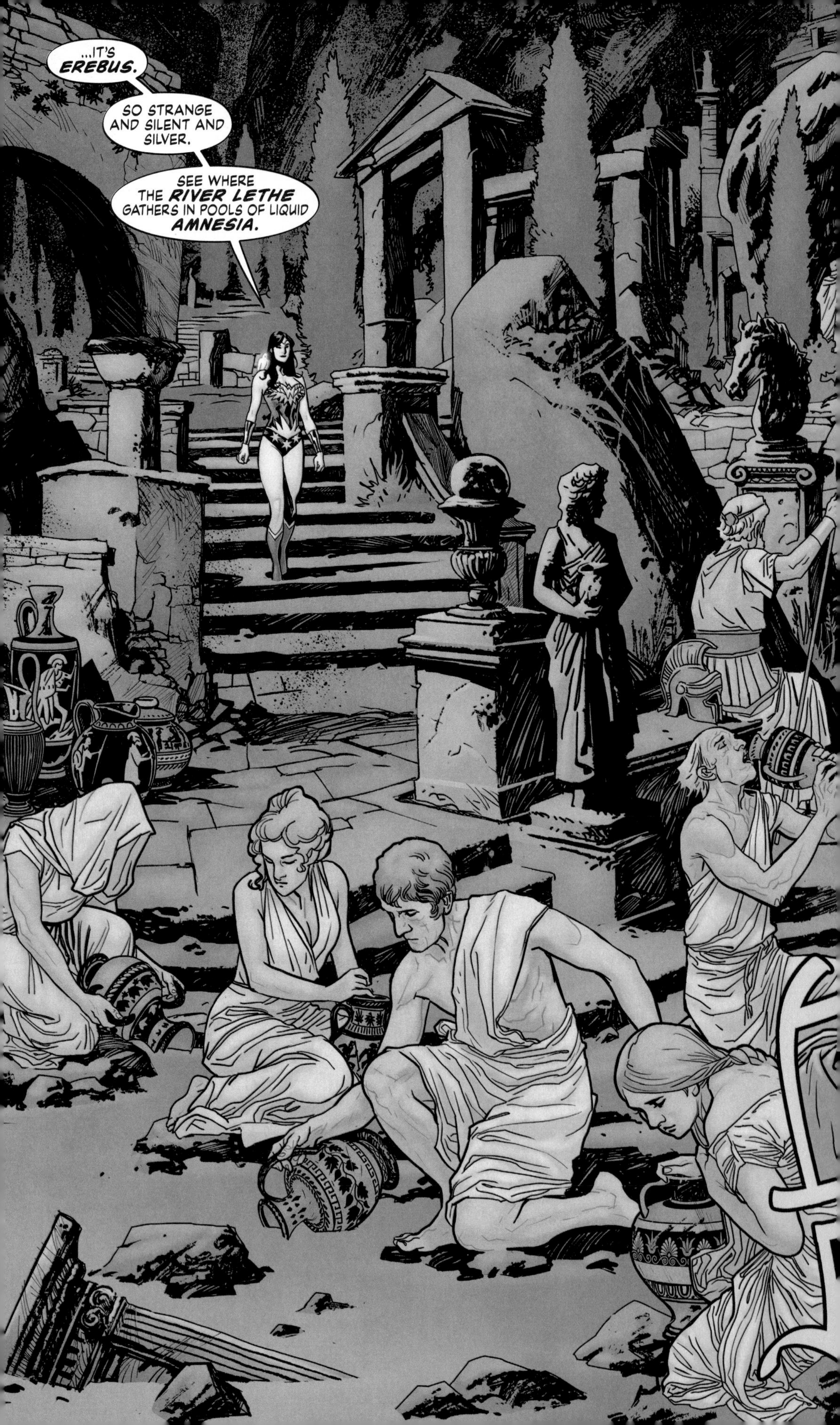
...IT'S EREBUS.
SO STRANGE AND SILENT AND SILVER.
SEE WHERE THE RIVER LETHE GATHERS IN POOLS OF LIQUID AMNESIA.

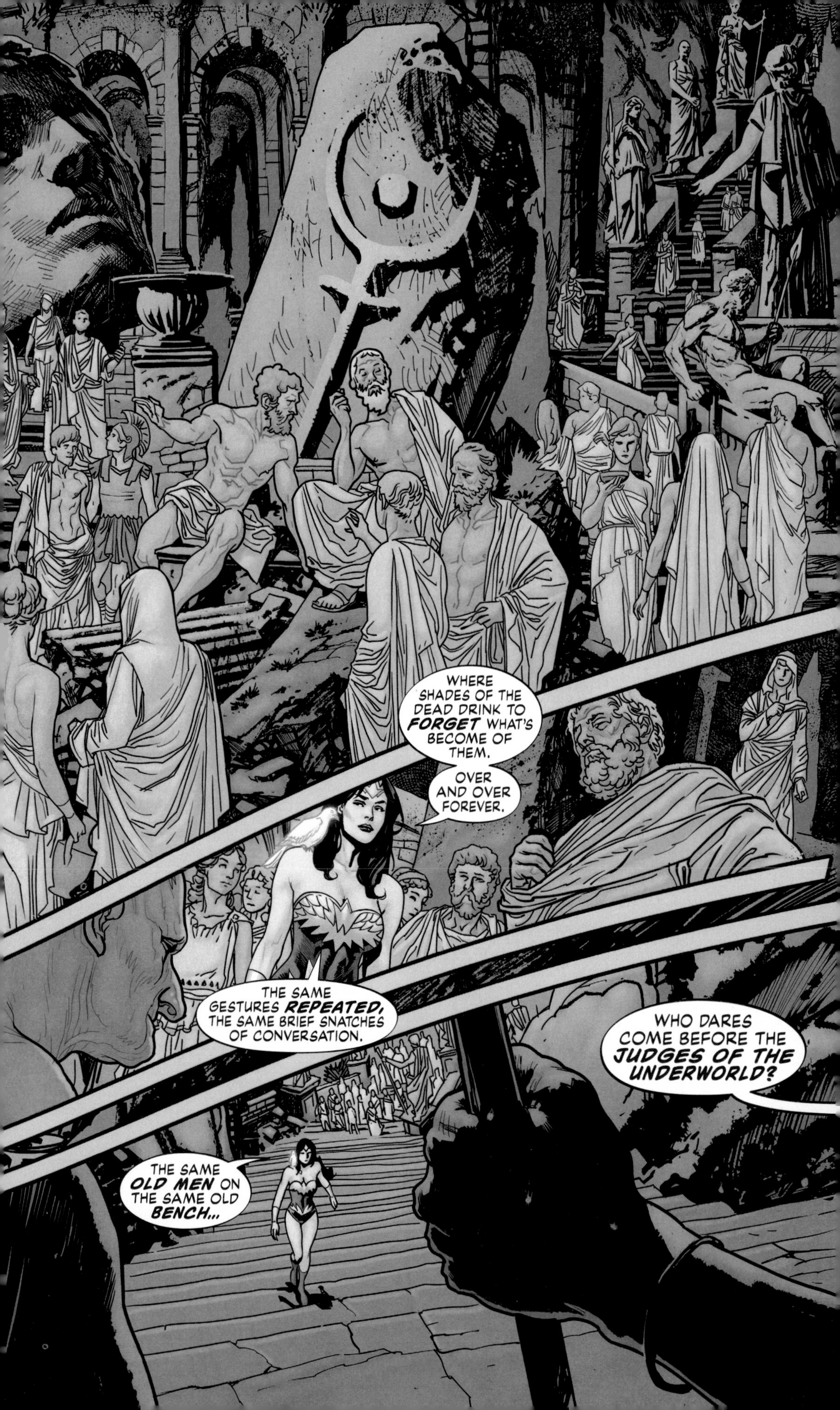
WHERE SHADES OF THE DEAD DRINK TO FORGET WHAT'S BECOME OF THEM.
OVER AND OVER FOREVER.
THE SAME GESTURES REPEATED, THE SAME BRIEF SNATCHES OF CONVERSATION.
WHO DARES COME BEFORE THE JUDGES OF THE UNDERWORLD?
THE SAME OLD MEN ON THE SAME OLD BENCH...

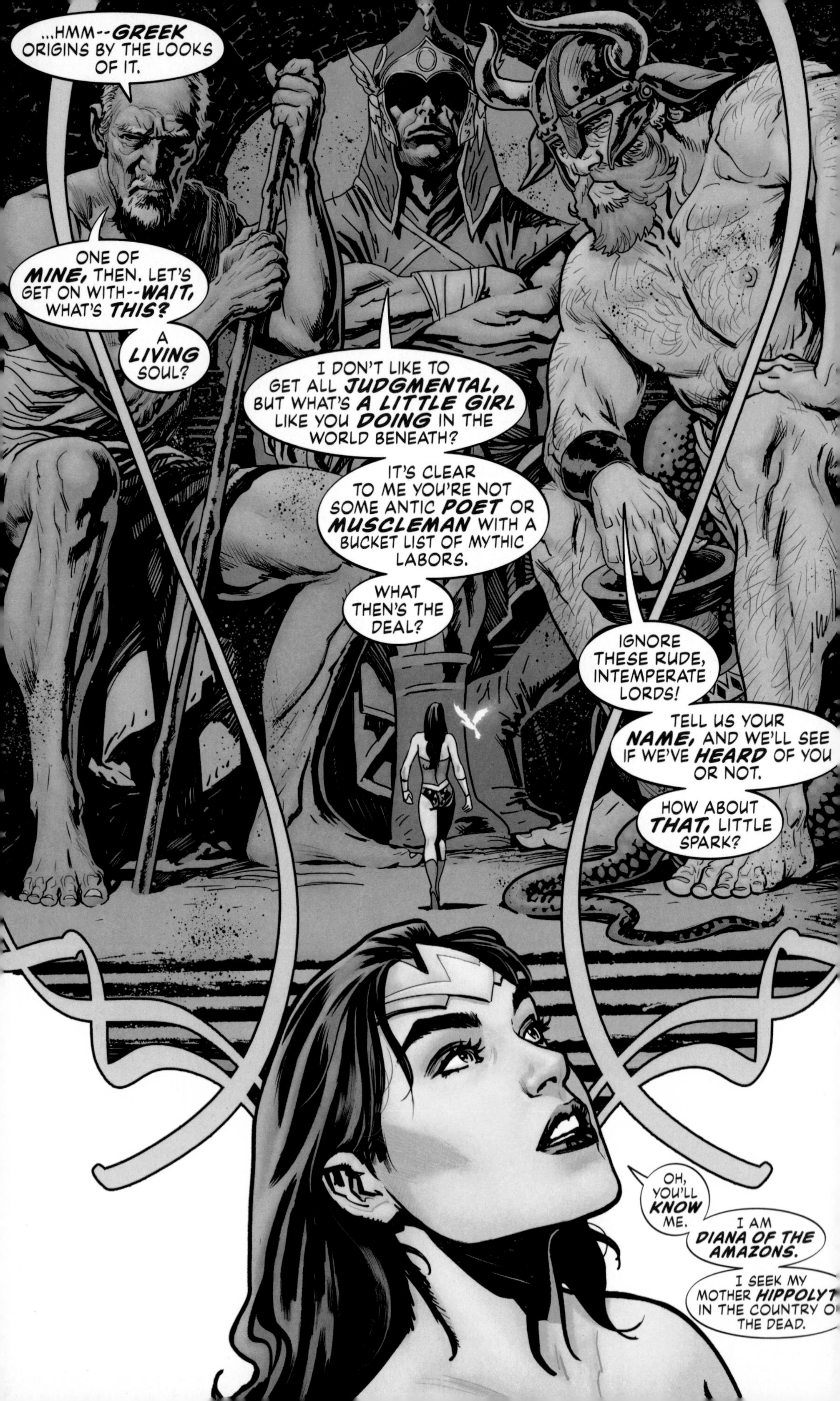
...HMM--GREEK ORIGINS BY THE LOOKS OF IT.
ONE OF MINE, THEN. LET'S GET ON WITH--WAIT, WHAT'S THIS?
A LIVING SOUL?
I DON'T LIKE TO GET ALL JUDGMENTAL, BUT WHAT'S A LITTLE GIRL LIKE YOU DOING IN THE WORLD BENEATH?
IT'S CLEAR TO ME YOU'RE NOT SOME ANTIC POET OR MUSCLEMAN WITH A BUCKET LIST OF MYTHIC LABORS.
WHAT THEN'S THE DEAL?
IGNORE THESE RUDE, INTEMPERATE LORDS!
TELL US YOUR NAME, AND WE'LL SEE IF WE'VE HEARD OF YOU OR NOT.
HOW ABOUT THAT, LITTLE SPARK?
OH, YOU'LL KNOW ME.
I AM DIANA OF THE AMAZONS.
I SEEK MY MOTHER HIPPOLYT IN THE COUNTRY O THE DEAD.

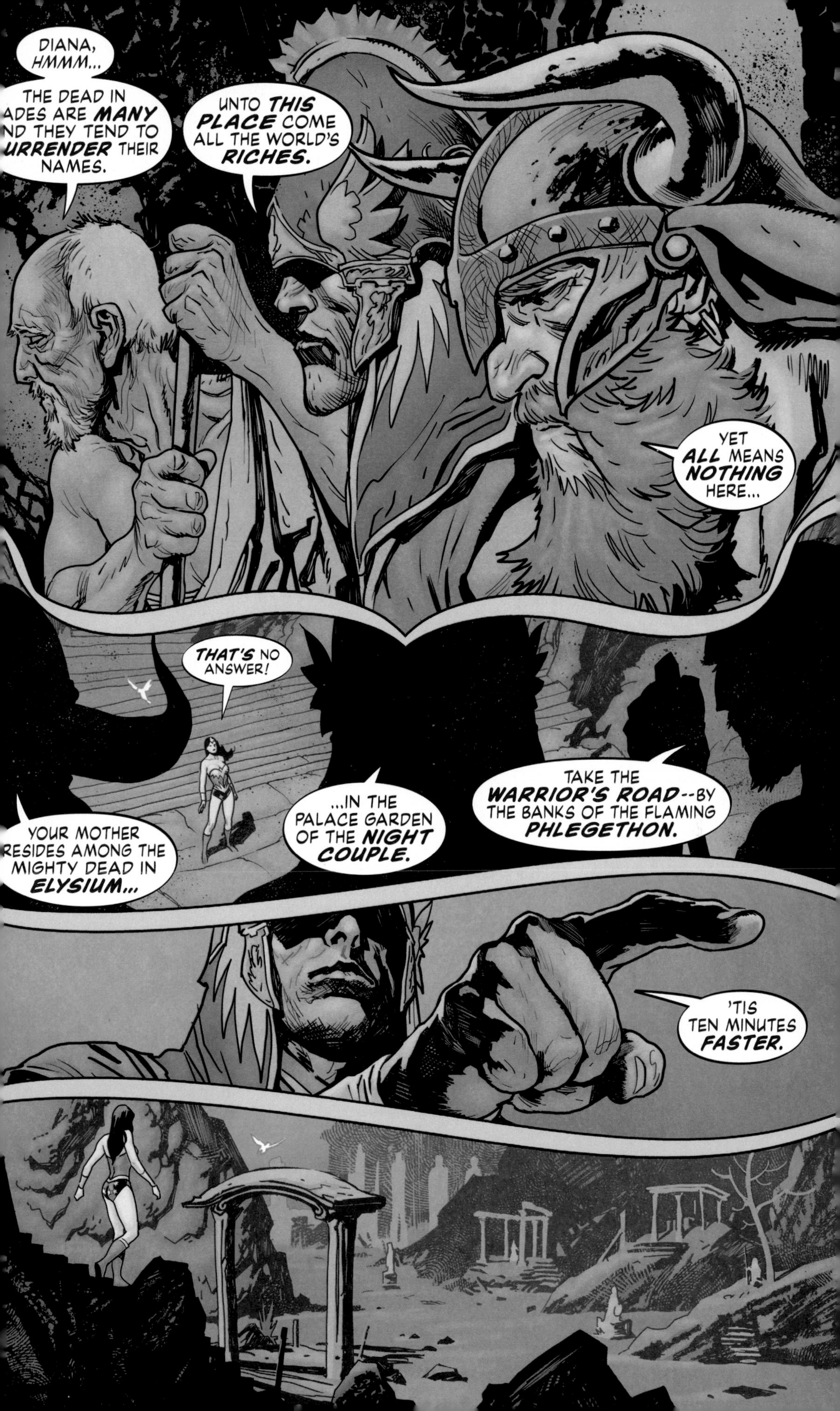
DIANA, HMMM...
THE DEAD IN ADES ARE MANY ND THEY TEND TO URRENDER THEIR NAMES.
UNTO THIS PLACE COME ALL THE WORLD'S RICHES.
YET ALL MEANS NOTHING HERE...
THAT'S NO ANSWER!
YOUR MOTHER RESIDES AMONG THE MIGHTY DEAD IN ELYSIUM...
...IN THE PALACE GARDEN OF THE NIGHT COUPLE.
TAKE THE WARRIOR'S ROAD--BY THE BANKS OF THE FLAMING PHLEGETHON.
'TIS TEN MINUTES FASTER.

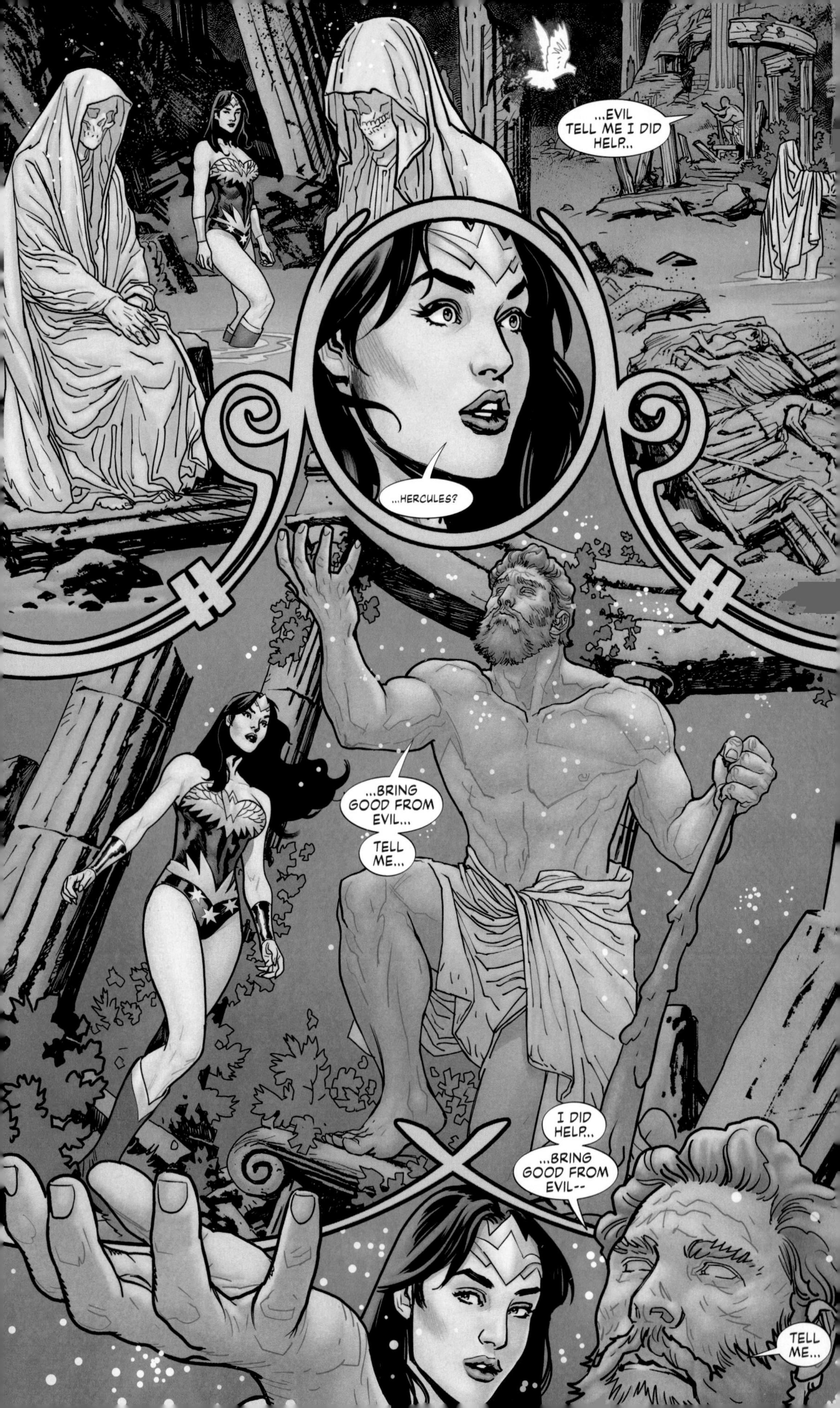
...EVIL TELL ME I DID HELP...
...HERCULES?
...BRING GOOD FROM EVIL...
TELL ME...
I DID HELP...
...BRING GOOD FROM EVIL--
TELL ME...

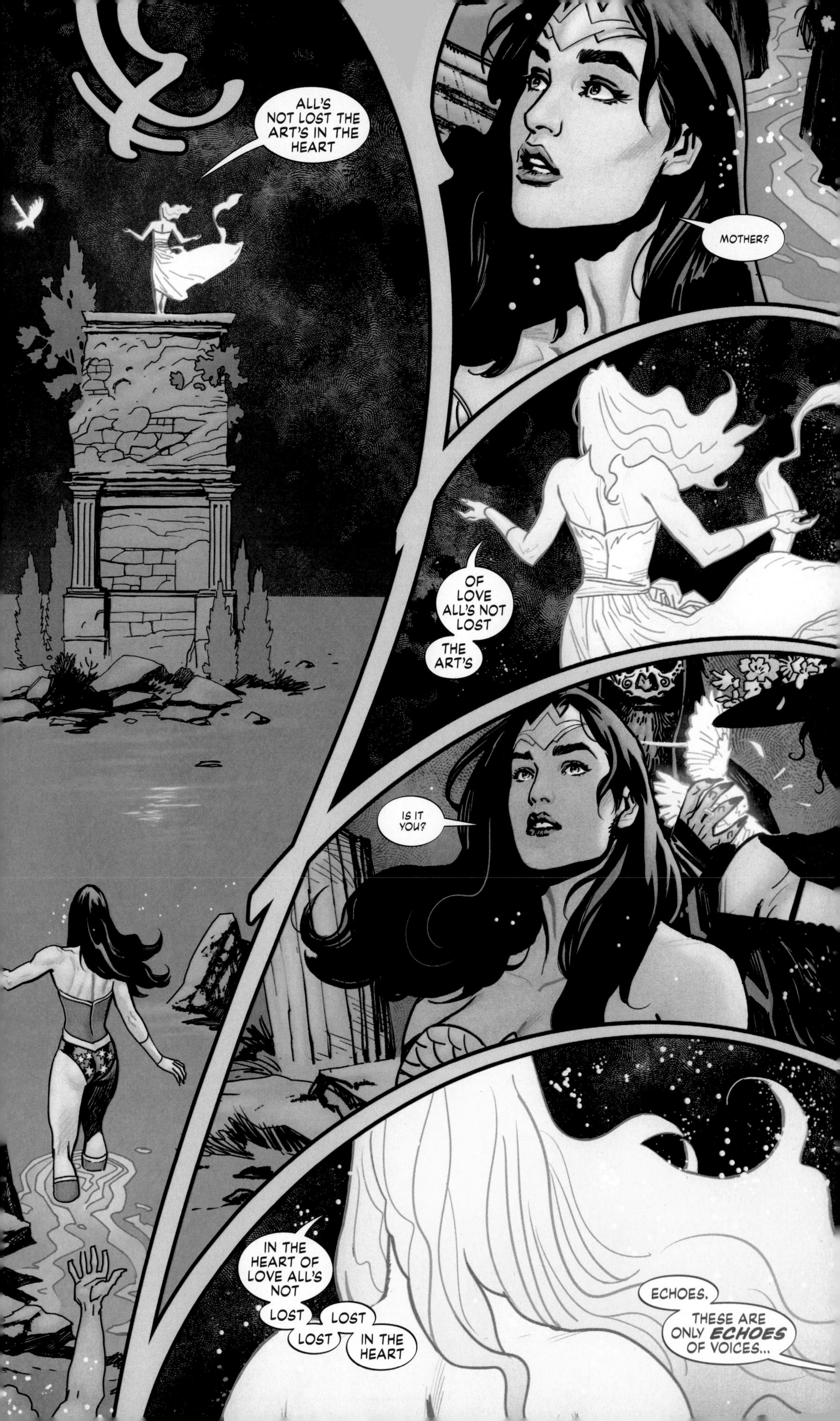
ALL'S NOT LOST THE ART'S IN THE HEART
MOTHER?
OF LOVE ALL'S NOT LOST
THE ART'S
IS IT YOU?
IN THE HEART OF LOVE ALL'S NOT
LOST
LOST
LOST
IN THE HEART
ECHOES.
THESE ARE ONLY ECHOES OF VOICES...

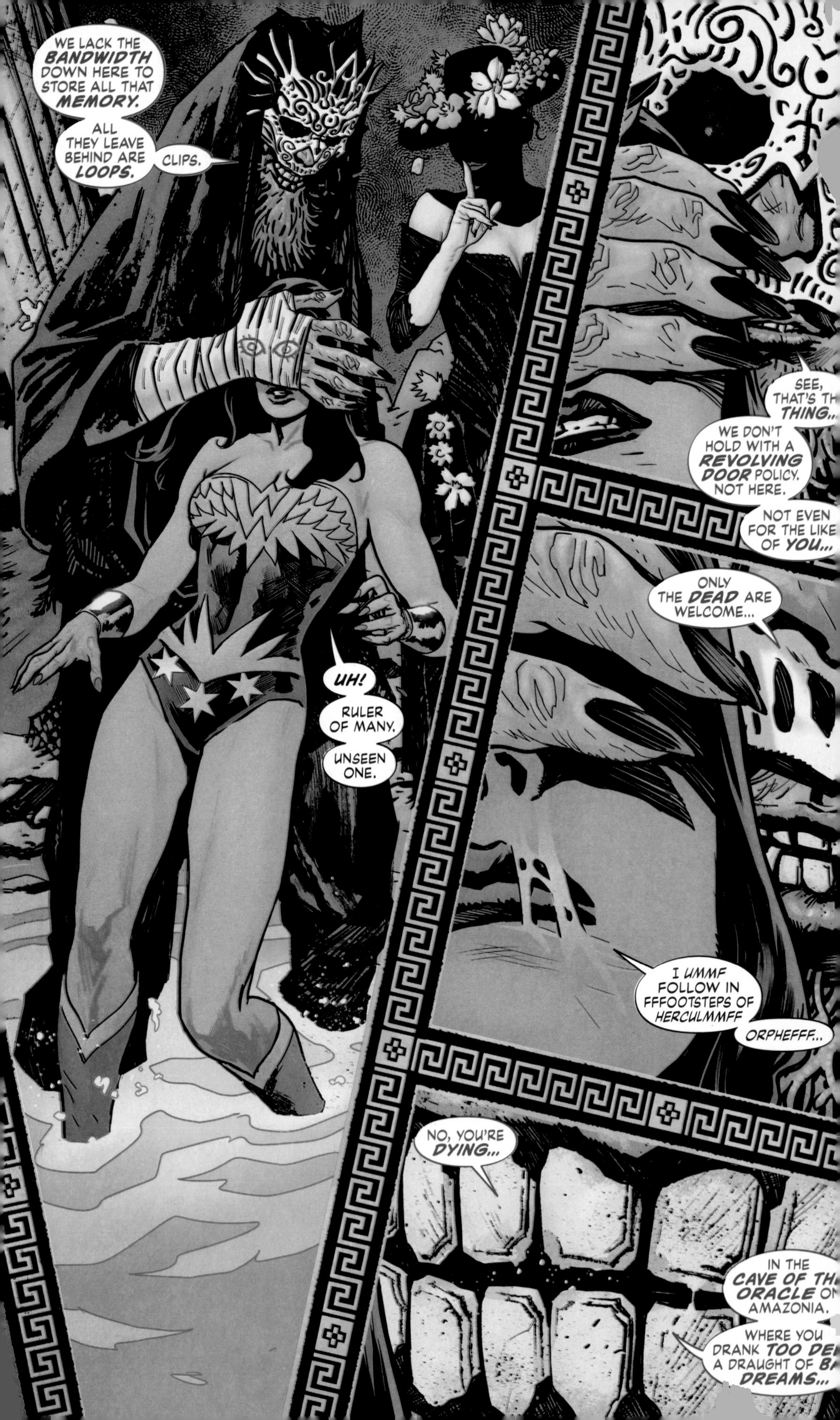
WE LACK THE BANDWIDTH DOWN HERE TO STORE ALL THAT MEMORY.
ALL THEY LEAVE BEHIND ARE LOOPS.
CLIPS.
UH!
RULER OF MANY.
UNSEEN ONE.
SEE, THAT'S TH THING...
WE DON'T HOLD WITH A REVOLVING DOOR POLICY. NOT HERE.
NOT EVEN FOR THE LIKE OF YOU...
ONLY THE DEAD ARE WELCOME...
I UMMF FOLLOW IN FFFOOTSTEPS OF HERCULMMFF
ORPHEFFF...
NO, YOU'RE DYING...
IN THE CAVE OF TH ORACLE O AMAZONIA.
WHERE YOU DRANK TOO DE A DRAUGHT OF B DREAMS...

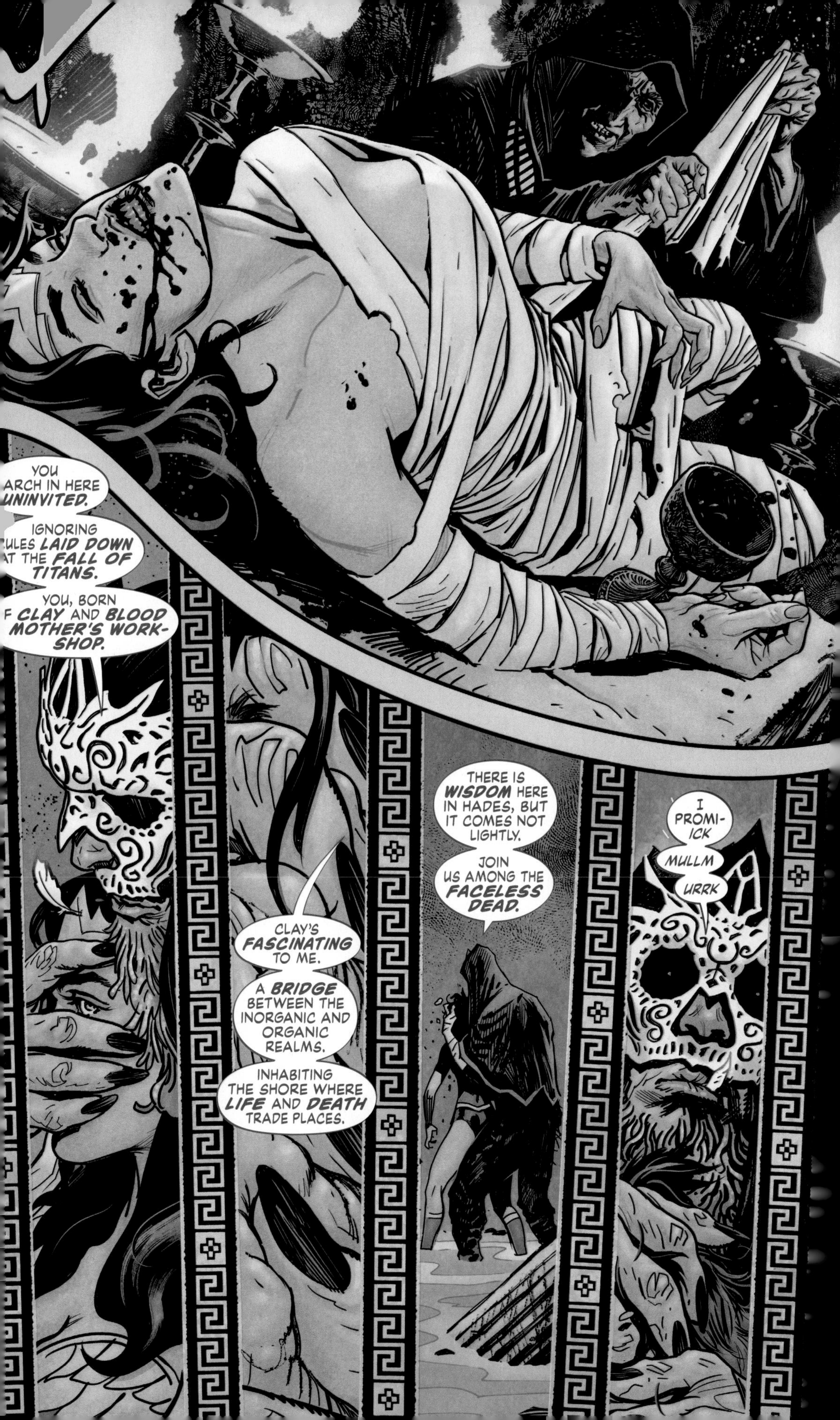
YOU ARCH IN HERE UNINVITED.
IGNORING ULES LAID DOWN AT THE FALL OF TITANS.
YOU, BORN F CLAY AND BLOOD MOTHER'S WORK-SHOP.
CLAY'S FASCINATING TO ME.
A BRIDGE BETWEEN THE INORGANIC AND ORGANIC REALMS.
INHABITING THE SHORE WHERE LIFE AND DEATH TRADE PLACES.
THERE IS WISDOM HERE IN HADES, BUT IT COMES NOT LIGHTLY.
JOIN US AMONG THE FACELESS DEAD.
I PROMI-ICK
MULLM
URRK

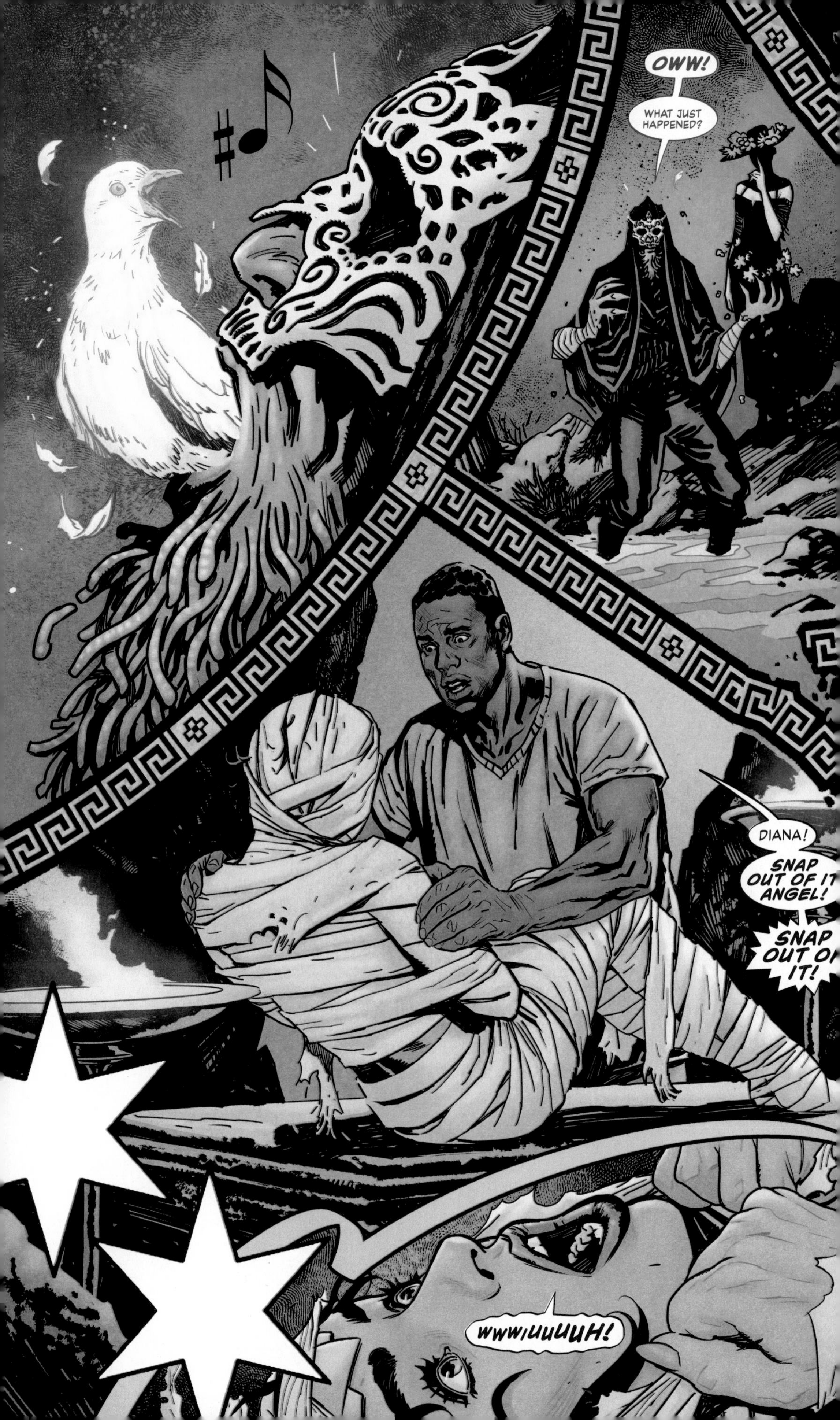
OWW!
WHAT JUST HAPPENED?
DIANA!
SNAP OUT OF IT ANGEL!
SNAP OUT OF IT!
WWWIUUUUH!

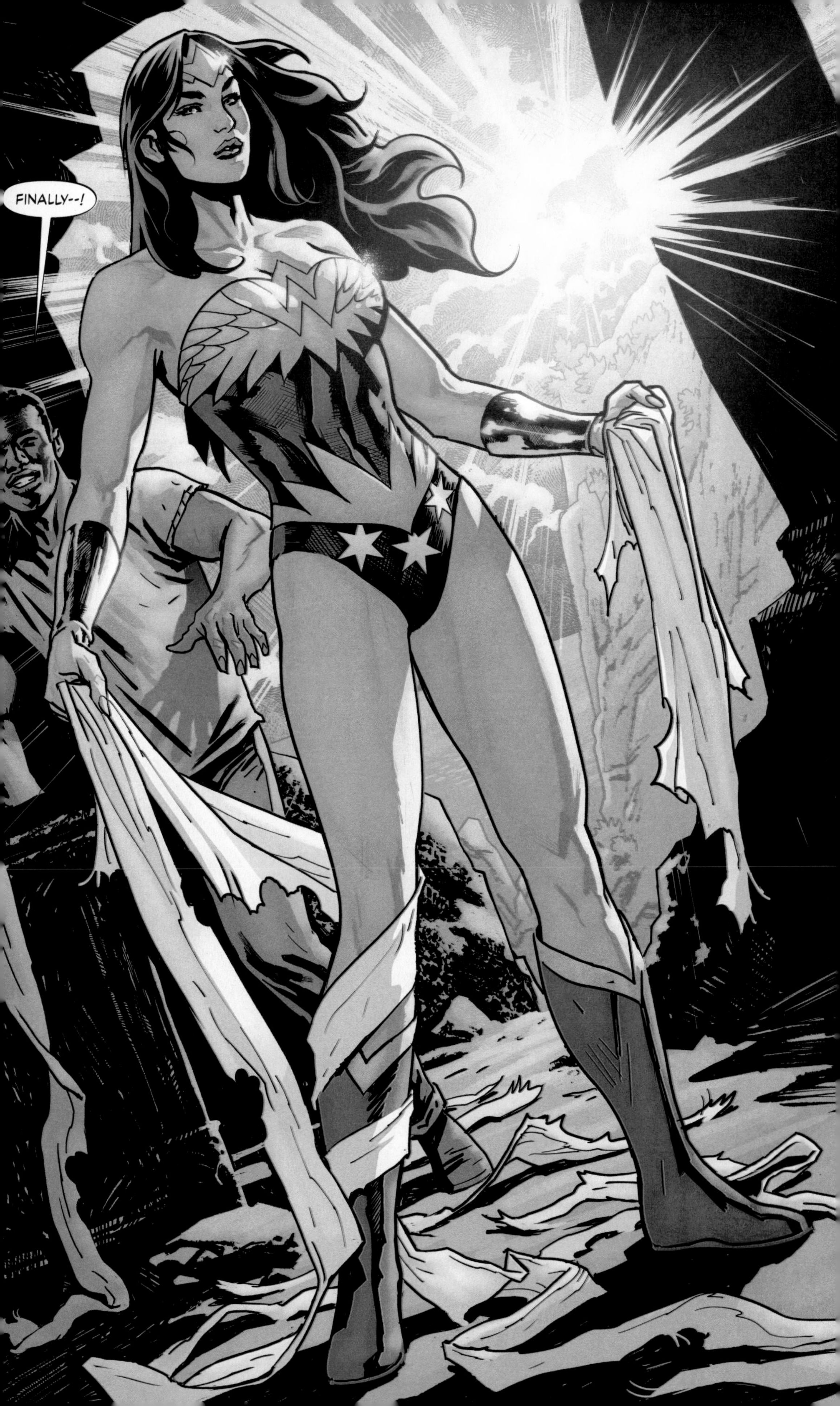
FINALLY--!

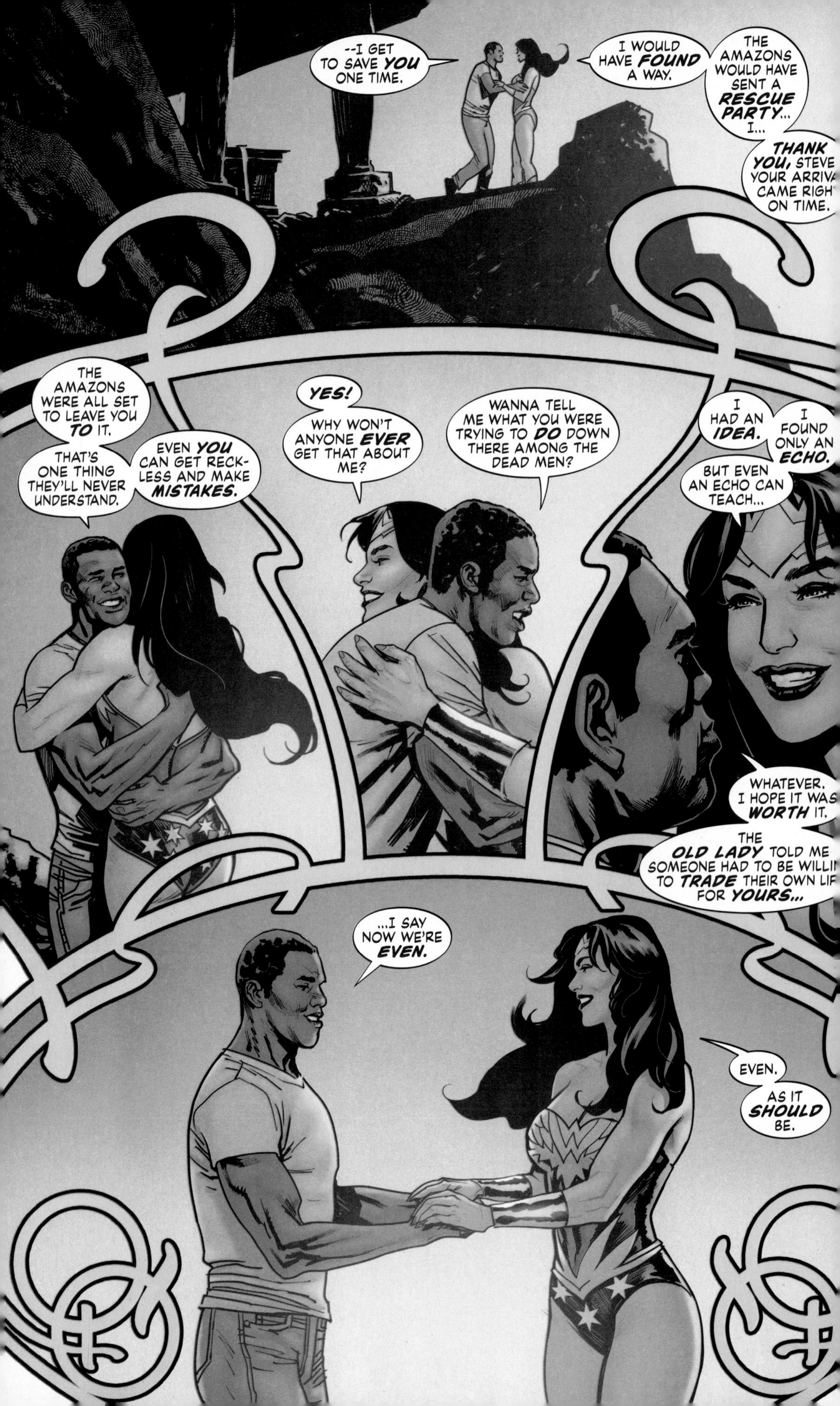
--I GET TO SAVE YOU ONE TIME.
I WOULD HAVE FOUND A WAY.
THE AMAZONS WOULD HAVE SENT A RESCUE PARTY... I...
THANK YOU, STEVE YOUR ARRIVA CAME RIGHT ON TIME.
THE AMAZONS WERE ALL SET TO LEAVE YOU TO IT.
THAT'S ONE THING THEY'LL NEVER UNDERSTAND.
EVEN YOU CAN GET RECKLESS AND MAKE MISTAKES.
YES!
WHY WON'T ANYONE EVER GET THAT ABOUT ME?
WANNA TELL ME WHAT YOU WERE TRYING TO DO DOWN THERE AMONG THE DEAD MEN?
I HAD AN IDEA.
I FOUND ONLY AN ECHO.
BUT EVEN AN ECHO CAN TEACH...
WHATEVER. I HOPE IT WAS WORTH IT.
THE OLD LADY TOLD ME SOMEONE HAD TO BE WILLIN TO TRADE THEIR OWN LIF FOR YOURS...
...I SAY NOW WE'RE EVEN.
EVEN.
AS IT SHOULD BE.

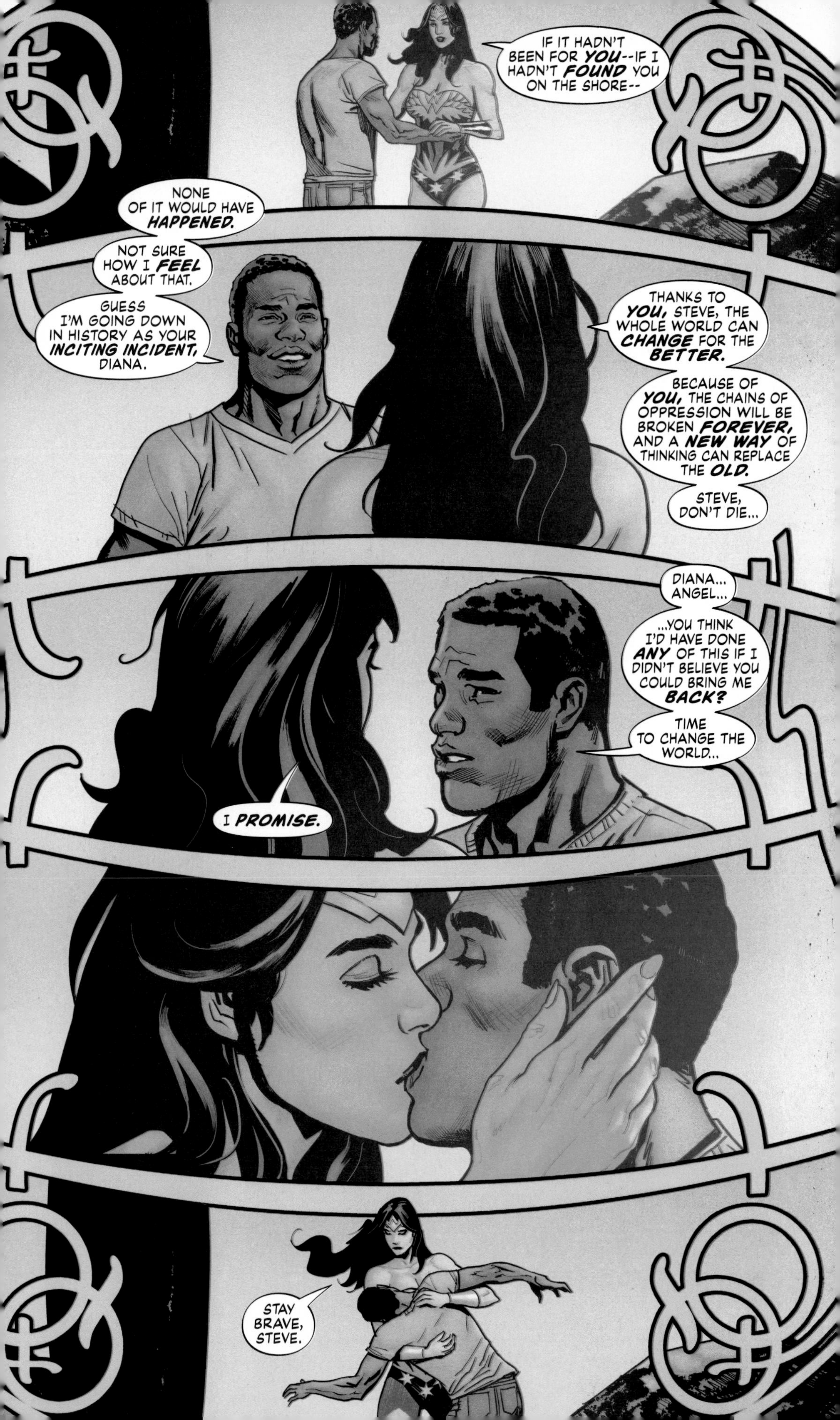
IF IT HADN'T BEEN FOR YOU--IF I HADN'T FOUND YOU ON THE SHORE--
NONE OF IT WOULD HAVE HAPPENED.
NOT SURE HOW I FEEL ABOUT THAT.
GUESS I'M GOING DOWN IN HISTORY AS YOUR INCITING INCIDENT, DIANA.
THANKS TO YOU, STEVE, THE WHOLE WORLD CAN CHANGE FOR THE BETTER.
BECAUSE OF YOU, THE CHAINS OF OPPRESSION WILL BE BROKEN FOREVER, AND A NEW WAY OF THINKING CAN REPLACE THE OLD.
STEVE, DON'T DIE...
DIANA... ANGEL...
...YOU THINK I'D HAVE DONE ANY OF THIS IF I DIDN'T BELIEVE YOU COULD BRING ME BACK?
TIME TO CHANGE THE WORLD...
I PROMISE.
STAY BRAVE, STEVE.

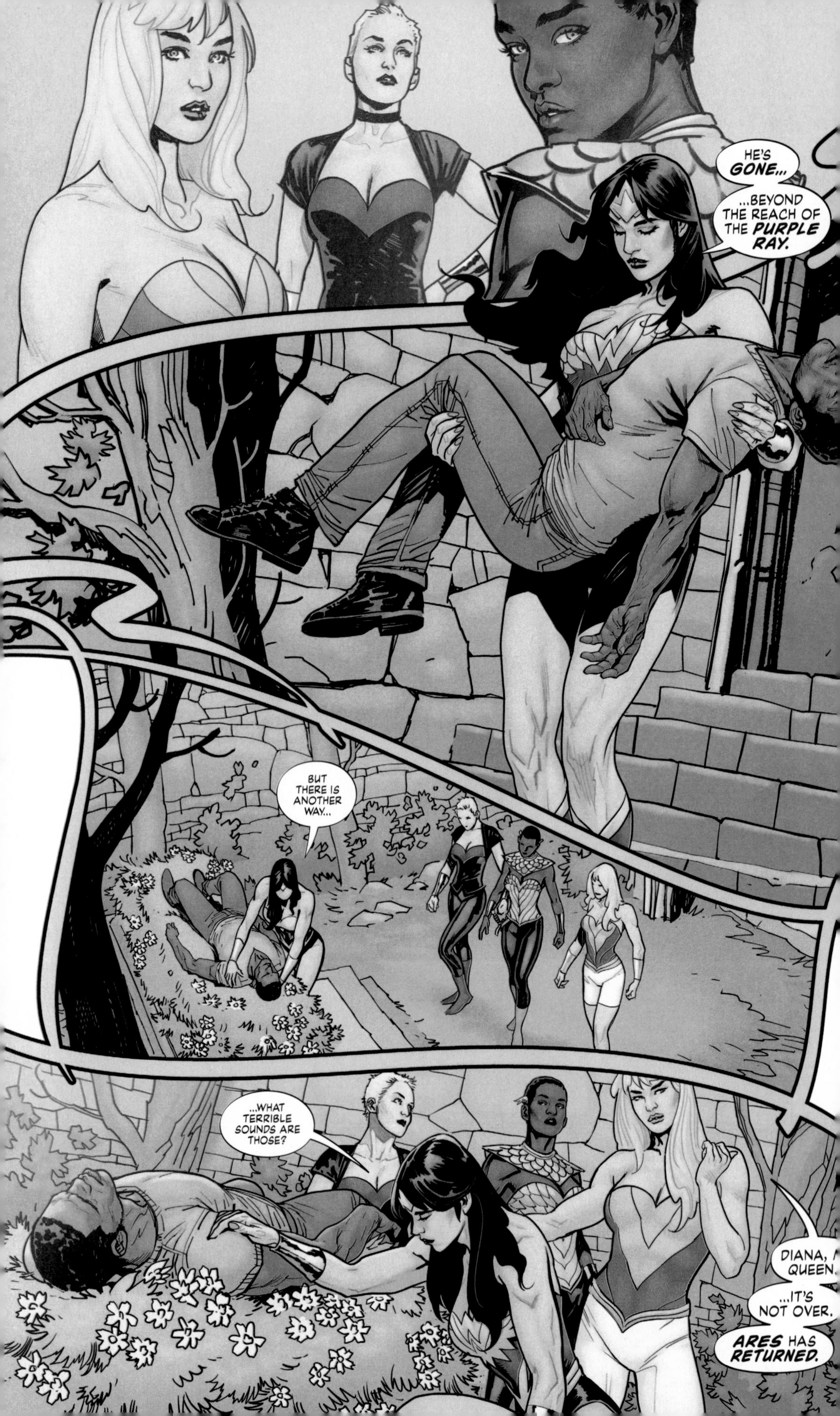
HE'S GONE...
...BEYOND THE REACH OF THE PURPLE RAY.
BUT THERE IS ANOTHER WAY...
...WHAT TERRIBLE SOUNDS ARE THOSE?
DIANA, QUEEN.
...IT'S NOT OVER.
ARES HAS RETURNED.

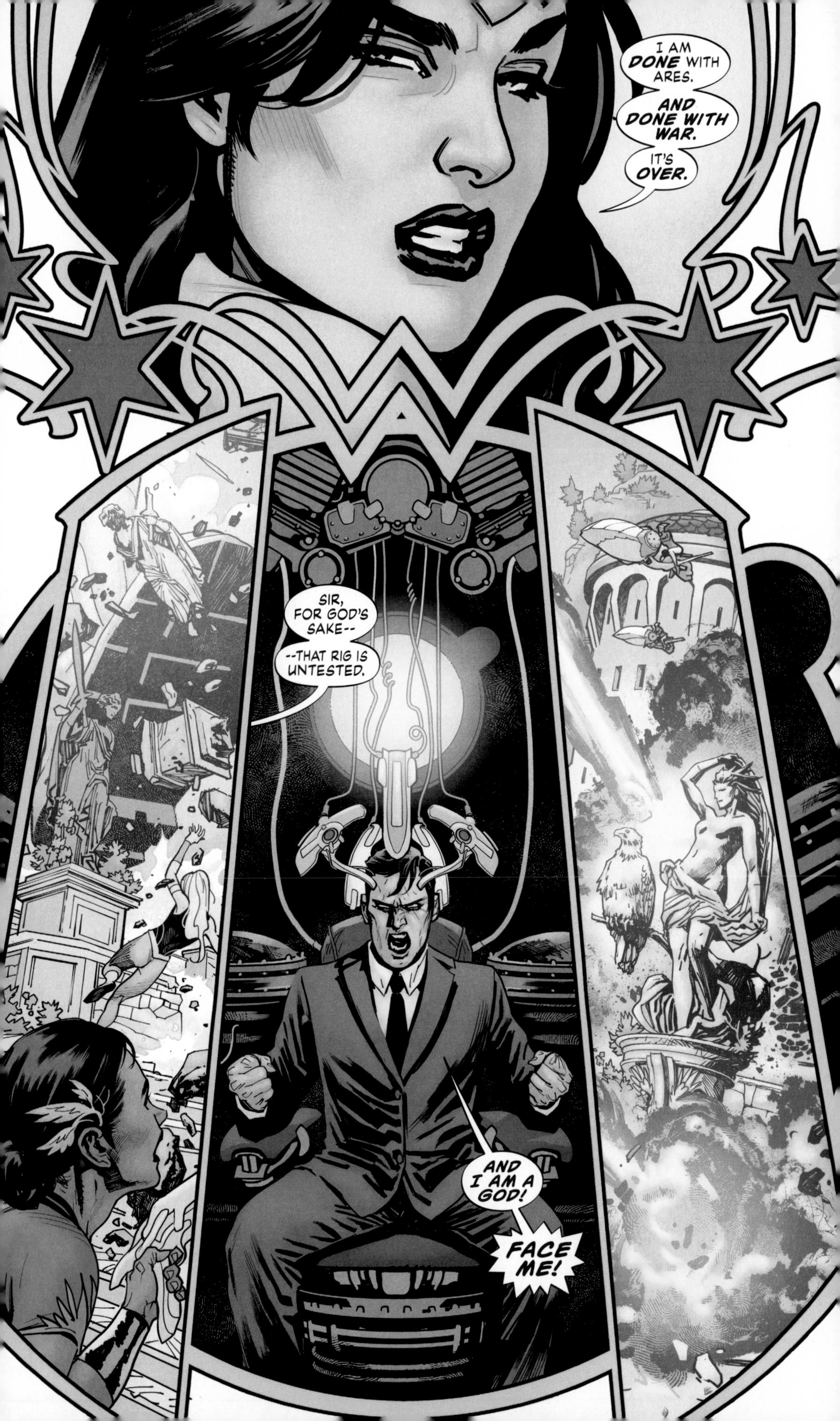
I AM DONE WITH ARES.
AND DONE WITH WAR.
IT'S OVER.
SIR, FOR GOD'S SAKE--
--THAT RIG IS UNTESTED.
AND I AM A GOD!
FACE ME!

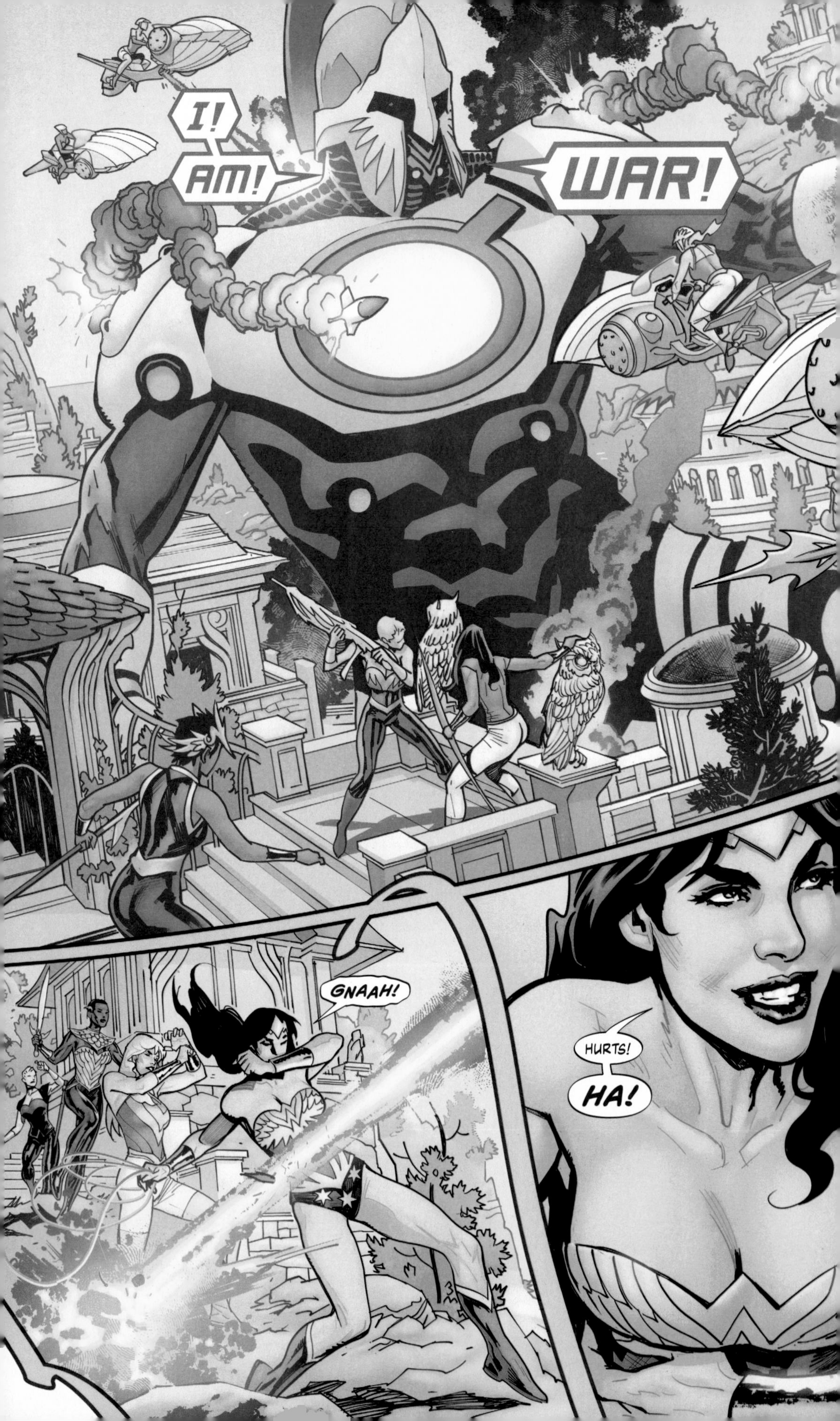
I!
AM!
WAR!
GNAAH!
HURTS!
HA!

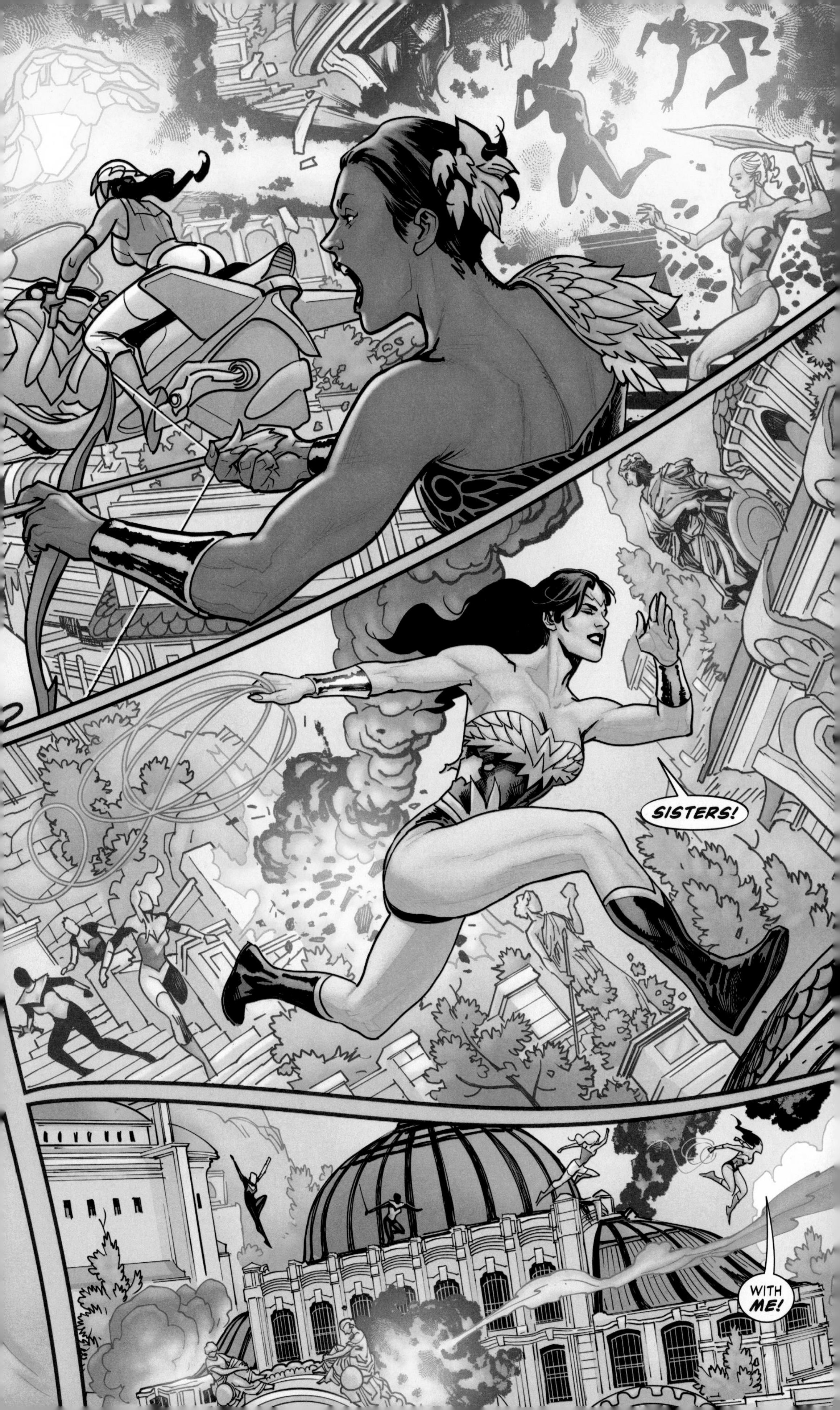
SISTERS!
WITH ME!

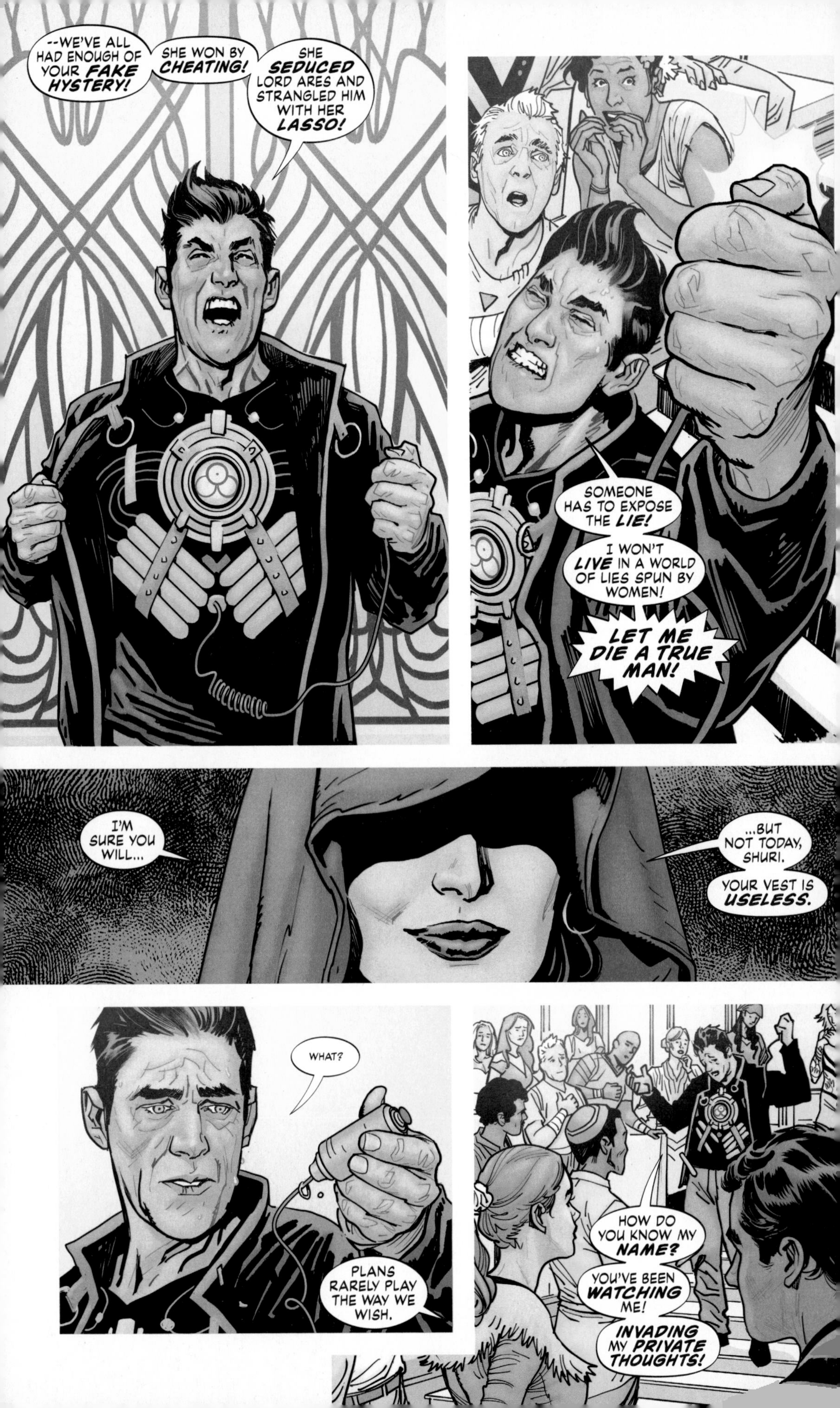
--WE'VE ALL HAD ENOUGH OF YOUR FAKE HYSTERY!
SHE WON BY CHEATING!
SHE SEDUCED LORD ARES AND STRANGLED HIM WITH HER LASSO!
SOMEONE HAS TO EXPOSE THE LIE!
I WON'T LIVE IN A WORLD OF LIES SPUN BY WOMEN!
LET ME DIE A TRUE MAN!
I'M SURE YOU WILL...
...BUT NOT TODAY, SHURI.
YOUR VEST IS USELESS.
WHAT?
PLANS RARELY PLAY THE WAY WE WISH.
HOW DO YOU KNOW MY NAME?
YOU'VE BEEN WATCHING ME!
INVADING MY PRIVATE THOUGHTS!

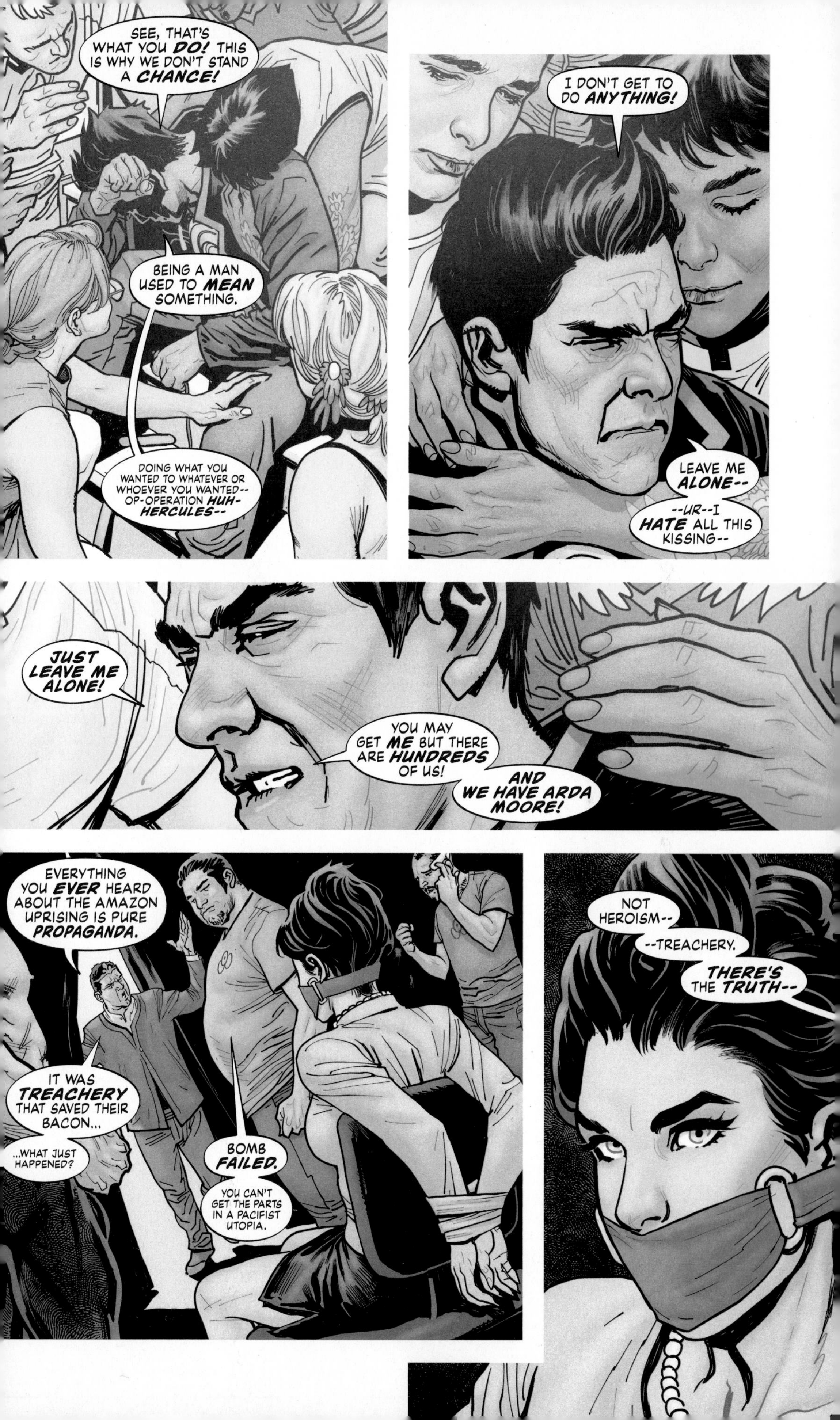
SEE, THAT'S WHAT YOU DO! THIS IS WHY WE DON'T STAND A CHANCE!
BEING A MAN USED TO MEAN SOMETHING.
DOING WHAT YOU WANTED TO WHATEVER OR WHOEVER YOU WANTED-- OP-OPERATION HUH-HERCULES--
I DON'T GET TO DO ANYTHING!
LEAVE ME ALONE--
--UR--I HATE ALL THIS KISSING--
JUST LEAVE ME ALONE!
YOU MAY GET ME BUT THERE ARE HUNDREDS OF US!
AND WE HAVE ARDA MOORE!
EVERYTHING YOU EVER HEARD ABOUT THE AMAZON UPRISING IS PURE PROPAGANDA.
IT WAS TREACHERY THAT SAVED THEIR BACON...
...WHAT JUST HAPPENED?
BOMB FAILED.
YOU CAN'T GET THE PARTS IN A PACIFIST UTOPIA.
NOT HEROISM--
--TREACHERY.
THERE'S THE TRUTH--

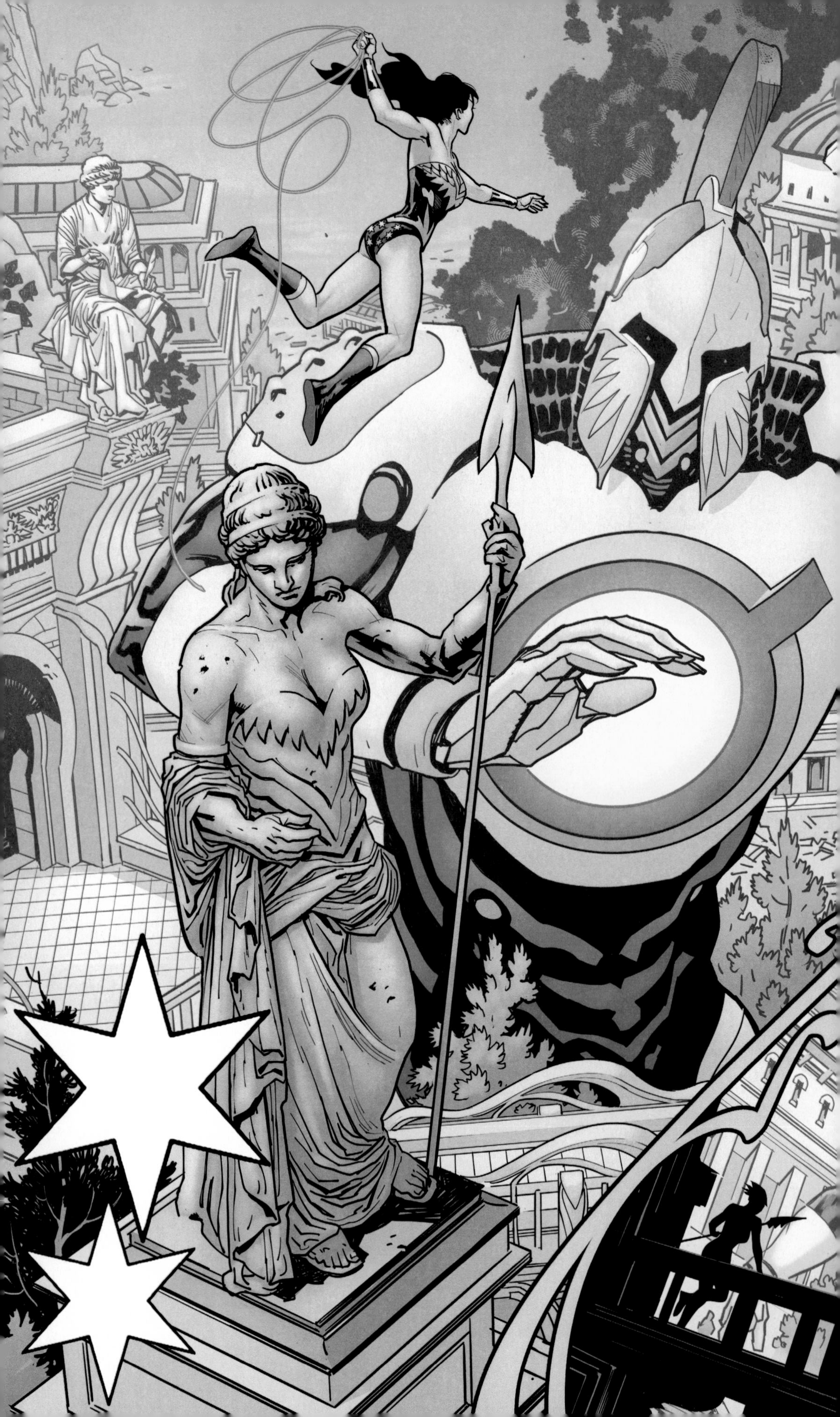

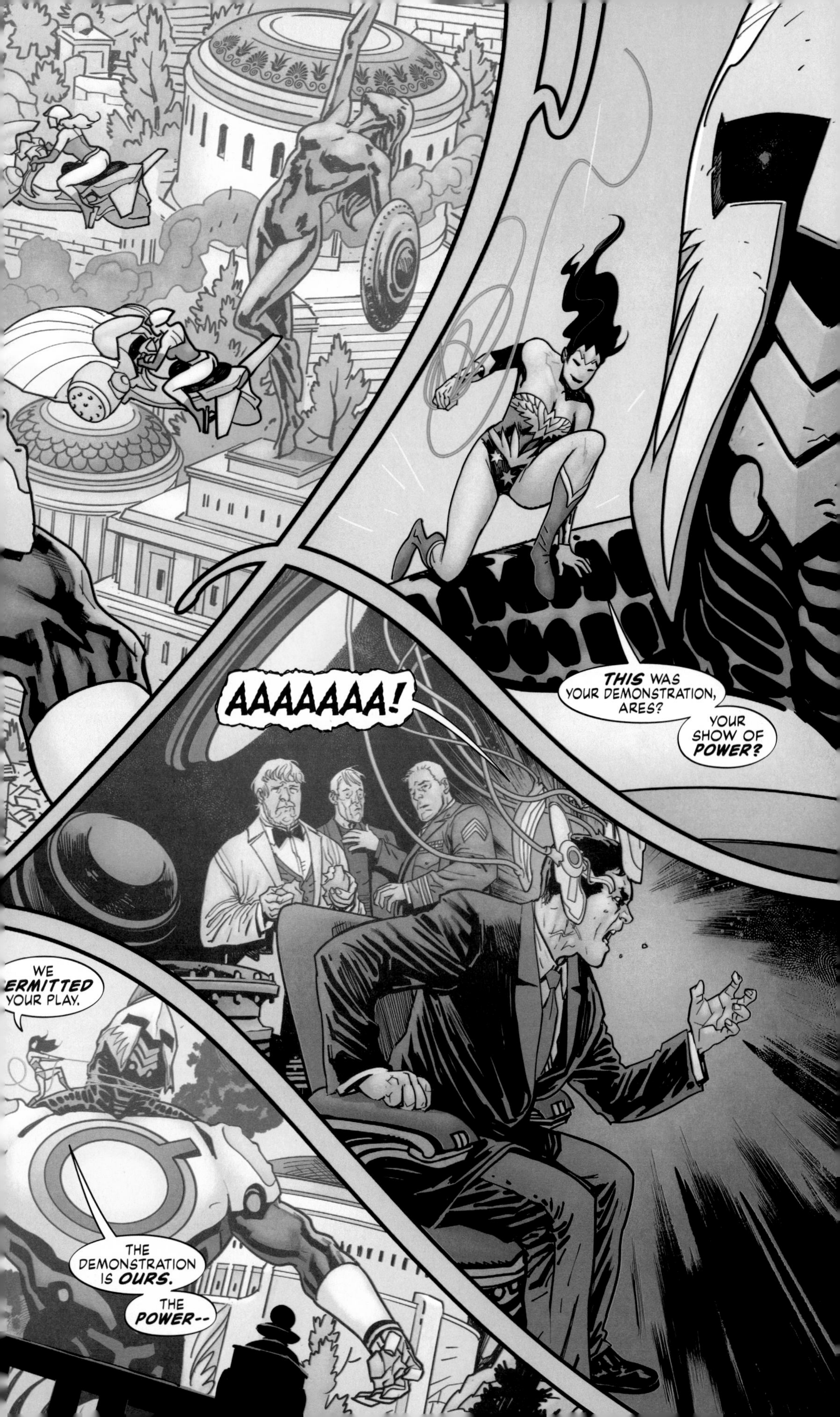
THIS WAS YOUR DEMONSTRATION, ARES?
YOUR SHOW OF POWER?
AAAAAAA!
WE ERMITTED YOUR PLAY.
THE DEMONSTRATION IS OURS.
THE POWER--

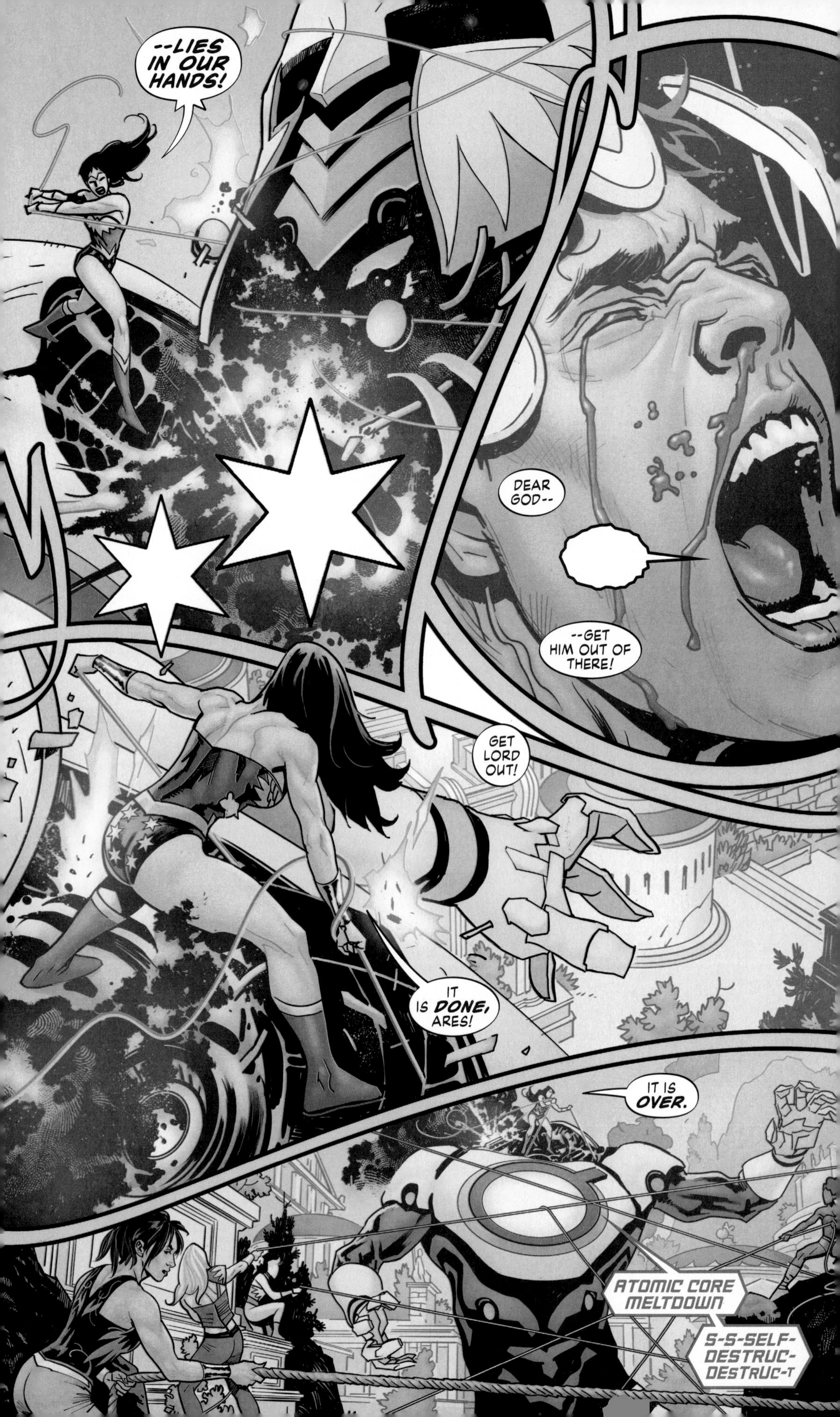

--LIES IN OUR HANDS!
DEAR GOD--
--GET HIM OUT OF THERE!
GET LORD OUT!
IT IS *DONE,* ARES!
IT IS *OVER.*
ATOMIC CORE MELTDOWN
S-S-SELF-DESTRUC-DESTRUC-T

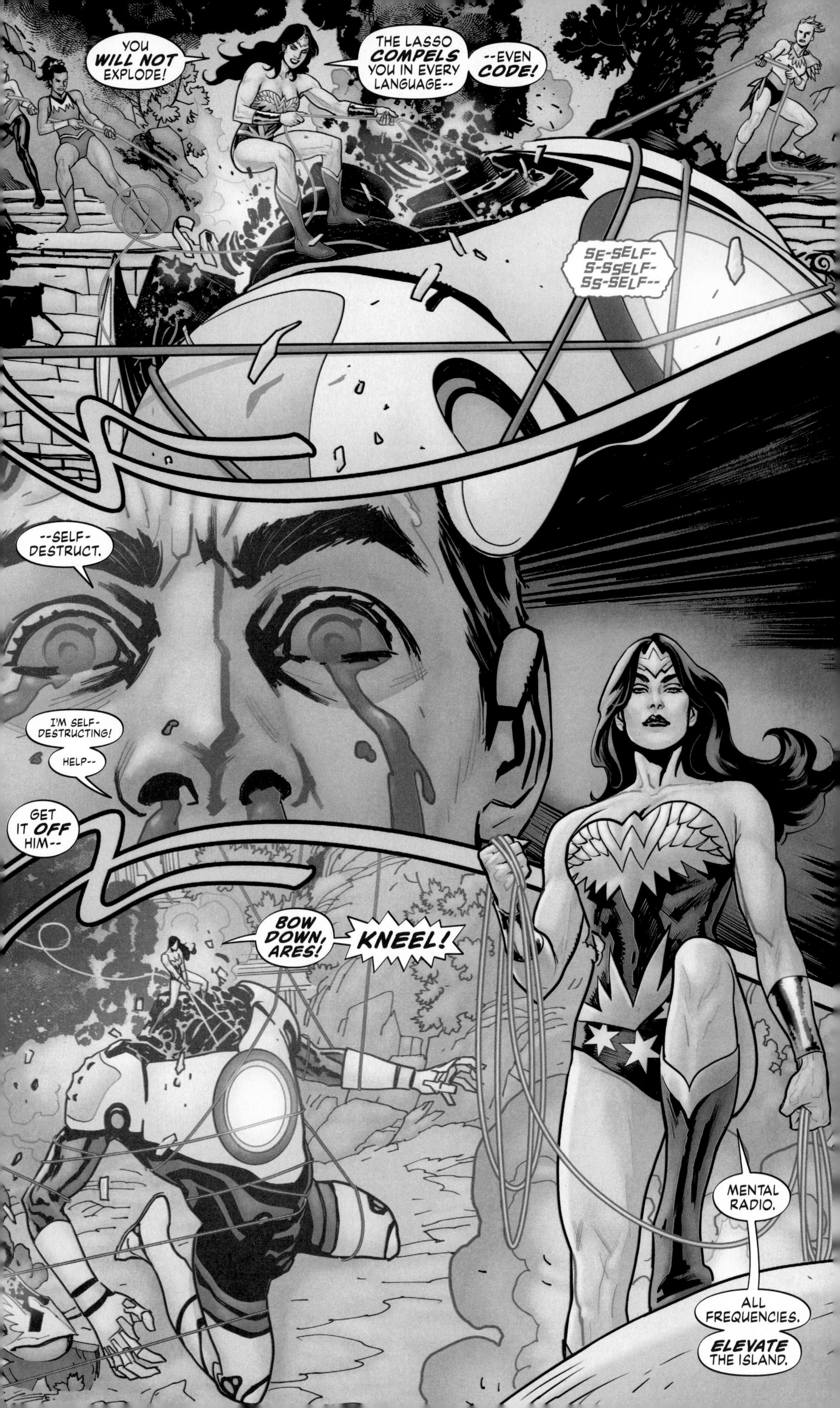

YOU WILL NOT EXPLODE!
THE LASSO COMPELS YOU IN EVERY LANGUAGE--
--EVEN CODE!
SE-SELF- S-SSELF- SS-SELF--
--SELF-DESTRUCT.
I'M SELF-DESTRUCTING!
HELP--
GET IT OFF HIM--
BOW DOWN, ARES!
KNEEL!
MENTAL RADIO.
ALL FREQUENCIES.
ELEVATE THE ISLAND.

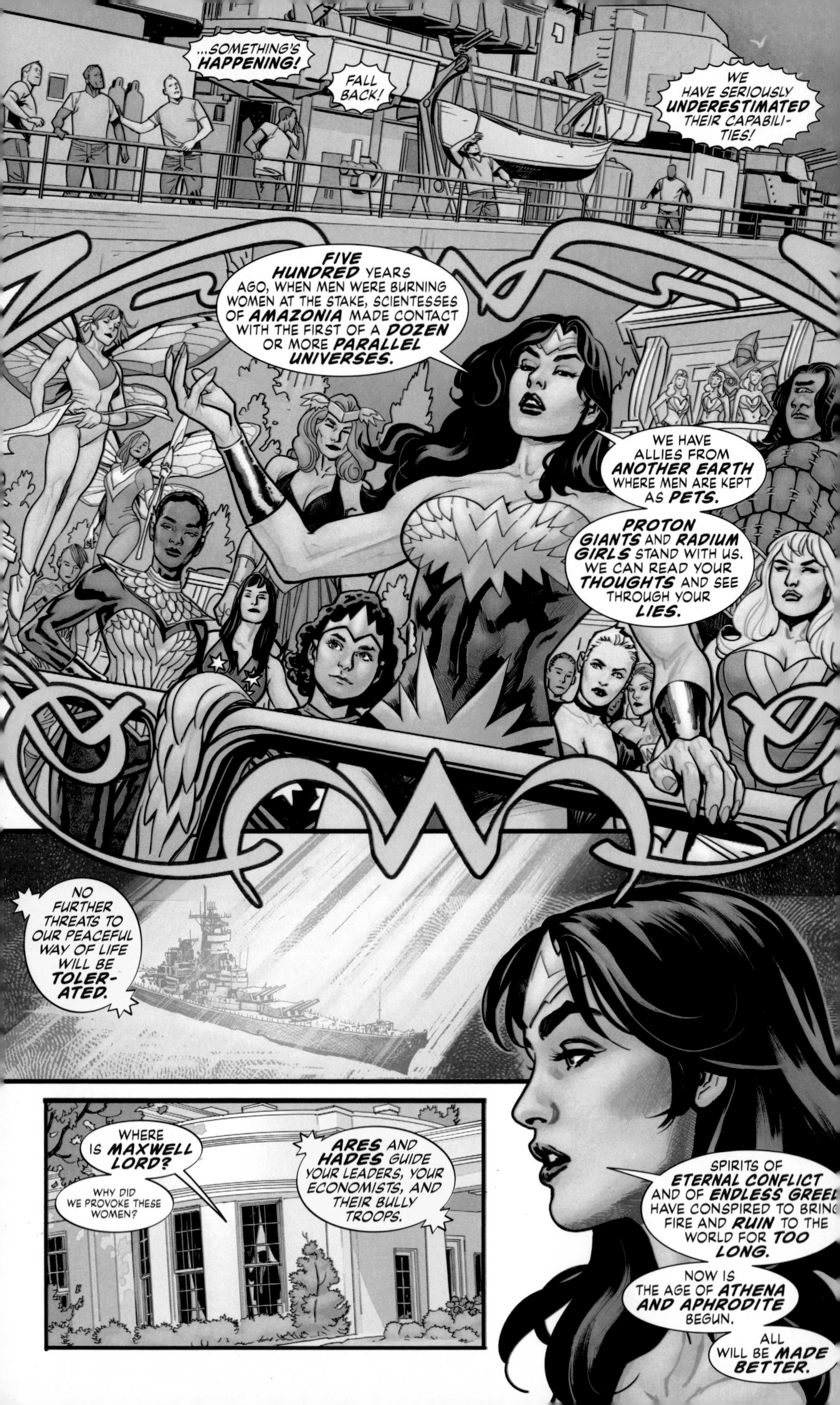
...SOMETHING'S HAPPENING!
FALL BACK!
WE HAVE SERIOUSLY UNDERESTIMATED THEIR CAPABILI-TIES!
FIVE HUNDRED YEARS AGO, WHEN MEN WERE BURNING WOMEN AT THE STAKE, SCIENTESSES OF AMAZONIA MADE CONTACT WITH THE FIRST OF A DOZEN OR MORE PARALLEL UNIVERSES.
WE HAVE ALLIES FROM ANOTHER EARTH WHERE MEN ARE KEPT AS PETS.
PROTON GIANTS AND RADIUM GIRLS STAND WITH US. WE CAN READ YOUR THOUGHTS AND SEE THROUGH YOUR LIES.
NO FURTHER THREATS TO OUR PEACEFUL WAY OF LIFE WILL BE TOLER-ATED.
WHERE IS MAXWELL LORD?
WHY DID WE PROVOKE THESE WOMEN?
ARES AND HADES GUIDE YOUR LEADERS, YOUR ECONOMISTS, AND THEIR BULLY TROOPS.
SPIRITS OF ETERNAL CONFLICT AND OF ENDLESS GREED HAVE CONSPIRED TO BRING FIRE AND RUIN TO THE WORLD FOR TOO LONG.
NOW IS THE AGE OF ATHENA AND APHRODITE BEGUN.
ALL WILL BE MADE BETTER.

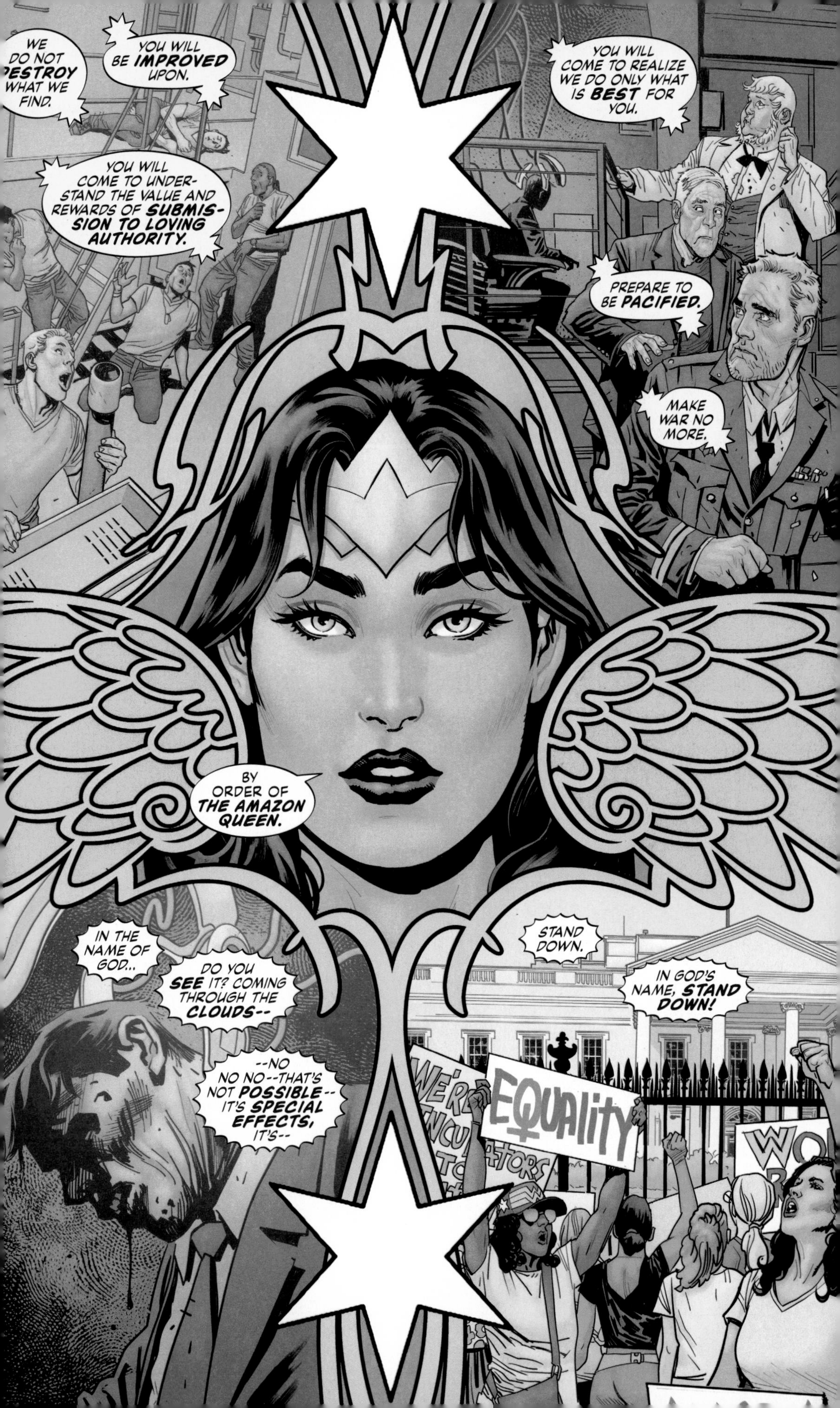

WE DO NOT DESTROY WHAT WE FIND.
YOU WILL BE IMPROVED UPON.
YOU WILL COME TO UNDER-STAND THE VALUE AND REWARDS OF SUBMIS-SION TO LOVING AUTHORITY.
YOU WILL COME TO REALIZE WE DO ONLY WHAT IS BEST FOR YOU.
PREPARE TO BE PACIFIED.
MAKE WAR NO MORE.
BY ORDER OF THE AMAZON QUEEN.
IN THE NAME OF GOD...
DO YOU SEE IT? COMING THROUGH THE CLOUDS--
--NO NO NO--THAT'S NOT POSSIBLE--IT'S SPECIAL EFFECTS, IT'S--
STAND DOWN.
IN GOD'S NAME, STAND DOWN!
EQUALITY

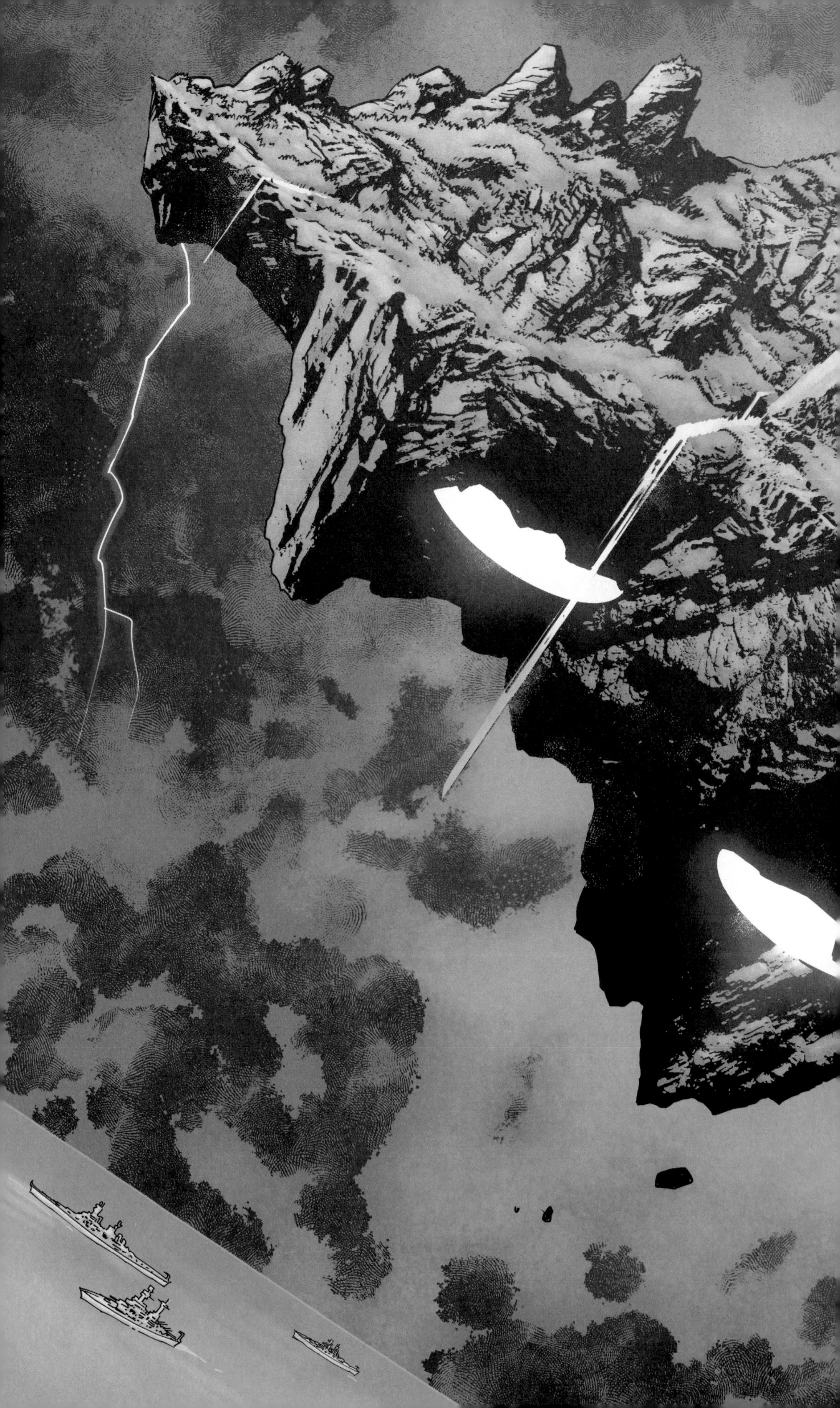

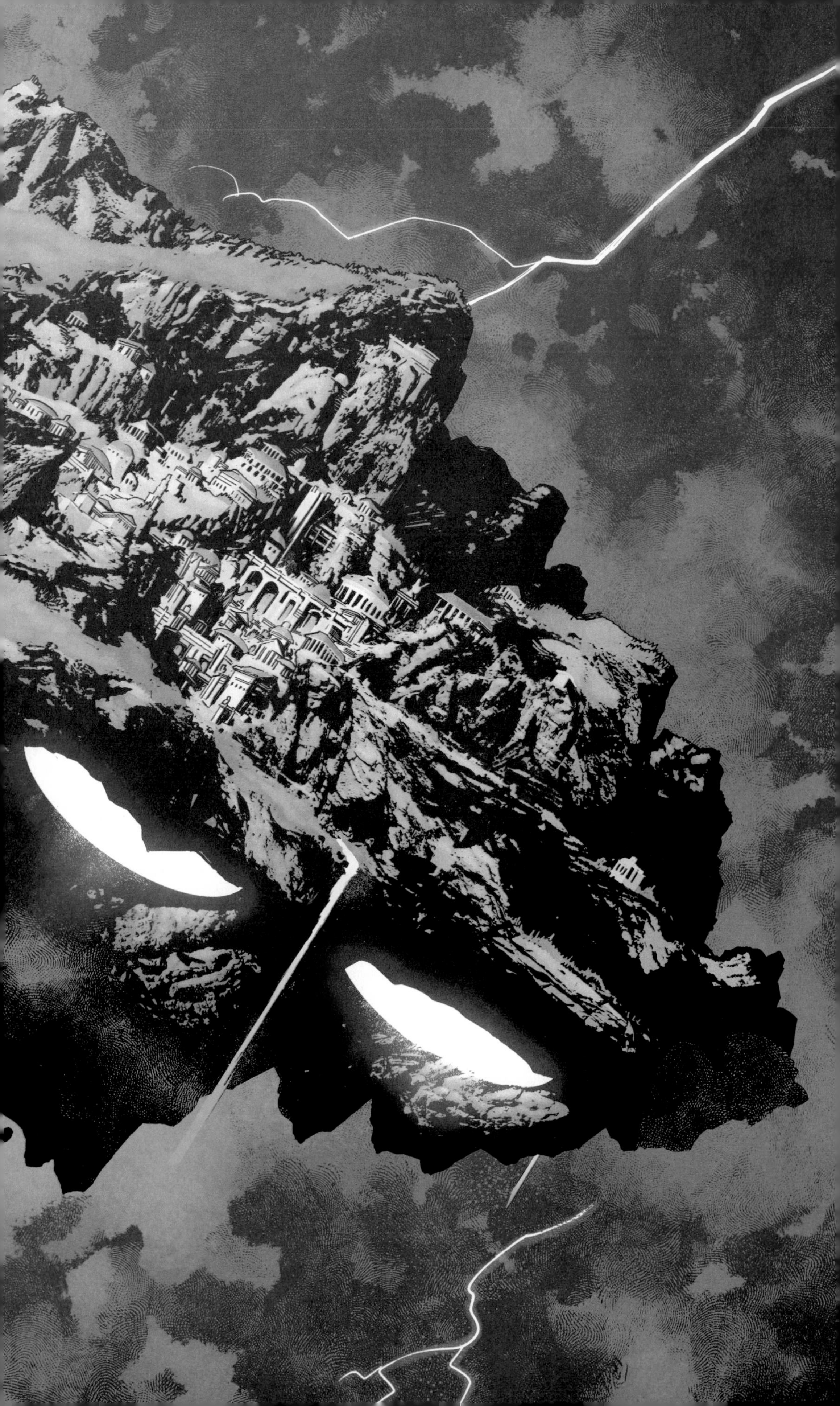

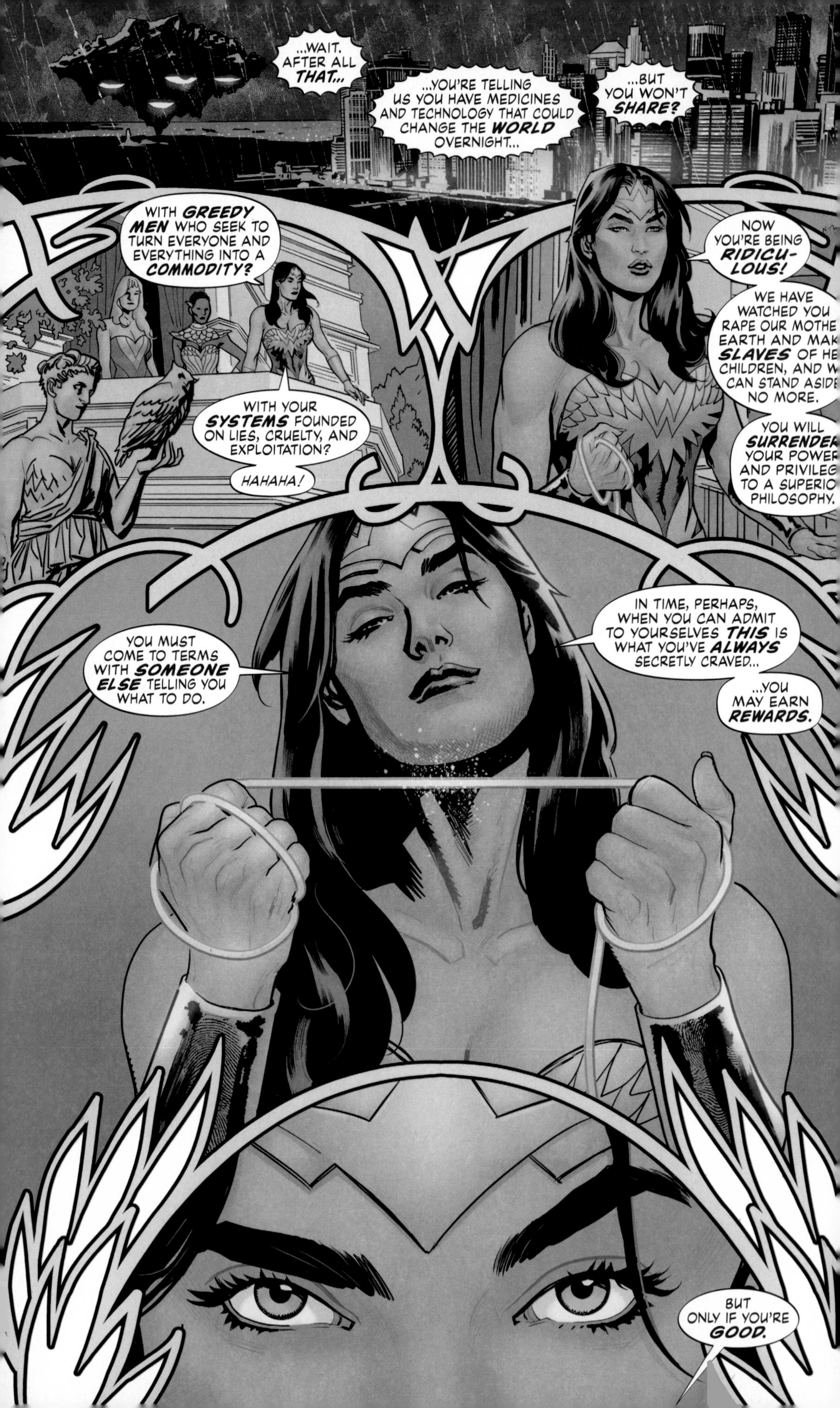

...WAIT. AFTER ALL THAT...
...YOU'RE TELLING US YOU HAVE MEDICINES AND TECHNOLOGY THAT COULD CHANGE THE WORLD OVERNIGHT...
...BUT YOU WON'T SHARE?
WITH GREEDY MEN WHO SEEK TO TURN EVERYONE AND EVERYTHING INTO A COMMODITY?
WITH YOUR SYSTEMS FOUNDED ON LIES, CRUELTY, AND EXPLOITATION?
HAHAHA!
NOW YOU'RE BEING RIDICU-LOUS!
WE HAVE WATCHED YOU RAPE OUR MOTHE EARTH AND MAK SLAVES OF HE CHILDREN, AND W CAN STAND ASIDE NO MORE.
YOU WILL SURRENDER YOUR POWER AND PRIVILEG TO A SUPERIO PHILOSOPHY.
YOU MUST COME TO TERMS WITH SOMEONE ELSE TELLING YOU WHAT TO DO.
IN TIME, PERHAPS, WHEN YOU CAN ADMIT TO YOURSELVES THIS IS WHAT YOU'VE ALWAYS SECRETLY CRAVED...
...YOU MAY EARN REWARDS.
BUT ONLY IF YOU'RE GOOD.

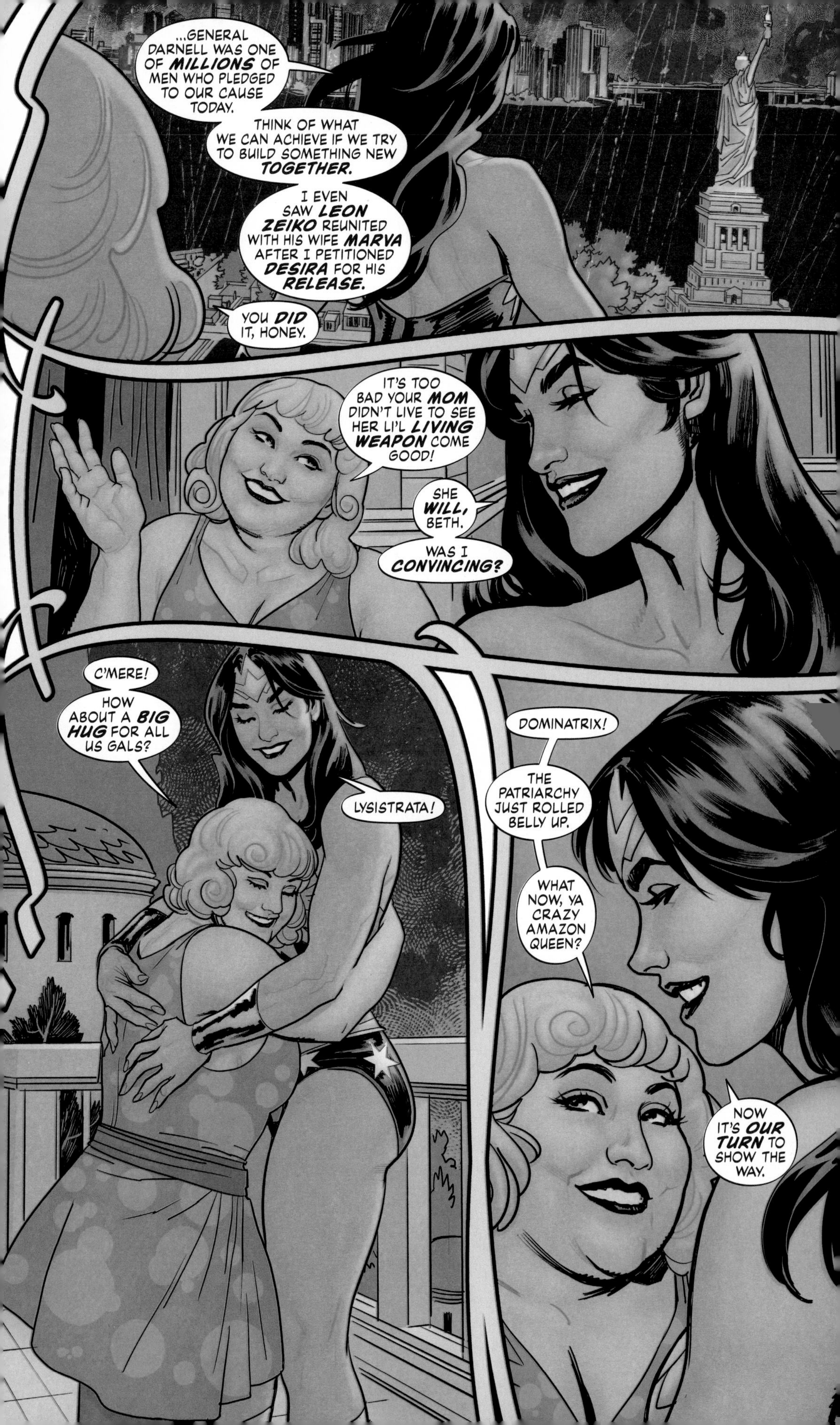
...GENERAL DARNELL WAS ONE OF MILLIONS OF MEN WHO PLEDGED TO OUR CAUSE TODAY.
THINK OF WHAT WE CAN ACHIEVE IF WE TRY TO BUILD SOMETHING NEW TOGETHER.
I EVEN SAW LEON ZEIKO REUNITED WITH HIS WIFE MARVA AFTER I PETITIONED DESIRA FOR HIS RELEASE.
YOU DID IT, HONEY.
IT'S TOO BAD YOUR MOM DIDN'T LIVE TO SEE HER LI'L LIVING WEAPON COME GOOD!
SHE WILL, BETH.
WAS I CONVINCING?
C'MERE!
HOW ABOUT A BIG HUG FOR ALL US GALS?
LYSISTRATA!
DOMINATRIX!
THE PATRIARCHY JUST ROLLED BELLY UP.
WHAT NOW, YA CRAZY AMAZON QUEEN?
NOW IT'S OUR TURN TO SHOW THE WAY.

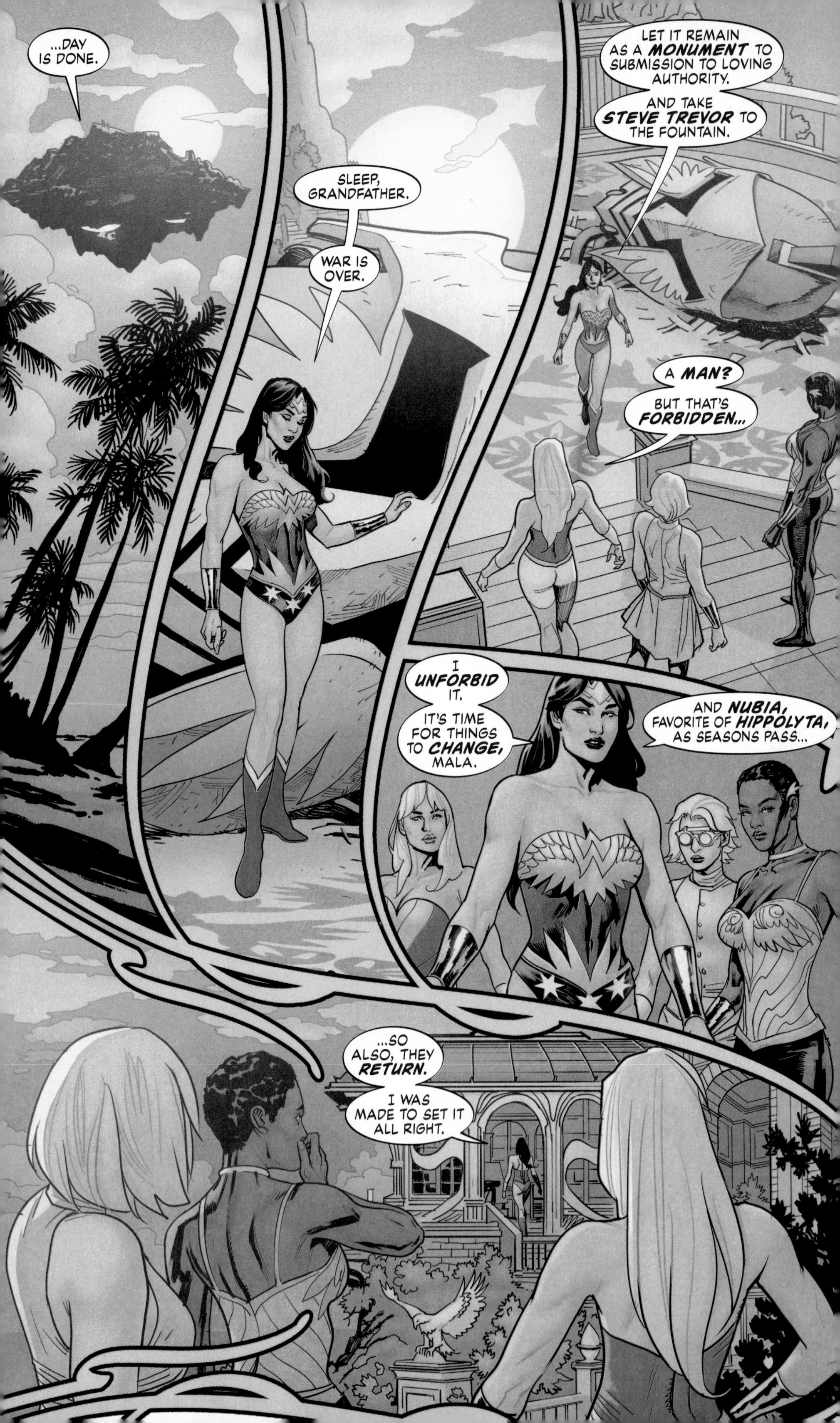
...DAY IS DONE.
SLEEP, GRANDFATHER.
WAR IS OVER.
LET IT REMAIN AS A MONUMENT TO SUBMISSION TO LOVING AUTHORITY.
AND TAKE STEVE TREVOR TO THE FOUNTAIN.
A MAN?
BUT THAT'S FORBIDDEN...
I UNFORBID IT.
IT'S TIME FOR THINGS TO CHANGE, MALA.
AND NUBIA, FAVORITE OF HIPPOLYTA, AS SEASONS PASS...
...SO ALSO, THEY RETURN.
I WAS MADE TO SET IT ALL RIGHT.

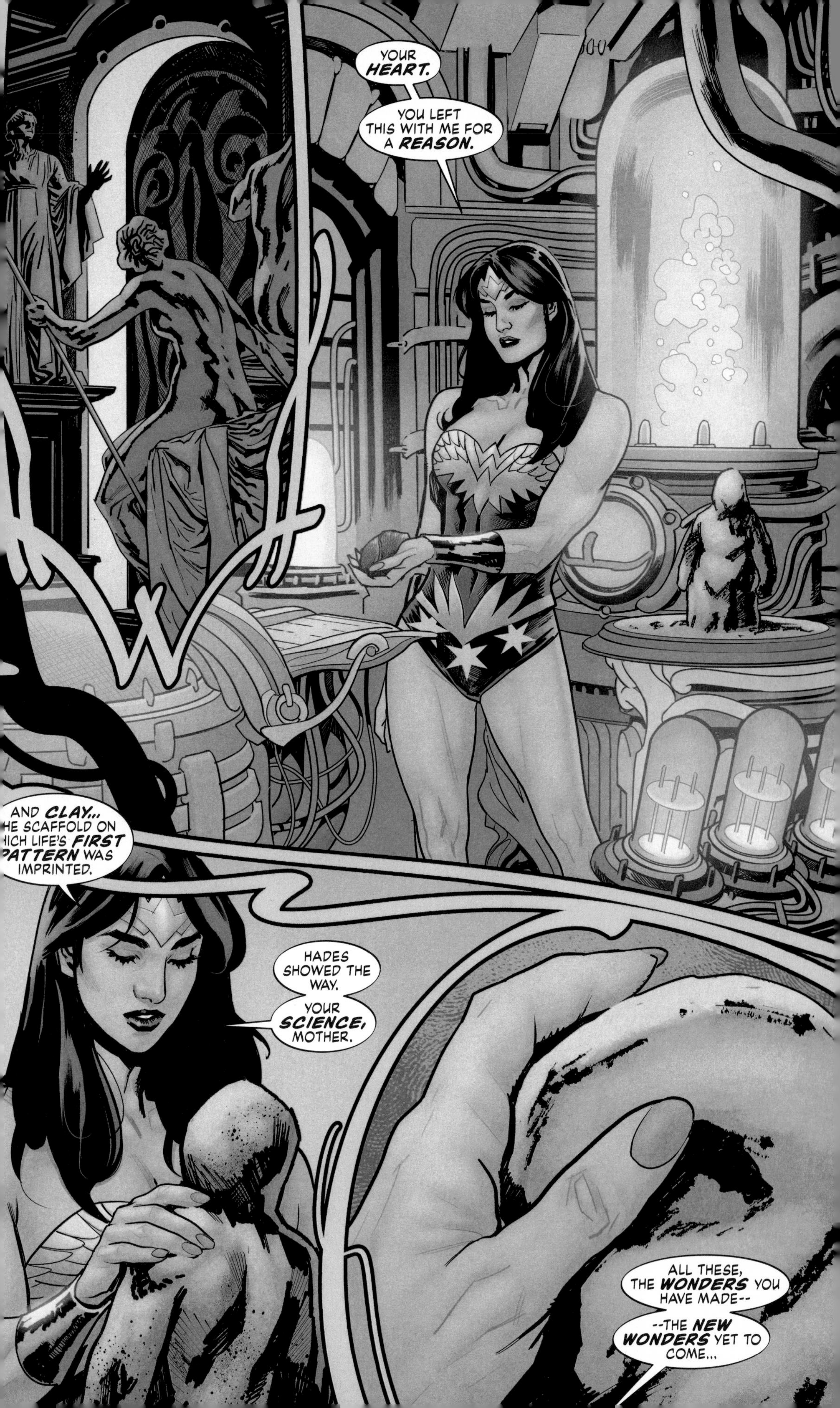
YOUR HEART.
YOU LEFT THIS WITH ME FOR A REASON.
AND CLAY... HE SCAFFOLD ON HICH LIFE'S FIRST PATTERN WAS IMPRINTED.
HADES SHOWED THE WAY.
YOUR SCIENCE, MOTHER.
ALL THESE, THE WONDERS YOU HAVE MADE--
--THE NEW WONDERS YET TO COME...

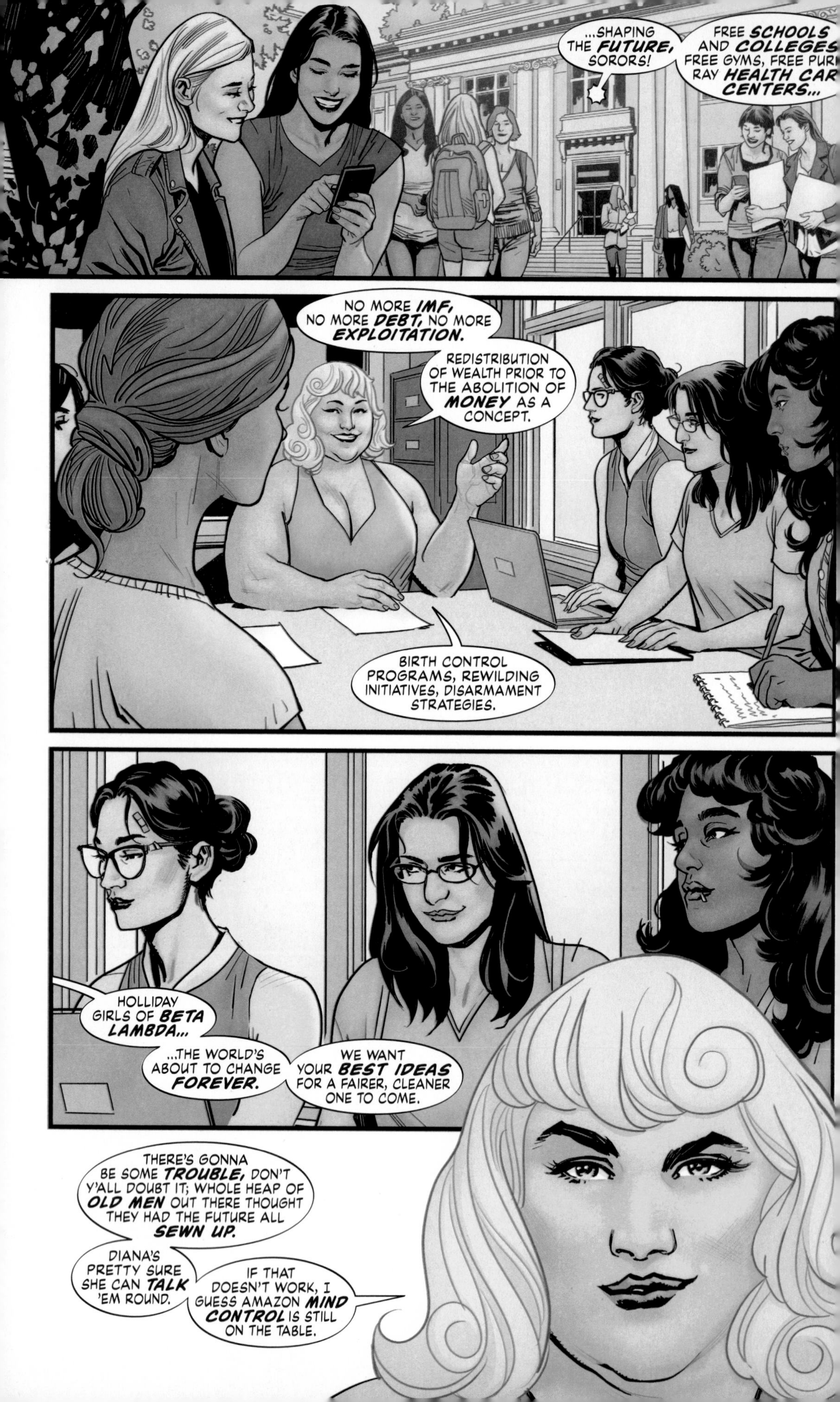

...SHAPING THE FUTURE, SORORS!
FREE SCHOOLS AND COLLEGES, FREE GYMS, FREE PURI RAY HEALTH CAR CENTERS...
NO MORE IMF, NO MORE DEBT, NO MORE EXPLOITATION.
REDISTRIBUTION OF WEALTH PRIOR TO THE ABOLITION OF MONEY AS A CONCEPT.
BIRTH CONTROL PROGRAMS, REWILDING INITIATIVES, DISARMAMENT STRATEGIES.
HOLLIDAY GIRLS OF BETA LAMBDA...
...THE WORLD'S ABOUT TO CHANGE FOREVER.
WE WANT YOUR BEST IDEAS FOR A FAIRER, CLEANER ONE TO COME.
THERE'S GONNA BE SOME TROUBLE, DON'T Y'ALL DOUBT IT; WHOLE HEAP OF OLD MEN OUT THERE THOUGHT THEY HAD THE FUTURE ALL SEWN UP.
DIANA'S PRETTY SURE SHE CAN TALK 'EM ROUND.
IF THAT DOESN'T WORK, I GUESS AMAZON MIND CONTROL IS STILL ON THE TABLE.

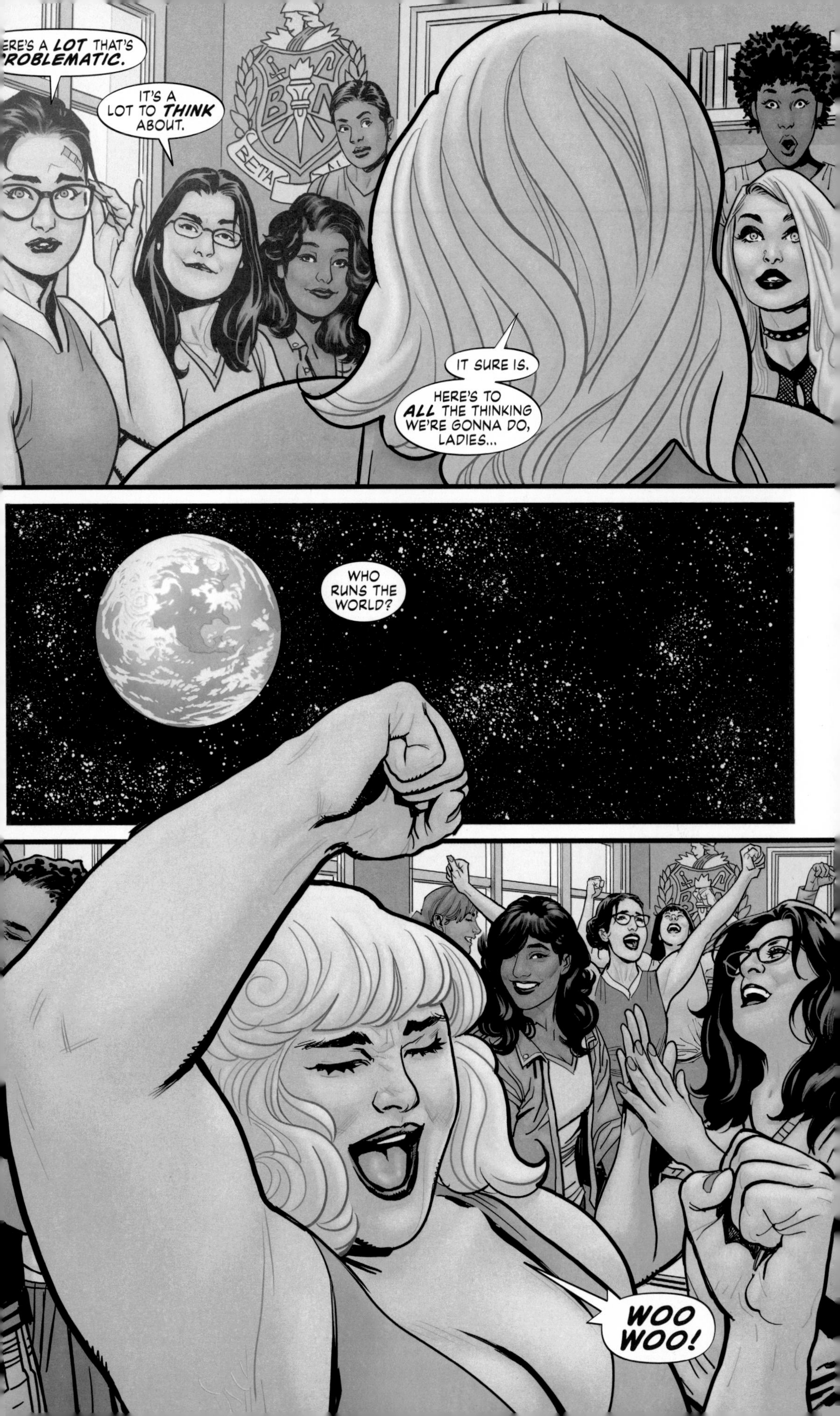
ERE'S A LOT THAT'S ROBLEMATIC.
IT'S A LOT TO THINK ABOUT.
IT SURE IS.
HERE'S TO ALL THE THINKING WE'RE GONNA DO, LADIES...
WHO RUNS THE WORLD?
WOO WOO!

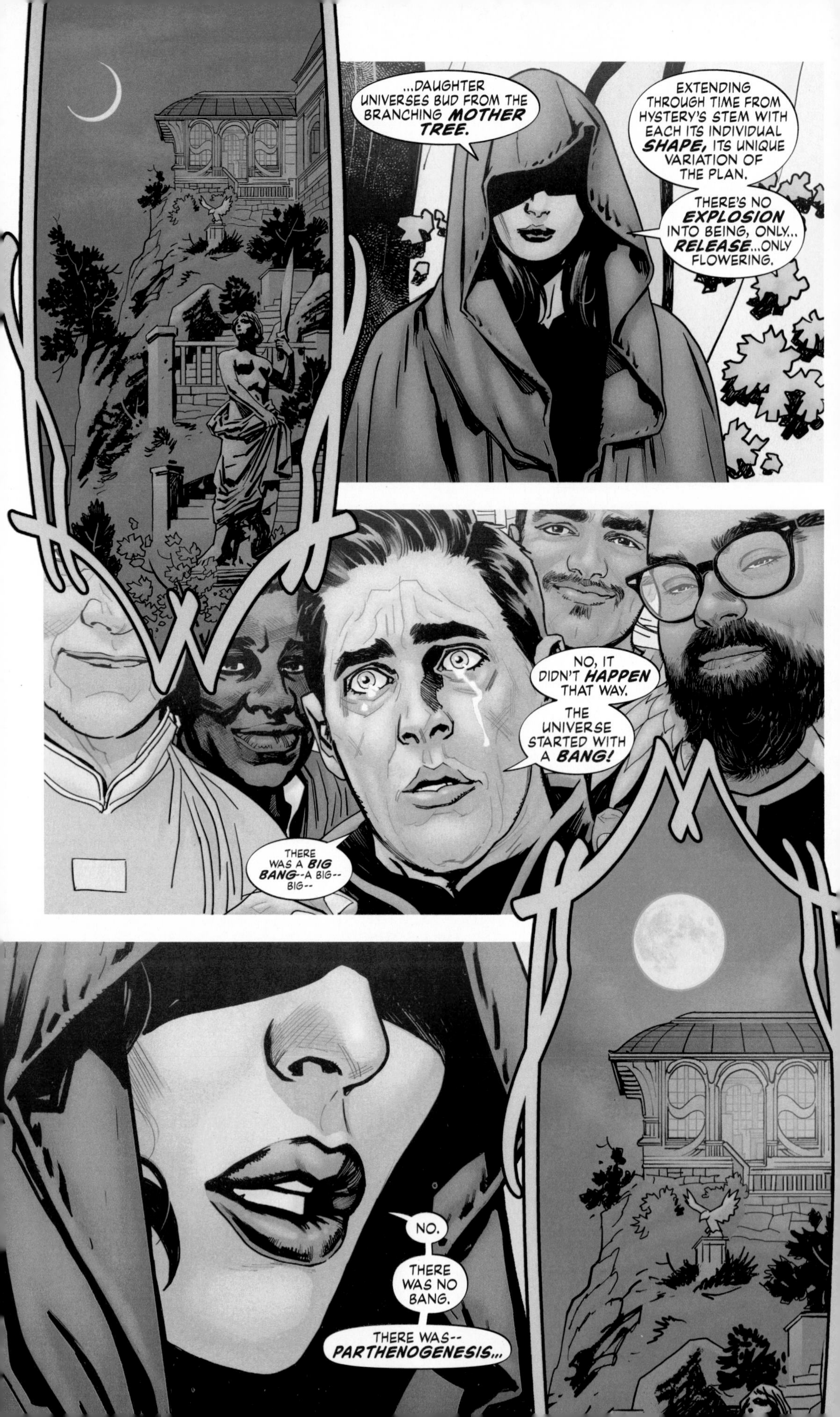
...DAUGHTER UNIVERSES BUD FROM THE BRANCHING MOTHER TREE.
EXTENDING THROUGH TIME FROM HYSTERY'S STEM WITH EACH ITS INDIVIDUAL SHAPE, ITS UNIQUE VARIATION OF THE PLAN.
THERE'S NO EXPLOSION INTO BEING, ONLY... RELEASE...ONLY FLOWERING.
NO, IT DIDN'T HAPPEN THAT WAY.
THE UNIVERSE STARTED WITH A BANG!
THERE WAS A BIG BANG--A BIG-- BIG--
NO.
THERE WAS NO BANG.
THERE WAS-- PARTHENOGENESIS...

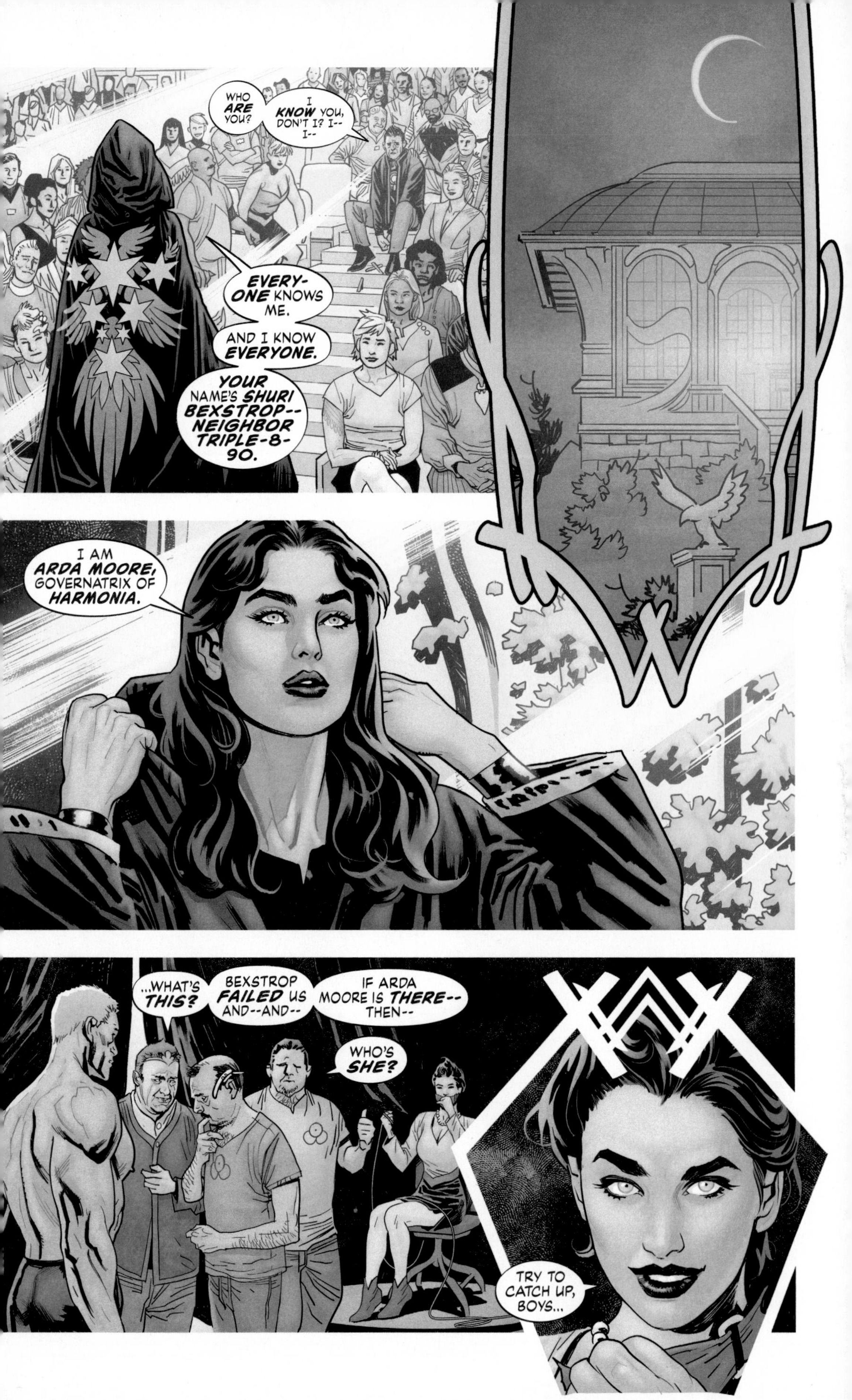

WHO ARE YOU?
I KNOW YOU, DON'T I? I-- I--
EVERY-ONE KNOWS ME.
AND I KNOW EVERYONE.
YOUR NAME'S SHURI BEXSTROP-- NEIGHBOR TRIPLE-8-90.
I AM ARDA MOORE, GOVERNATRIX OF HARMONIA.
...WHAT'S THIS?
BEXSTROP FAILED US AND--AND--
IF ARDA MOORE IS THERE-- THEN--
WHO'S SHE?
TRY TO CATCH UP, BOYS...

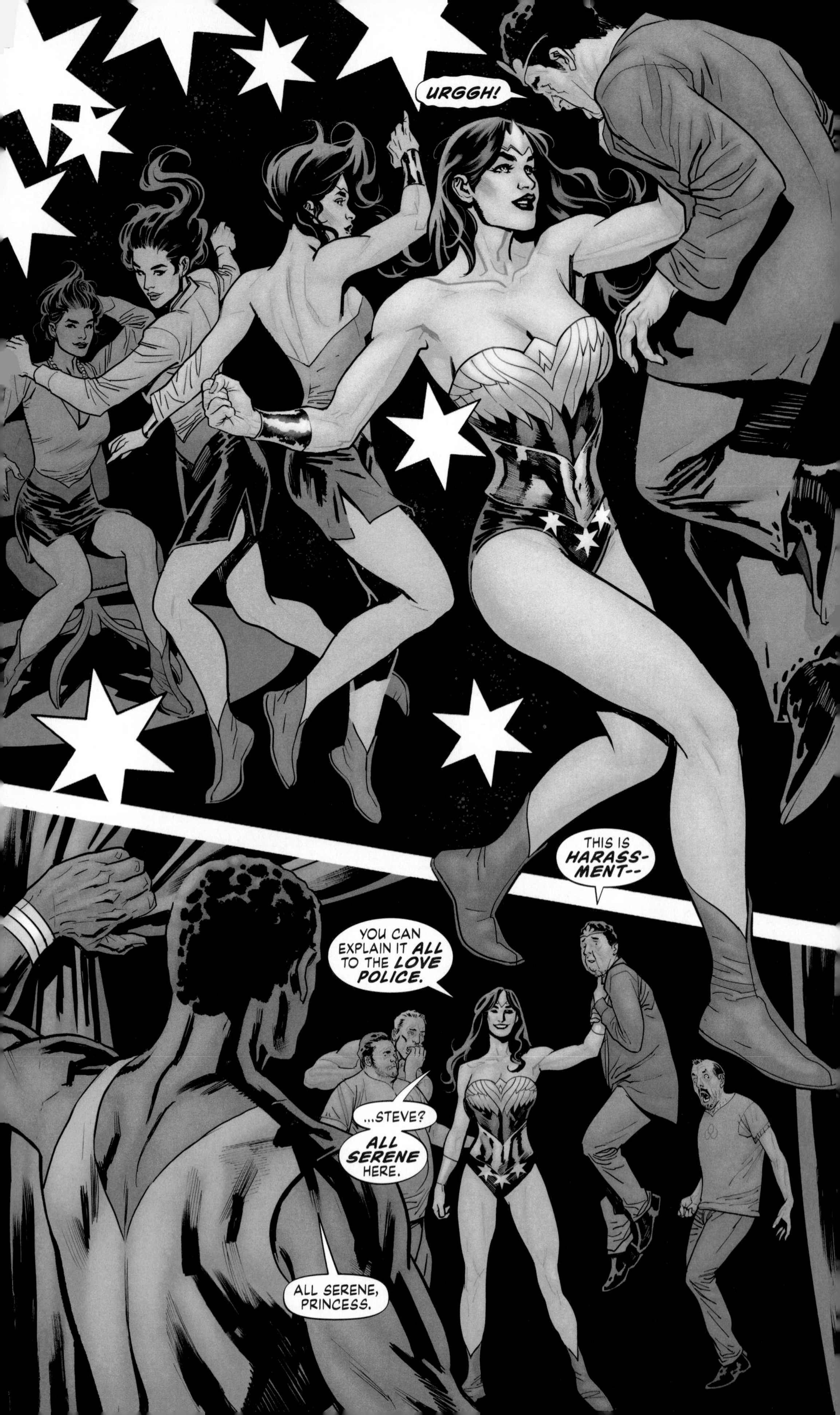
URGGH!
THIS IS HARASS- MENT--
YOU CAN EXPLAIN IT ALL TO THE LOVE POLICE.
...STEVE? ALL SERENE HERE.
ALL SERENE, PRINCESS.

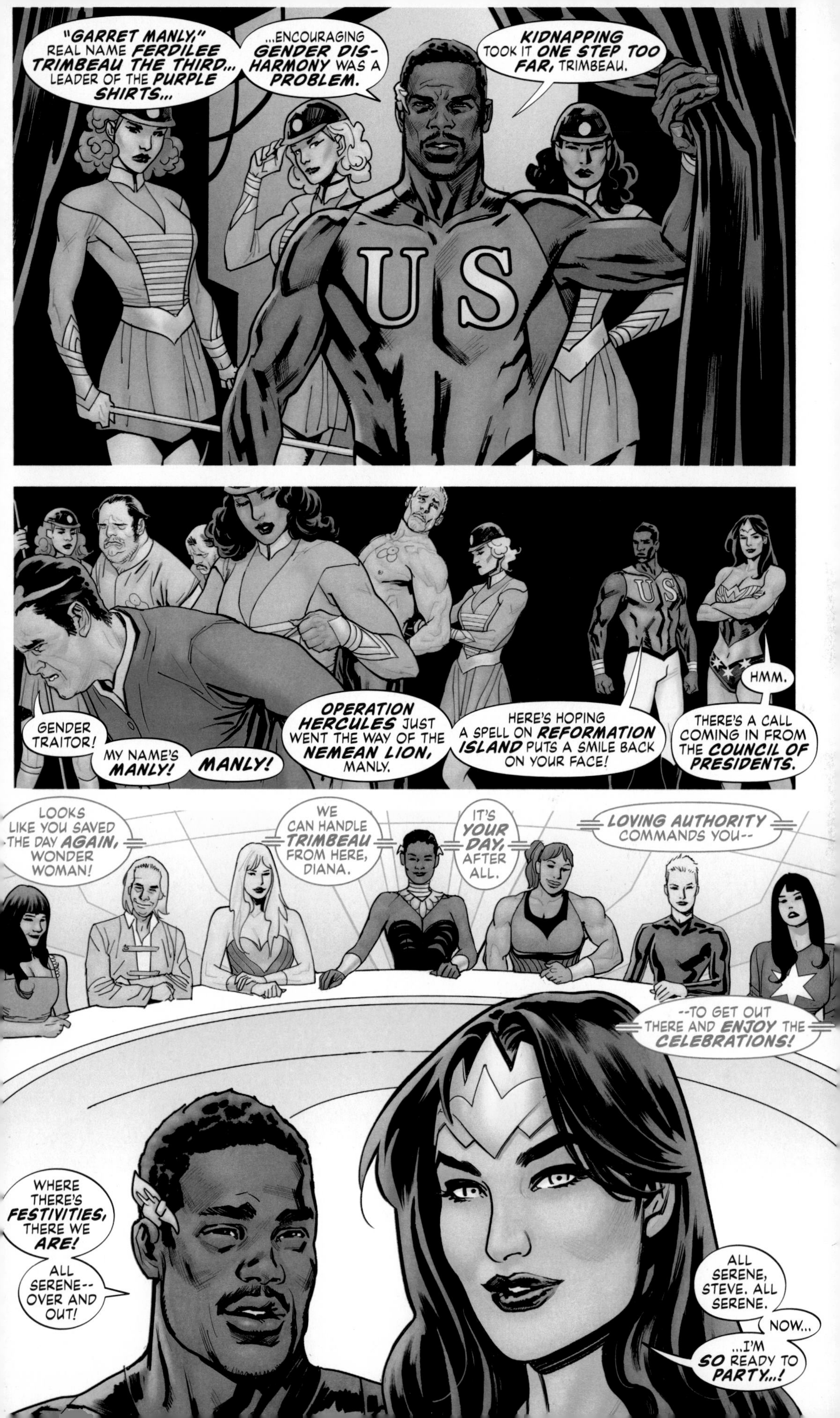
"GARRET MANLY," REAL NAME FERDILEE TRIMBEAU THE THIRD... LEADER OF THE PURPLE SHIRTS...
...ENCOURAGING GENDER DIS-HARMONY WAS A PROBLEM.
KIDNAPPING TOOK IT ONE STEP TOO FAR, TRIMBEAU.
GENDER TRAITOR!
MY NAME'S MANLY!
MANLY!
OPERATION HERCULES JUST WENT THE WAY OF THE NEMEAN LION, MANLY.
HERE'S HOPING A SPELL ON REFORMATION ISLAND PUTS A SMILE BACK ON YOUR FACE!
HMM.
THERE'S A CALL COMING IN FROM THE COUNCIL OF PRESIDENTS.
LOOKS LIKE YOU SAVED THE DAY AGAIN, WONDER WOMAN!
WE CAN HANDLE TRIMBEAU FROM HERE, DIANA.
IT'S YOUR DAY, AFTER ALL.
LOVING AUTHORITY COMMANDS YOU--
--TO GET OUT THERE AND ENJOY THE CELEBRATIONS!
WHERE THERE'S FESTIVITIES, THERE WE ARE!
ALL SERENE--OVER AND OUT!
ALL SERENE, STEVE. ALL SERENE.
NOW...
...I'M SO READY TO PARTY...!

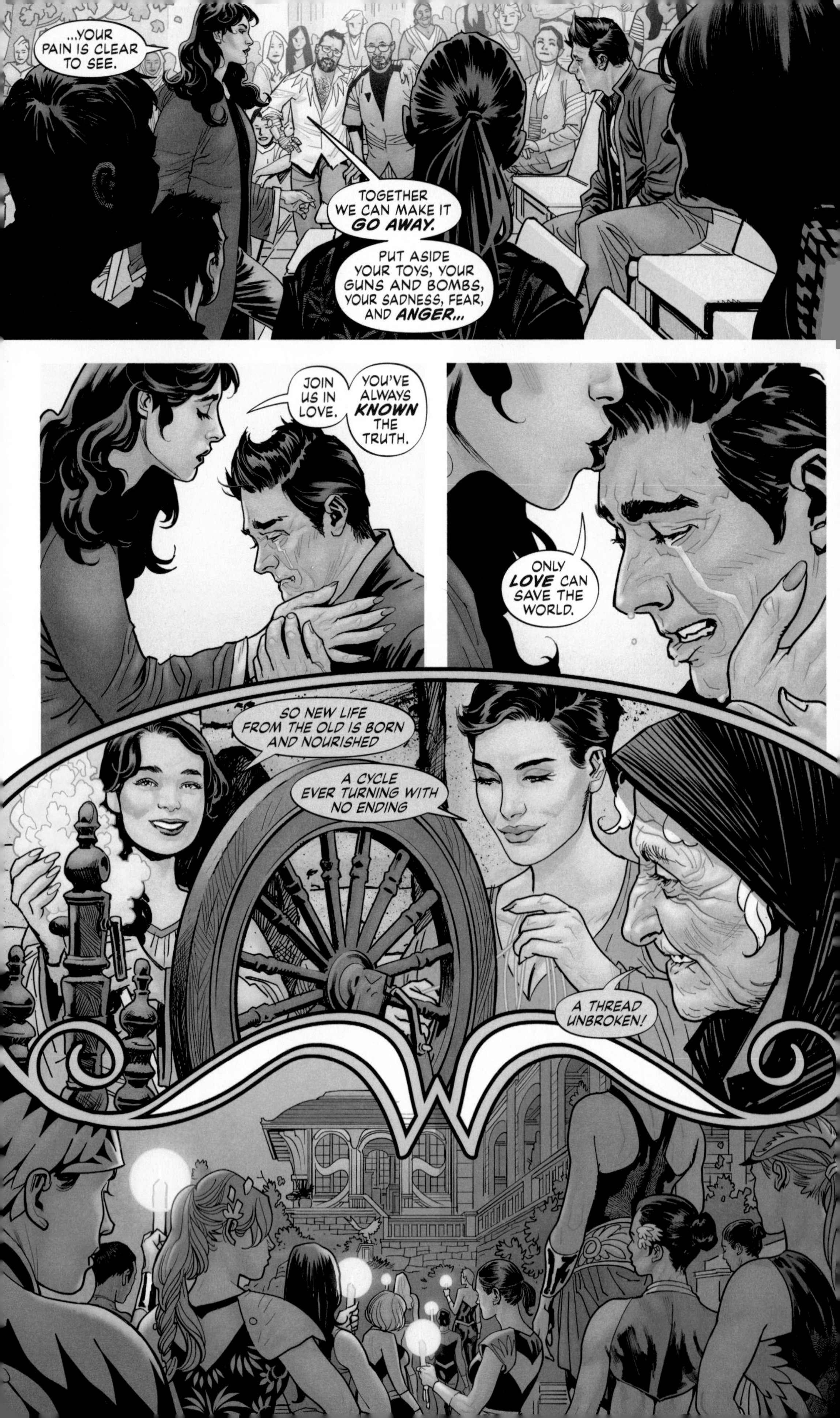
...YOUR PAIN IS CLEAR TO SEE.
TOGETHER WE CAN MAKE IT GO AWAY.
PUT ASIDE YOUR TOYS, YOUR GUNS AND BOMBS, YOUR SADNESS, FEAR, AND ANGER...
JOIN US IN LOVE.
YOU'VE ALWAYS KNOWN THE TRUTH.
ONLY LOVE CAN SAVE THE WORLD.
SO NEW LIFE FROM THE OLD IS BORN AND NOURISHED
A CYCLE EVER TURNING WITH NO ENDING
A THREAD UNBROKEN!

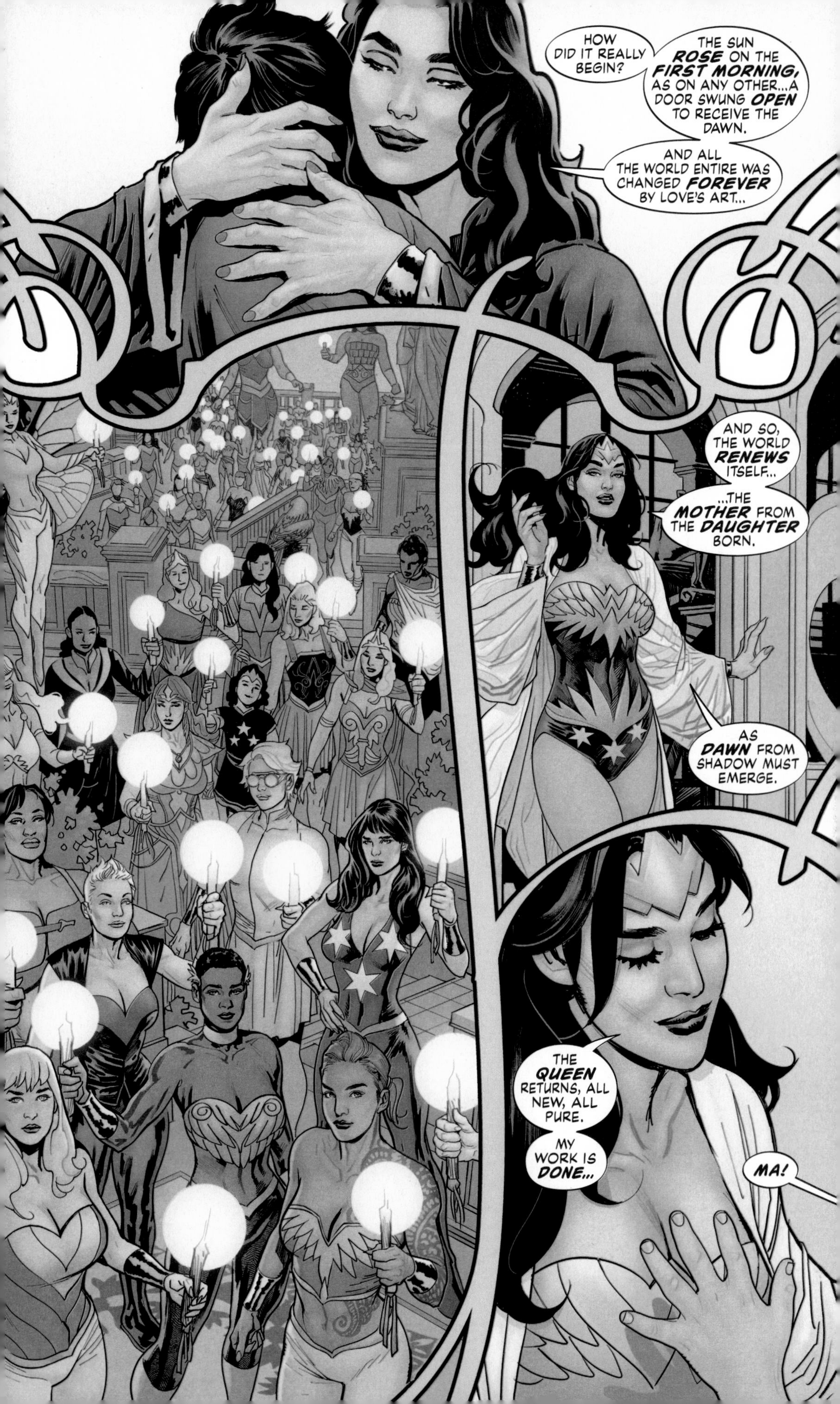

HOW DID IT REALLY BEGIN?
THE SUN ROSE ON THE FIRST MORNING, AS ON ANY OTHER...A DOOR SWUNG OPEN TO RECEIVE THE DAWN.
AND ALL THE WORLD ENTIRE WAS CHANGED FOREVER BY LOVE'S ART...
AND SO, THE WORLD RENEWS ITSELF...
...THE MOTHER FROM THE DAUGHTER BORN.
AS DAWN FROM SHADOW MUST EMERGE.
THE QUEEN RETURNS, ALL NEW, ALL PURE.
MY WORK IS DONE...
MA!

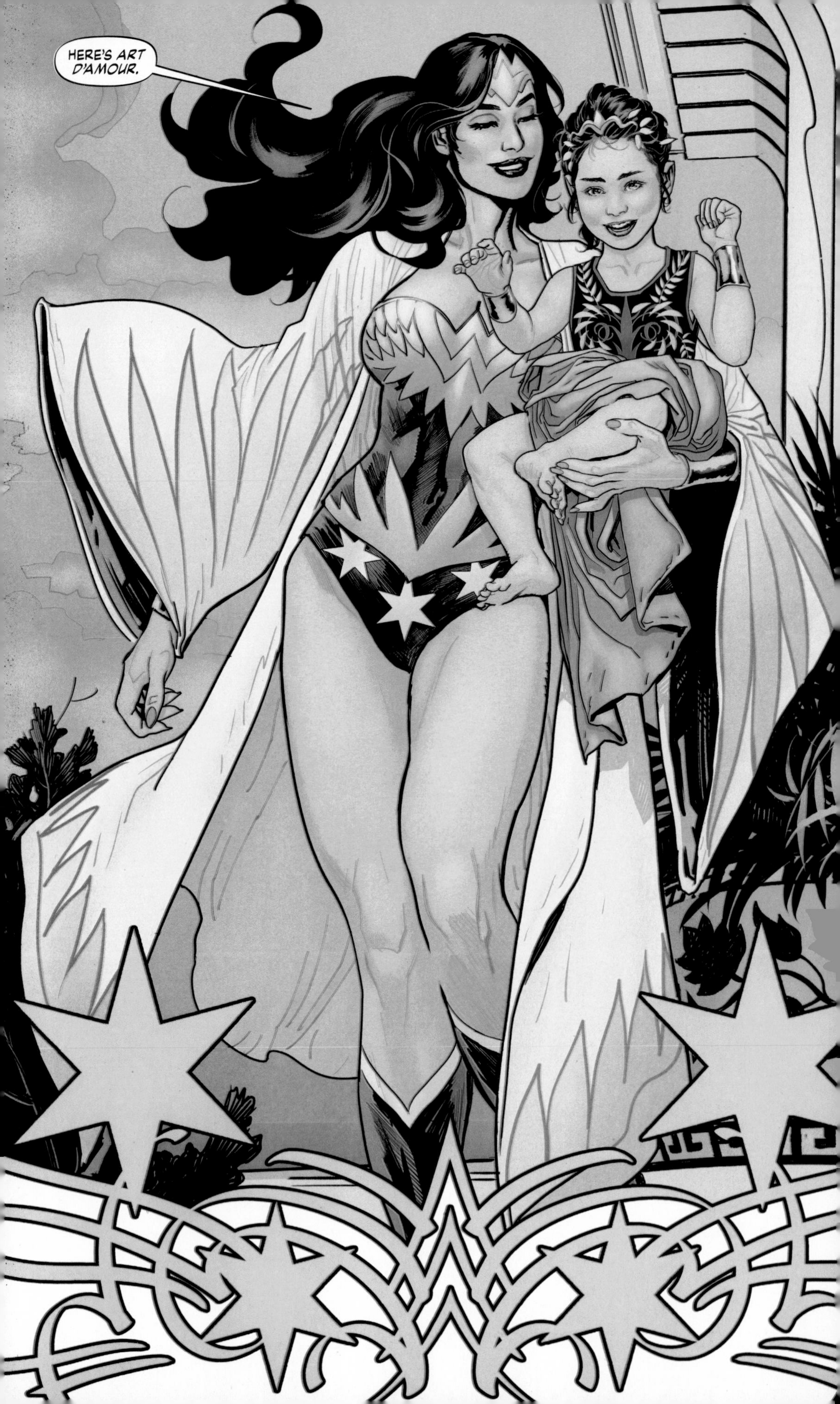
HERE'S ART D'AMOUR.

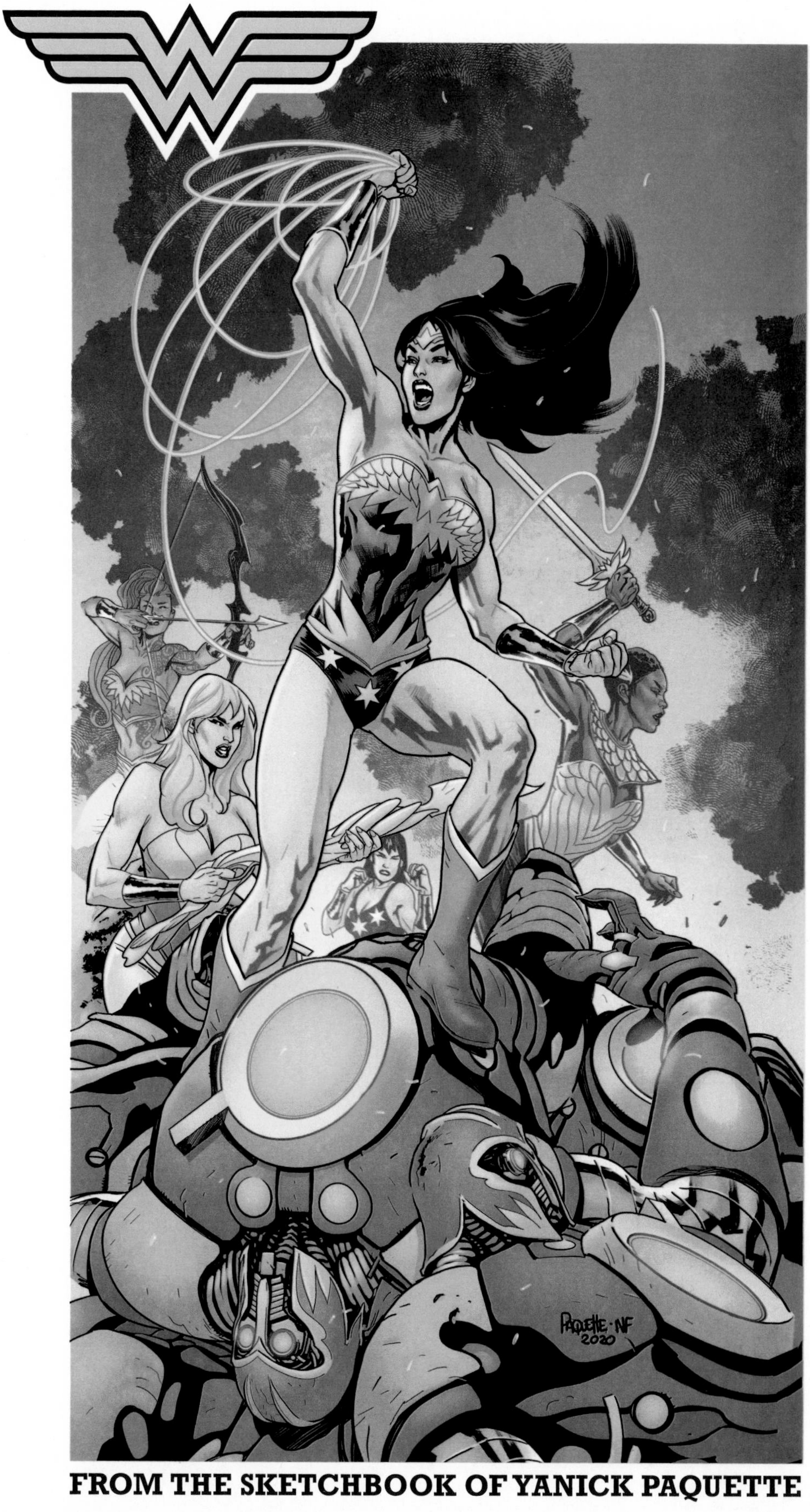
PAQUETTE · NF
2020

FROM THE SKETCHBOOK OF YANICK PAQUETTE

The Future, The Capital City of Harmonia

Whenever I could, I tried to go back to the rich source material for the design elements in the *Wonder Woman Earth One* series. Our utopian future is no exception and Harry G. Peter's remarkable illustrations for *Wonder Woman #7* (1943) have been a great inspiration.

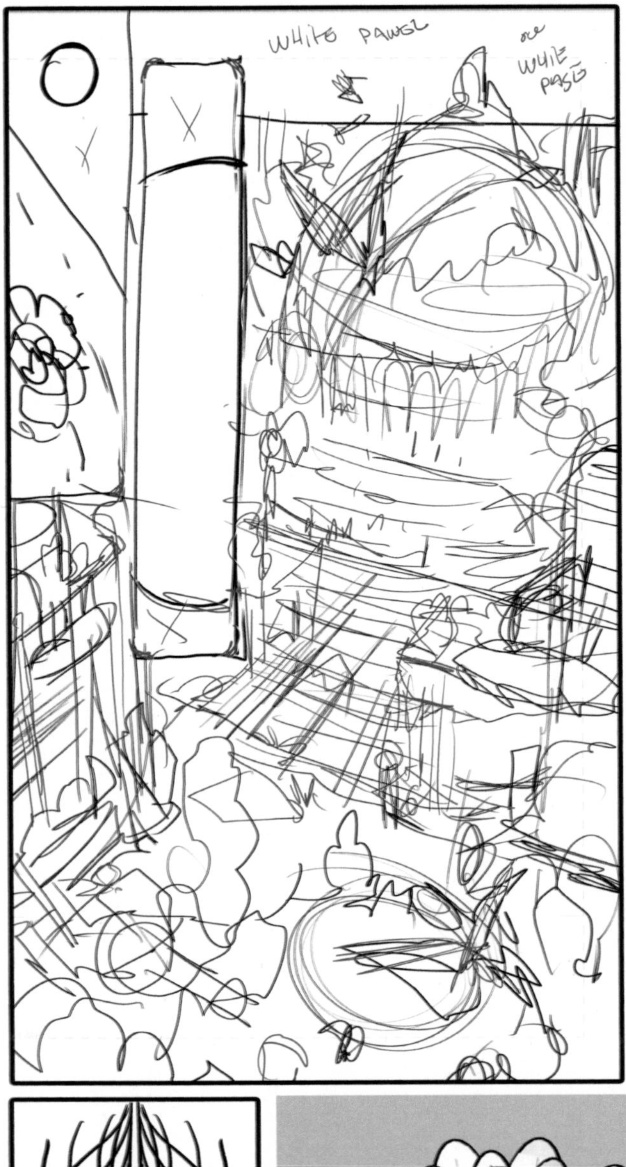

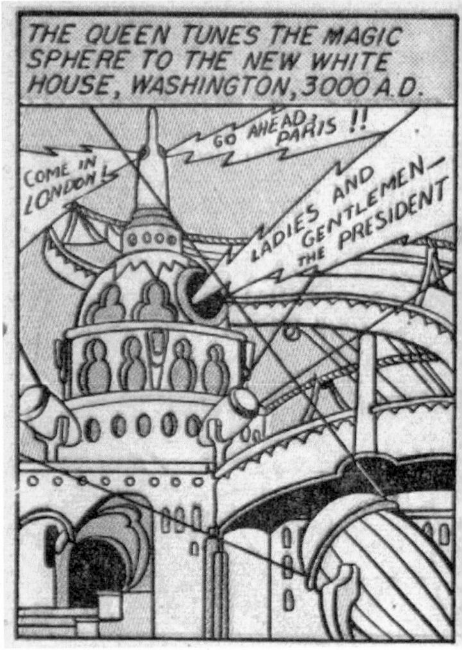
THE QUEEN TUNES THE MAGIC SPHERE TO THE NEW WHITE HOUSE, WASHINGTON, 3000 A.D.
COME IN LONDON!
GO AHEAD PARIS !!
LADIES AND GENTLEMEN— THE PRESIDENT

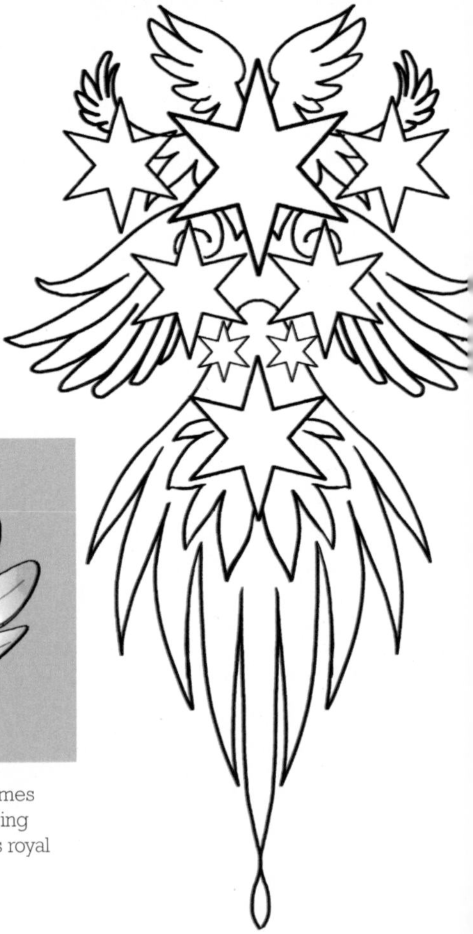

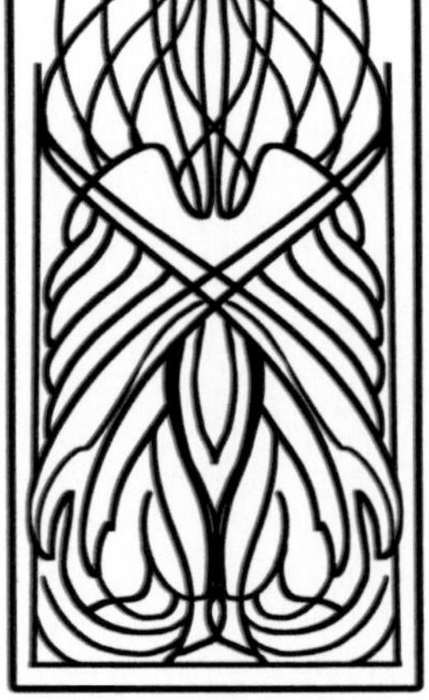

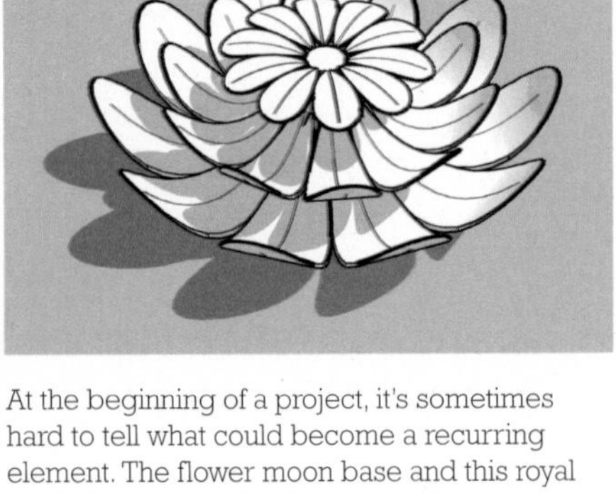

At the beginning of a project, it's sometimes hard to tell what could become a recurring element. The flower moon base and this royal symbol turn out to be barely used.

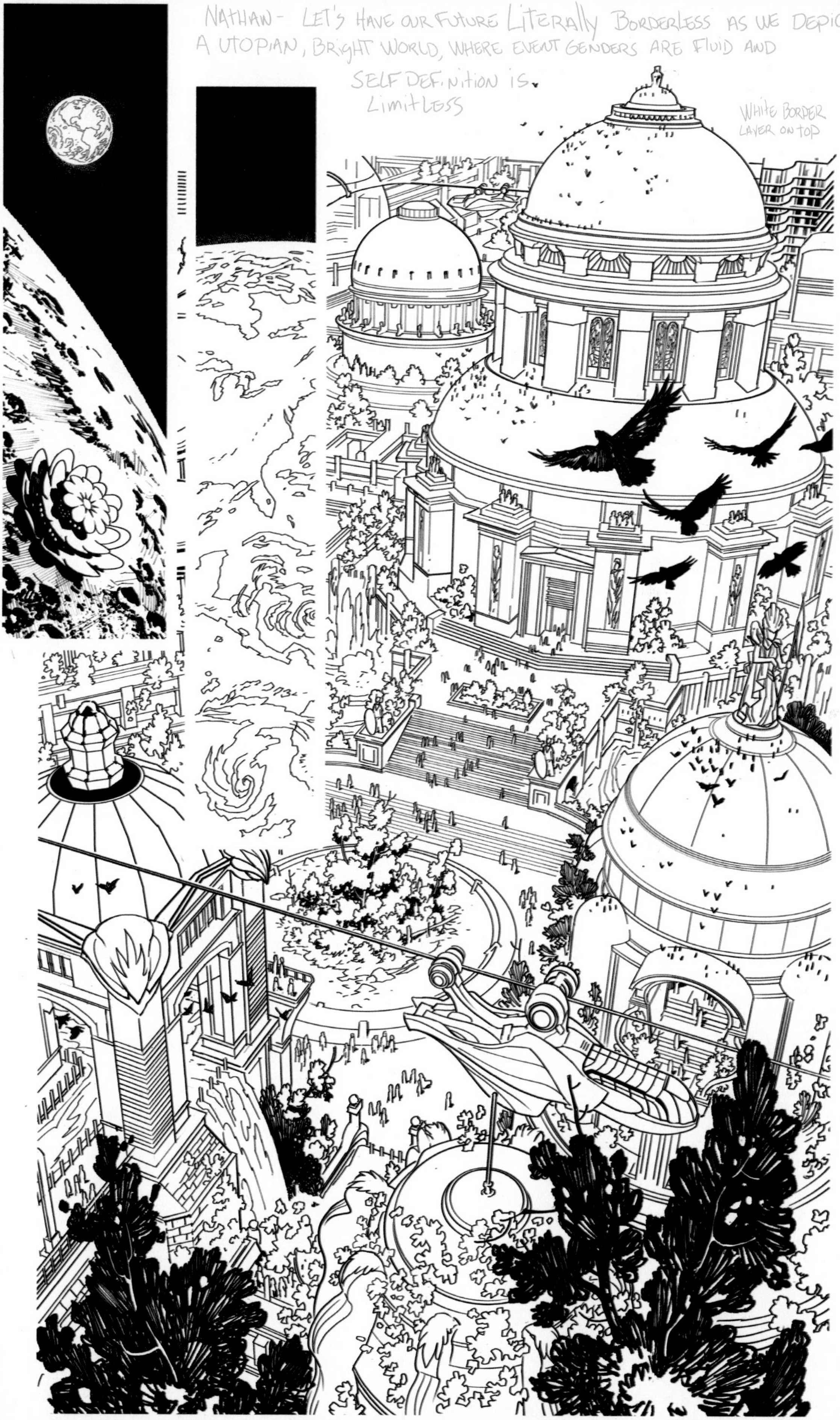
NATHAN- LET'S HAVE OUR FUTURE LITERALLY BORDERLESS AS WE DEPICT A UTOPIAN, BRIGHT WORLD, WHERE EVENT GENDERS ARE FLUID AND SELF DEFINITION IS LIMITLESS
WHITE BORDER LAYER ON TOP

Wonder Woman Earth One Evolution

It was Grant's intention to give Diana a vast, ever-changing wardrobe for all occasions. Here are some of the chest-piece variations occurring throughout the three ` volumes.

Young Diana (vol 1 & 2)

Holiday Girls's Big Band

Wonder Woman vol 1

Wonder Woman March speech vol 2

Manworld Military vol 2

Ares Wars vol 3

Year 3000 Wonder Woman

Queen Wonder Woman vol 3

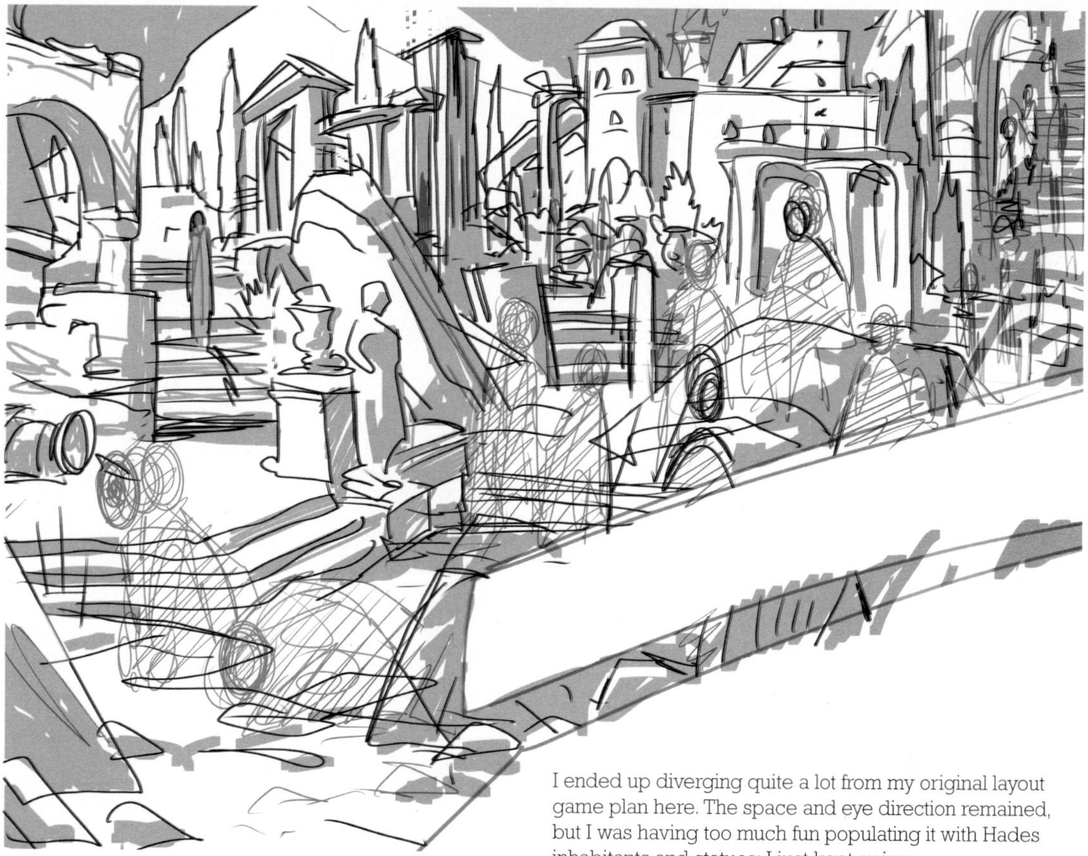

I ended up diverging quite a lot from my original layout game plan here. The space and eye direction remained, but I was having too much fun populating it with Hades inhabitants and statues; I just kept going.

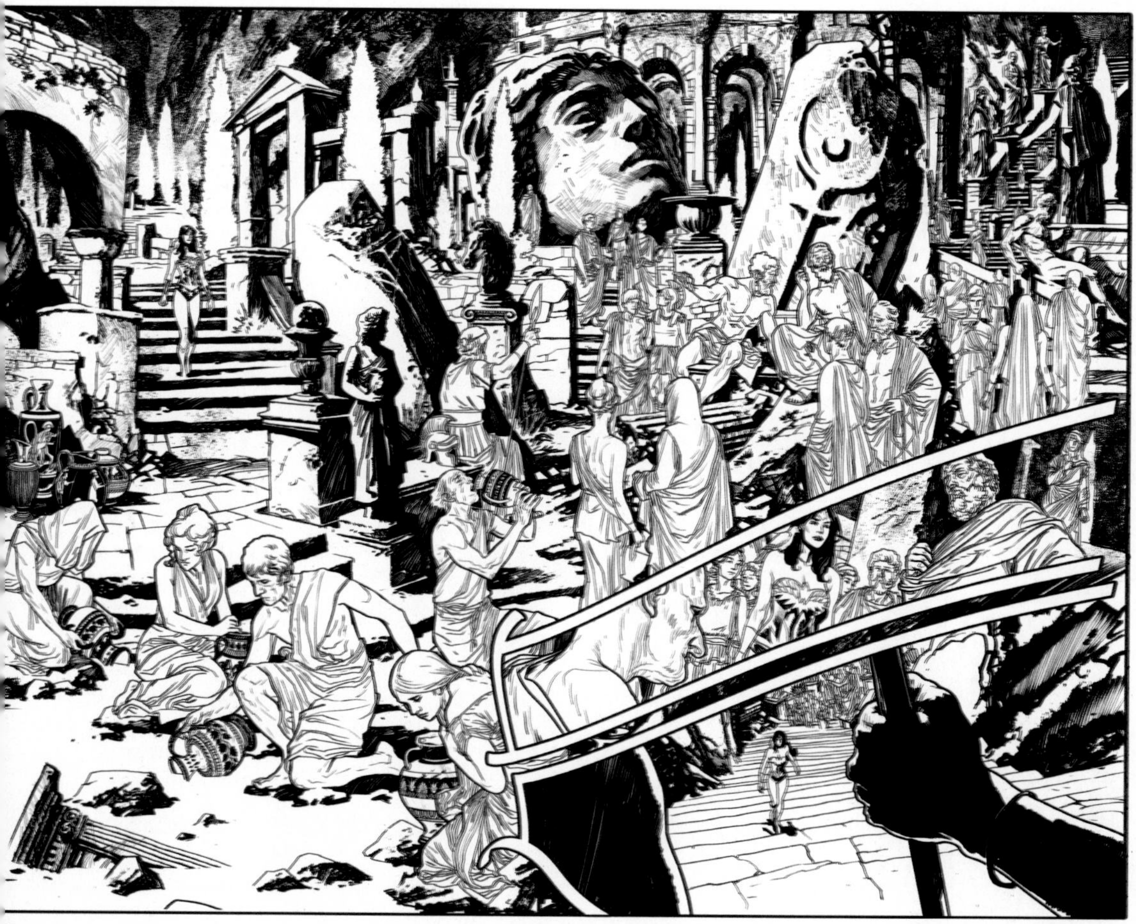

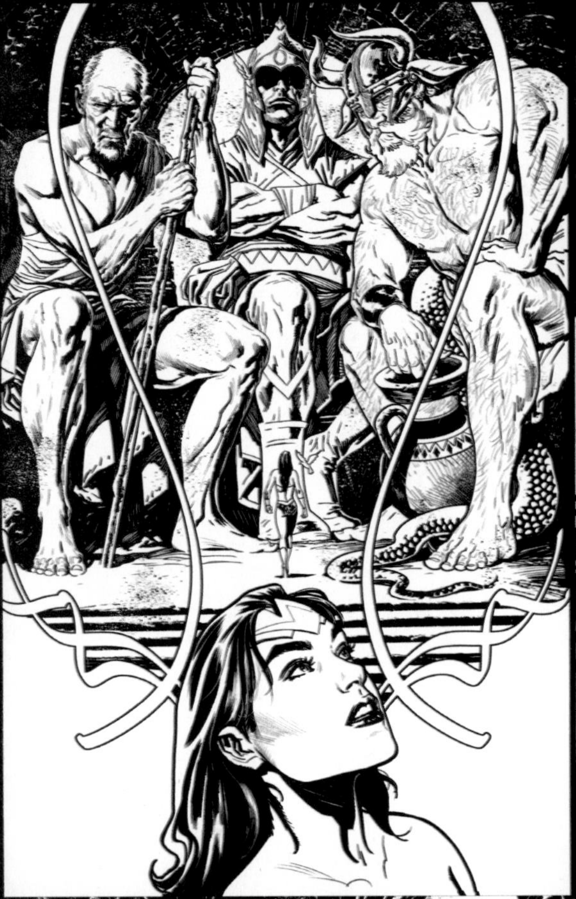

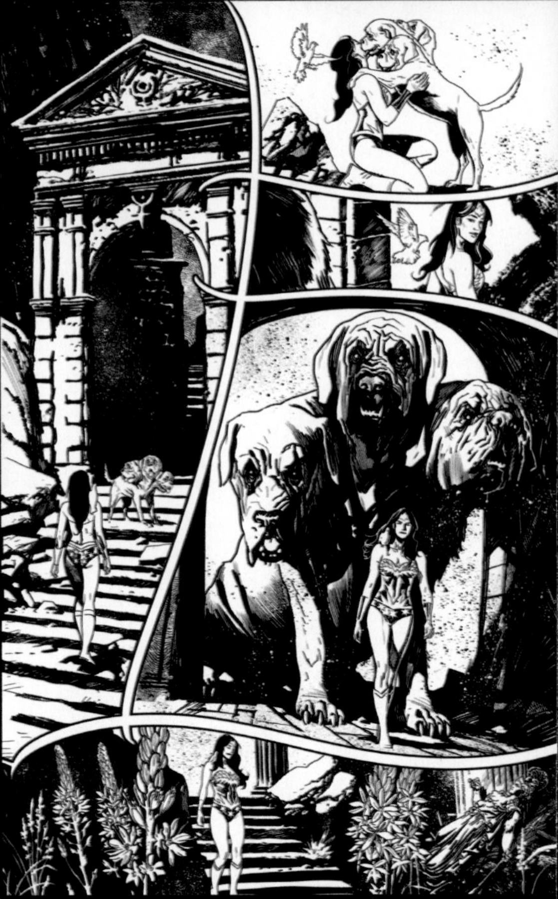

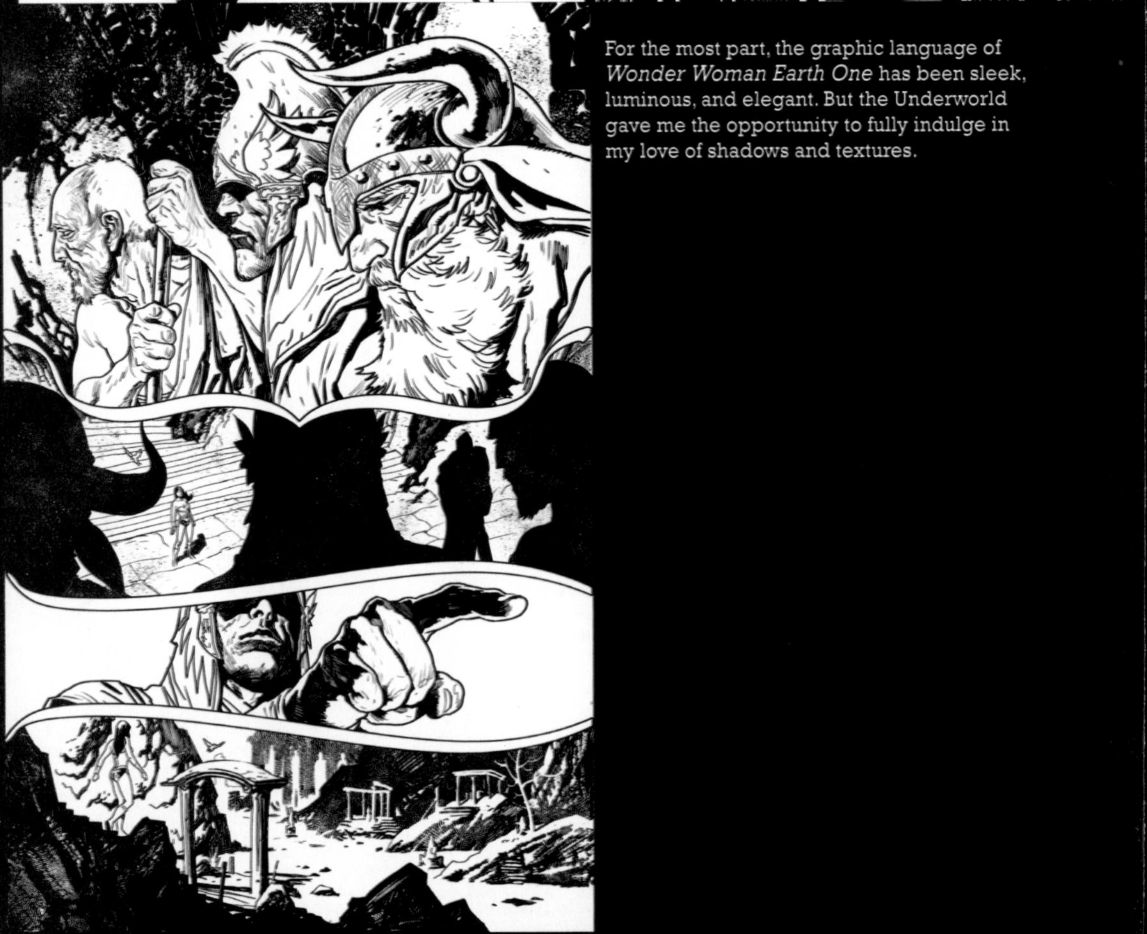

For the most part, the graphic language of *Wonder Woman Earth One* has been sleek, luminous, and elegant. But the Underworld gave me the opportunity to fully indulge in my love of shadows and textures.

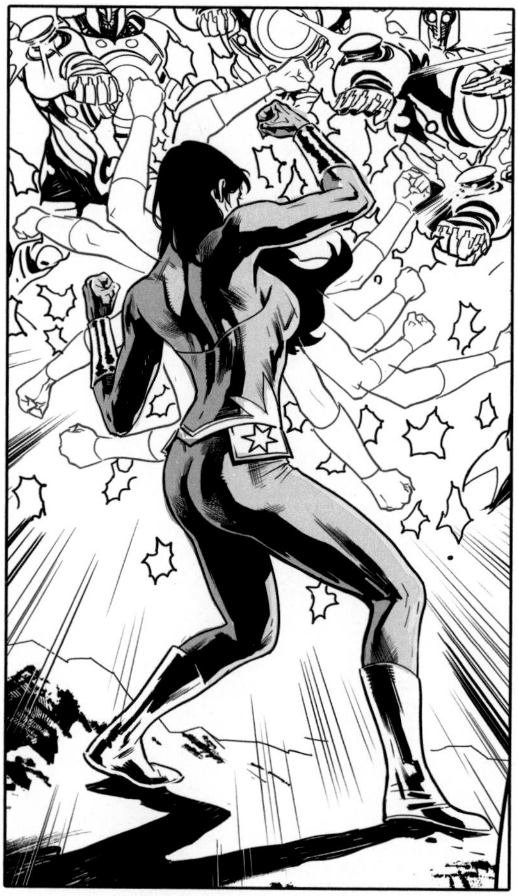

Nathan Fairbairn is easily one of the absolute best colorists in comics. After a decade of collaborations, he can easily decipher my most obscure light sourcing and always turn in better final pages than I could have imagined. Still, to make sure my own double-light math checks out, I sometimes work out shadow and light mapping on a separate layer.

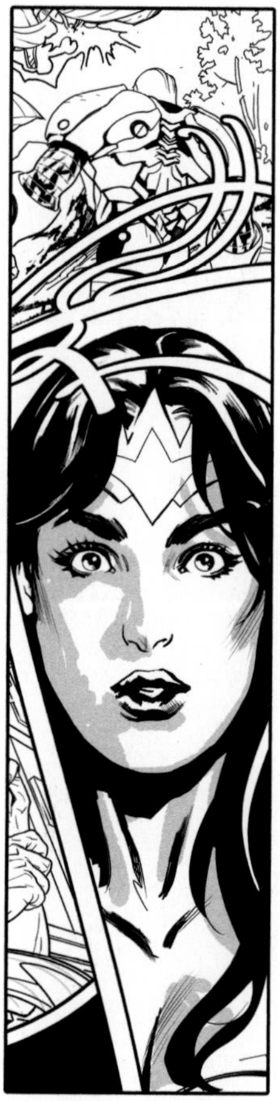

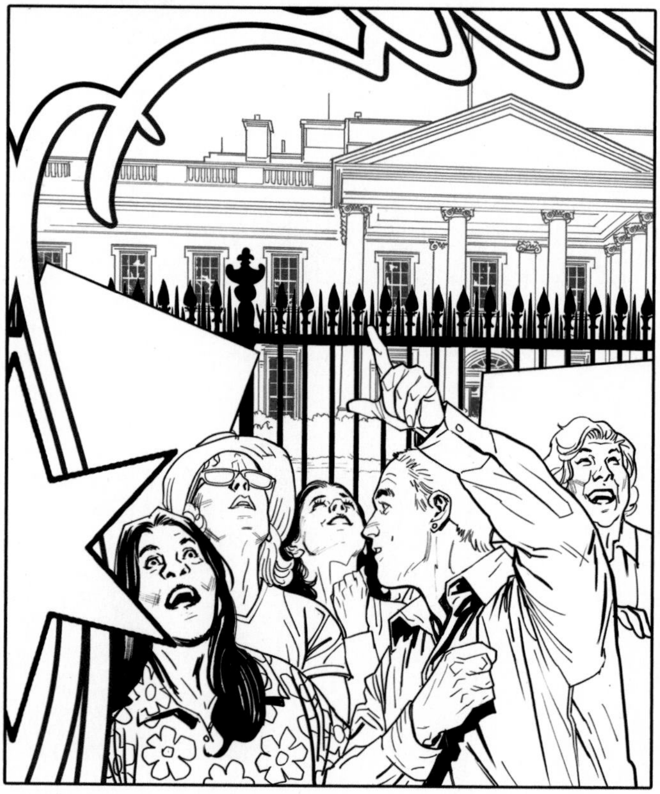

Unused Panel
This is what you get when you are drawing too late at night…a crowd of protesters reacting to a flying Amazonian island which is, in fact, thousands of miles away. Morning coffee saved my honor.

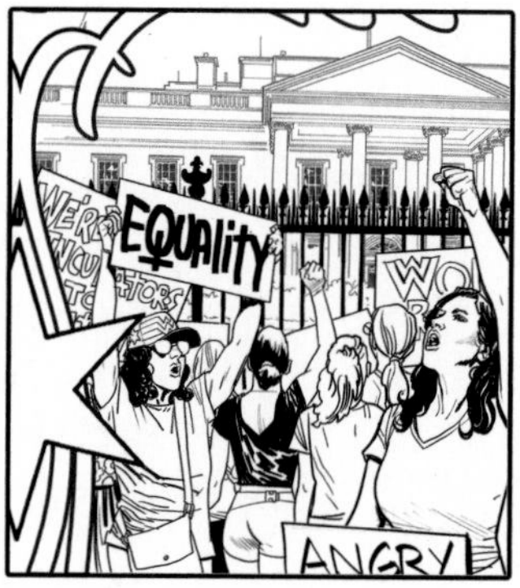
EQUALITY
ANGRY

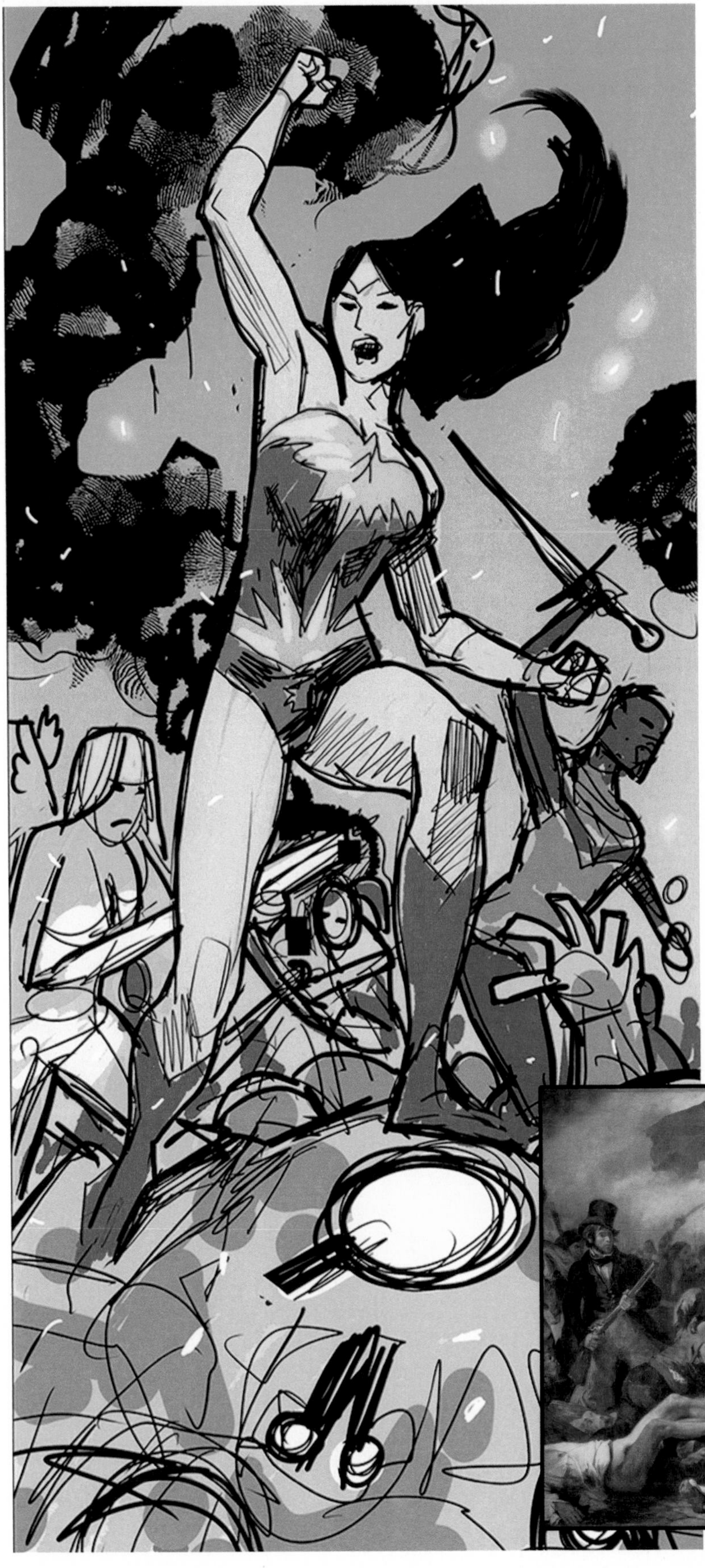

Cover Sketch
Finding a cover concept for the heroic finale of our Wonder Woman saga was much easier than for volumes 1 or 2. With the Amazons finally enacting their revolution and toppling the old patriarchal regime, the famous Eugène Delacroix painting *La Liberté guidant le peuple (Liberty Leading the People)* served as perfect inspiration. This was the only sketch I submitted.

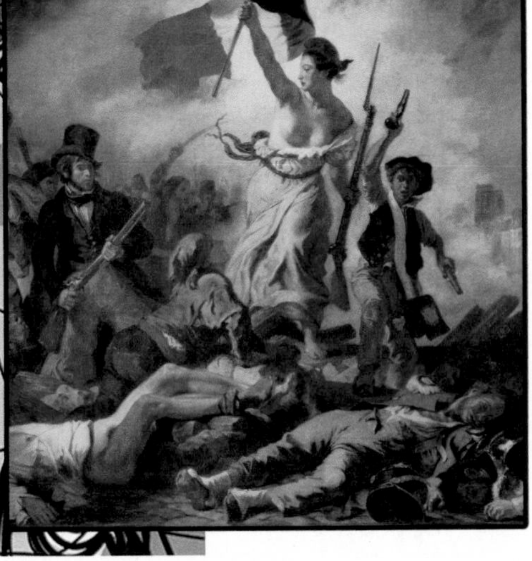

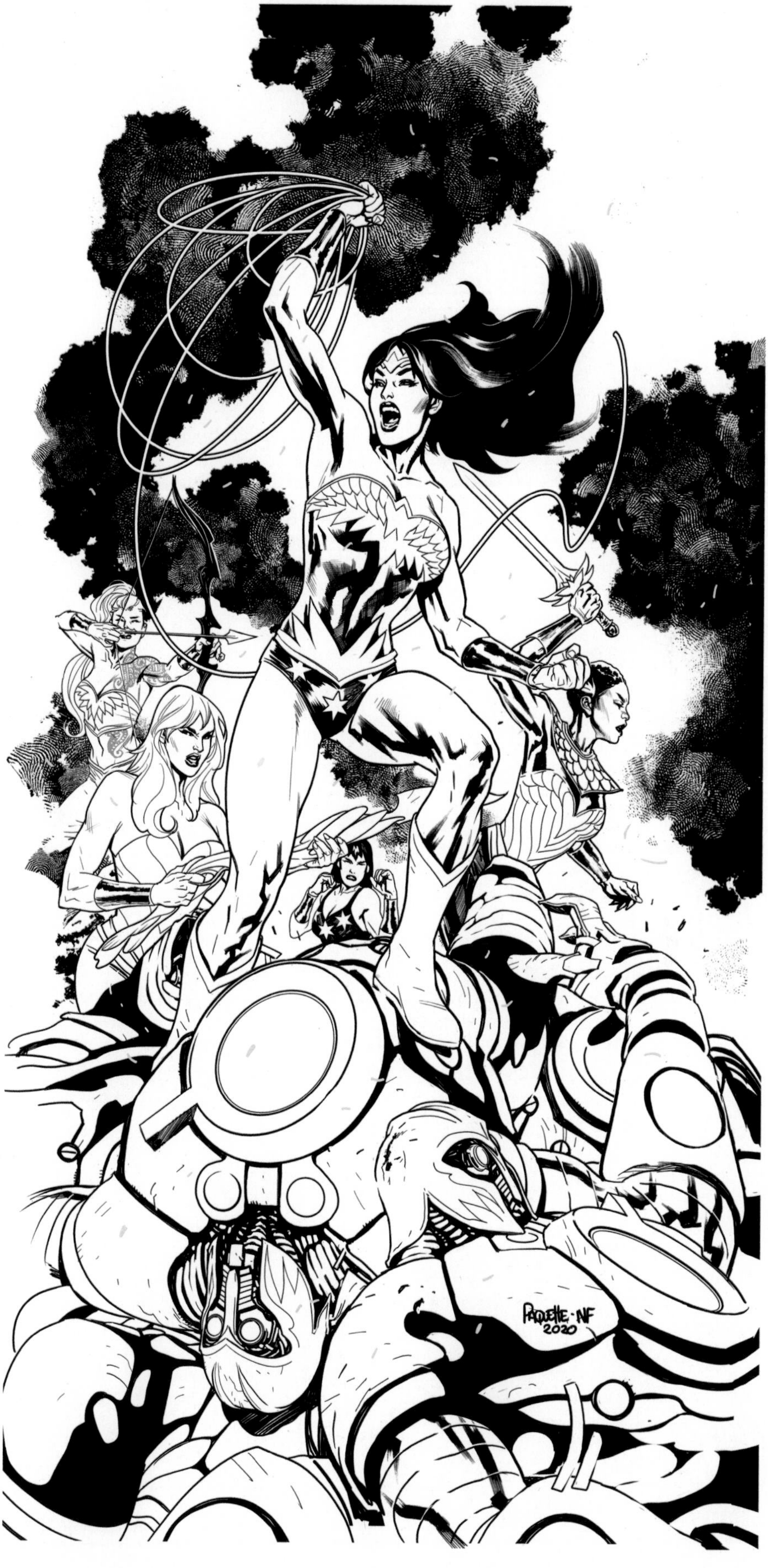
PAQUETTE · NF
2020

GRANT MORRISON has been working with DC Comics for more than twenty years, beginning with his legendary runs on the revolutionary titles *Animal Man* and *Doom Patrol*. Since then he has written numerous bestsellers—including *JLA*, *Batman*, and *New X-Men*—as well as the critically acclaimed creator-owned series *The Invisibles*, *Seaguy*, *The Filth*, *We3* and *Joe the Barbarian*. Morrison has also expanded the borders of the DC Universe in the award-winning pages of *Seven Soldiers*, *All-Star Superman*, *Final Crisis*, *Batman, Inc.*, *Action Comics* and *The Multiversity*. Currently, he is writing the epic space adventures of Hal Jordan in *The Green Lantern*.

He is the co-creator of the 2017 hit SyFY television series *Happy!* based on his comic book. Currently he is co-creator on a TV adaptation of Aldous Huxley's *Brave New World*, streaming on Peacock.

In his secret identity, Morrison is a "counterculture" spokesperson, a musician, an award-winning playwright, and a chaos magician. He is also the author of the *New York Times* bestseller *Supergods*, a groundbreaking psycho-historic mapping of the superhero as a cultural organism. He divides his time between his homes in Los Angeles and Scotland.

YANICK PAQUETTE is a Shuster Award-winning Canadian artist who has been drawing comics since the late '90s. He illustrated many comics for both Marvel and DC, including various X-Men titles; two *Terra Obscura* miniseries with Alan Moore; and *Seven Soldiers: The Bulleteer, Batman Incorporated,* and Wonder Woman Earth One with Grant Morrison. An avid insect collector and naturalist from childhood, Paquette's tenure on *Swamp Thing* allowed him a rare occasion to conjugate his passion for biology and lush comics.